CONTRARIAN JURISTS

This book presents a unique study of the field of comparative law examining the key differences between schools and approaches and examining their contradictions.

Comparative law is depicted in this book as a field of contrarians, jurists who tend to oppose or reject prevailing opinions or established practices. Contrarianism has made it exceedingly difficult to find one's way in the field where there are drastically varying views on the basic issues.

The book guides readers through divisive debates and disagreements and helps to draw useful conclusions. Instead of lamenting comparative law's feeble place in the legal academia or fantasising about the supposed great future of a unified discipline, the book highlights the collisions and tracks their influence on the field. By focusing on tensions underlying the field, this book encourages readers to think critically while studying law comparatively.

Contrarian Jurists

The Story of Comparative Law and How Collisions Shaped It

Jaakko Husa

•HART•

OXFORD • LONDON • NEW YORK • NEW DELHI • SYDNEY

HART PUBLISHING
Bloomsbury Publishing Plc
Kemp House, Chawley Park, Cumnor Hill, Oxford, OX2 9PH, UK
1385 Broadway, New York, NY 10018, USA
Bloomsbury Publishing Ireland Limited, 29 Earlsfort Terrace, Dublin 2, D02 AY28, Ireland

HART PUBLISHING, the Hart/Stag logo, BLOOMSBURY and the Diana logo are trademarks of Bloomsbury Publishing Plc
First published in Great Britain 2026

1

A catalogue record for this book is available from the British Library.

A catalogue record for this book is available from the Library of Congress.

Library of Congress Control Number: 2026934360.

ISBN: HB: 978-1-5099-8556-2
ePDF: 978-1-5099-8555-5
ePub: 978-1-5099-8557-9

Typeset by Lumina Datamatics Ltd

For product safety related questions contact productsafety@bloomsbury.com

To find out more about our authors and books visit www.hartpublishing.co.uk. Here you will find extracts, author information, details of forthcoming events and the option to sign up for our newsletters.

PREFACE

Books – even academic monographs – have reasons for their existence. This volume is a result of three influences. First, my interest in comparative law arose in the early years of the 1990s when I penned my doctoral thesis in public law. While doing research for the thesis, I came across comparative study of law, which has continued to fascinate me ever since. Comparative law remains an enigma despite the fact that I have constantly tried to get a hold of it as a form of legal scholarship.

Second, since the times of my doctoral research the story of comparative law has been slowly growing within me. I have become convinced that as an intellectual field it has distinctive features that influence how it is being done and how it transforms. It had never been my intention to write this book but if I am to believe William Faulkner 'If a story is in you, it has to come out'. More prosaically, years of experience and persistent internal drive caused this book to see the light of day. It was time to reap the harvest.

The third factor is Hart Publishing as they believed in the story and its narrator. I thank the people at Hart especially because stories need a little encouragement in order to be told. Of course, it goes without saying that the book project has been managed with great professionalism since the day I submitted the proposal.

I have no way of knowing if readers will like or hate the story I tell. In any case, I can say that it has been a pleasure to author the story of modern comparative law as I see it. If I am lucky, readers will find the story interesting and entertaining. If I am not lucky then, well, let us not go there. Regardless of the reception, special thanks go to Christopher Goddard, who helped to streamline the text and clarify my expression. Of course, I am indebted to others as well but in the writing of this book, I have incurred so many debts that I simply cannot acknowledge them all here. Family, friends, colleagues, and foes alike – you know who you are.

Jaakko Husa
Helsinki, November 2025

CONTENTS

1

Setting the Scene: Is Comparative Law Developing?

The title of this book refers to the disputes that have shaped comparative law. In order to address the comparative study of law through the prism of what can be labelled as collisions, one needs first to define what comparative law means. Defining comparative law is not as straightforward as one would perhaps expect, even in legal academia. This may come as a surprise as we tend to assume that legal scholars know what is meant by comparative law. In any case, so much ink has been spilled on the subject of comparative law as a form of legal scholarship that any assumption of scholars knowing – let alone agreeing – on what comparative law is, must simply be a myth. In other words, defining a field may seem to be a trivial issue at first. However, in the case of comparative law it is useful as many divisive issues have arisen through asking what comparative law means, or should mean.

In many ways, comparative law is a field that keeps defining and redefining itself. This is not necessarily a problem, but it reveals something essential about comparative law as an academic arena. In essence, comparative law appears to be always in the making, as it simply never merely 'is'. This state of affairs may be embarrassing to those who identify themselves as comparative law scholars, but it also reflects the dynamic nature of the field. Comparative law scholars resemble characters in a Samuel Beckett play as they are waiting for a Godot – a fully mature field of legal scholarship – who never arrives. But then the question arises whether this kind of field is able to develop.

I. An Arena of Dissenting Entrepreneurs?

Defining comparative law as a field of legal scholarship can be approached in several ways.[1] Despite certain differences, the core elements are nonetheless similar. For instance, scholars typically hold that comparative law expands study to

[1] What is meant by 'legal scholarship', see David Feldman, 'The Nature of Legal Scholarship' (1989) 52 *MLR* 498–517 ('involves curiosity about the world, which may be stimulated either by the need to achieve a goal or by desire to understand something for its own sake. It is the attempt to understand

more than one legal system. In other words, comparative law turns its focus away from domestic law. Moreover, a majority of scholars seem to agree that comparative study of law is about *differences* and *similarities* between the legal systems compared.[2] Unsurprisingly, this is where the feeble consensus ends. Comparative studies of law vary significantly in purpose, method, and style. Some believe that comparative law's key function is to help the comparatist to understand their own law better by engaging with foreign law. Others stress the importance of differences or similarities depending on the scholarly darlings of the comparatist. The overall picture gives an impression that is somewhat bewildering, at least for the uninitiated. As Mathias Siems says, 'Comparative law is a "strange animal"'.[3] To continue the animal metaphor, comparative law is like a platypus in that it combines things in ways that defy traditional boundaries between species. Regardless, comparative law certainly stands out as one of the legal disciplines.[4] Its aims are no different from the other branches of legal scholarship because, as Rodolfo Sacco puts it, 'It seeks knowledge of law'.[5] That much is clear even though sometimes its very existence has been questioned. To extend the animal metaphor further, rumour has it that zoologists thought that the first specimen of platypus they saw was so weird that it must have been a hoax. It is possible that similar sentiments about comparative law have been experienced by domestically focused doctrinal legal scholars.

Comparatists have constantly been keen to justify their existence, yet there is little doubt that comparative law exists to serve certain aims or purposes. Patrick Glenn usefully distinguished three main purposes of comparative law. First, it can be considered as an instrument of learning and knowledge about law in general. In this regard, it has significant similarities with legal theory and legal history as it provides information about the context of law. Second, it can be seen as an instrument of evolutionary and taxonomic science along the lines drawn during the mainstream scientific views of the nineteenth and twentieth centuries.[6] Third, it can be understood as a pragmatic and utilitarian tool for international

something, by a person who is guided by certain ideals, which distinguishes scholarship both from the single-minded pursuit of an end and from dilettantism', ibid 502–503).

[2] See, eg, Geoffrey Samuel, *An Introduction to Comparative Law Theory and Method* (Hart Publishing 2014); Günther Frankenberg, *Comparative Law as Critique* (Edward Elgar 2016); Catherine Valcke, *Comparing Law* (CUP 2018); Uwe Kischel, *Comparative Law* (OUP 2019); Pier Giuseppe Monateri, *Advanced Introduction to Comparative Legal Methods* (Edward Elgar 2021); Mathias Siems, *Comparative Law*, 3rd edn (CUP 2022); Pierre Legrand, *Negative Comparative Law* (CUP 2022); Jaakko Husa, *Introduction to Comparative Law*, 2nd edn (Hart Publishing 2023); Roberto Scarciglia, *Methods and Legal Comparison* (Edward Elgar 2023).

[3] Siems (n 2) 11.

[4] See Husa (n 2) 33–61; Kischel (n 2) 10–26. I assume that law in general is an academic discipline mainly because it enjoys institutional recognition and produces discourse of a scholarly nature (systemic study, theoretical foundations, use of sources, style of argumentation, research ethics, etc). See, eg, Finn Mäkelä, 'Is Law an Academic Discipline?' (2016) 50 *La Revue Thémis de l'Universite de Montréal* 422–52.

[5] Rodolfo Sacco, 'Legal Formants' (1991) 39 *AJCL* 1–34, 4.

[6] See Leontin-Jean Constantinesco, *Traité de droit comparé*, Tome III (Economica 1983). Taxonomic tradition is still alive, especially in French-speaking legal academia. See, eg, Gilles Cuniberti, *Grands Systèmes de droit contemporains*, 4th edn (LGDJ 2019).

harmonisation or improvement of national legislation.[7] For the present purpose it is beneficial to assume that these are the three broadly understood main aims of comparative law as a field of legal research.[8] However, the aims do not tell us what kind of a field of knowledge comparative law is. Beyond question, it is beneficial to be aware of the main aims of comparative law in order to be able to address the field through the framework of collisions.[9]

For the purposes of the present discussion it suffices to presume that comparative law is an academic field of research that studies organised human communities and their norms that are given special attention as something we typically recognise as 'the law'. For the comparatist, law is necessarily something that needs to be conceived broadly; hence, there is no point in addressing legal philosophy issues here.[10] In essence, scholars active in this kind of study use a comparative approach in order to draw conclusions about differences and similarities as they seek to understand the reasons lying behind their findings.[11] This is the kind of knowledge Sacco spoke about.

As a field, comparative law seems to have a number of constant features that make up its recognisable character. Lack of consensus is another feature that has continuously been a part of comparative law. Despite differences, it has been quite commonplace to pen the intellectual history of comparative law as a kind of unified narrative that depicts the story of a developing discipline moving from adolescence towards adulthood. In 1932, Walter Hug told the story of comparative law by starting from the ancient world and then walking the reader through the Middle Ages, the Renaissance, the seventeenth and eighteenth centuries and then the nineteenth century.[12] Tellingly, Hug noted that at the time of writing there was as yet no common opinion as to what were the goals, objects, and methods that comparative law should pursue.[13] The word 'yet' gives way to the underlying idea of an *evolving* field of scholarship, as if a distant dream would be looming in the future where comparative law would have reached its scholarly adulthood. Despite this underlying academic desire – shared by numerous comparatists – the field of comparative law was described 85 years after Hug as being varied, as 'critical

[7] H Patrick Glenn, 'Aims of Comparative Law' in Jan Smits, Jaakko Husa, Catherine Valcke & Madalena Narciso (eds), *Elgar Encyclopedia of Comparative Law*, 3rd edn (Edward Elgar 2023) 87–94. See also Kischel (n 2) 143–51; Siems (n 2) 2–5; Husa (n 2) 63–99.

[8] Of course comparative law has also a great value for law teaching, see eg Jaakko Husa, 'Turning the Curriculum Upside Down' (2009) 10 *German Law Journal* 913–26 and Fiona Cownie, 'Comparative Legal Education' in Smits et al (n 7) 350–57.

[9] Issues that concern comparative study of law are, of course, partially the same as in social sciences and humanist studies even though here the focus is on comparative study of law. See Maurice Adams & Mark Van Hoecke (eds), *Comparative Methods in Law, Humanities and Social Sciences* (Edward Elgar 2021).

[10] For further discussion see, eg, HLA Hart's classic *The Concept of Law* (Clarendon 1961) and Hans Kelsen's famous *Reine Rechtslehre*, 2nd edn (Deuticke 1960).

[11] Valcke (n 2) 1, says that the aim is 'to understand each legal system on its own terms'.

[12] Walther Hug, 'The History of Comparative Law' (1932) 45 *Harvard Law Review* 1027–70.

[13] ibid 1028. For a more recent shorter account of comparative law's history, see George Winterton, 'Comparative Law Teaching' (1975) 23 *AJCL* 69–118, 87–97.

scholars have divided it variably'.[14] This does not sound like the common opinion Hug talked about.

The divided nature of the field is easy to see as textbooks still seek to justify and explain the existence of comparative law as a form of legal scholarship.[15] According to this view – which indeed seems to hold water – comparative law scholars have typically lamented over their field as it is said to suffer from 'malaise'.[16] As an indication of this malaise, comparatists are divided into camps with differing diagnoses and remedies.[17] Along these lines, it has even been argued that comparative law suffers from an inferiority syndrome, which is why it has been regarded as the Cinderella of legal disciplines.[18] The prince with the glass slipper is still missing, despite aspirations.

Much comparative law scholarship of recent decades has been – if seen against the backdrop of 'malaise' – critical as to its nature as it has sought to reject what the 'canon' (real or imagined) has offered.[19] Even though scholars do not necessarily explicitly say what they mean by expressions such as 'canon' or 'mainstream', it seems more than likely that they refer to the predominance of doctrinal scholarship or what can be labelled as 'legal expertise'.[20] Legal doctrine in this context generally means a certain way to understand and practise legal scholarship. In turn, this understanding is considered as influencing all forms of legal scholarship even if it would not be strictly speaking doctrinal as to its nature. Indeed, comparative law has been living most of its existence under the shadow of doctrinal study of law, a setting that explains a considerable part of theoretically oriented scholarship's motivations.

Deep-rooted among comparatists is the idea that comparative law is still in the making because it is not mature. The intellectual atmosphere of comparative law reflects a famous quote from Antiquity attributed to Heraclitus: 'Everything flows, nothing stays still' (τὰ πάντα ῥεῖ καὶ οὐδὲν μένει).[21] Often, a whiff of desperation

[14] Robert Leckey, 'Review of Comparative Law' (2017) 26 *Social & Legal Studies* 3–24, 4.

[15] cf Stephen A Smith, 'Comparative Legal Scholarship as Ordinary Legal Scholarship' (2010) 5 *JCL* 331–56, 332.

[16] See also Mathias Reimann, 'The Progress and Failure of Comparative Law in the Second Half of the Twentieth Century' (2002) 50 *AJCL* 671–700 ('Comparative law will probably not make serious progress until it bids farewell to its current laissez faire approach to theoretical and methodological basics. The discipline would be better off if comparatists gathered the courage to define a common canon of knowledge…', ibid 700).

[17] cf Valcke (n 2) 6.

[18] Frankenberg (n 2) 3–5.

[19] See for more detailed discussion Ugo Mattei, 'Comparative Law and Critical Legal Studies' in Mathias Reimann & Reinhard Zimmermann (eds), *The Oxford Handbook of Comparative Law*, 2nd edn (OUP 2019) 805–25 (speaks of assault on the traditional 'canon', ibid 813–14). See also Thomas Coendet, 'Critical Methods' in Mathias Siems & Po Jen Yap (eds), *Cambridge Handbook of Comparative Law* (CUP 2024) 48–71 (suggests that critical comparative law should be conceived being 'against the mainstream as a matter of principle', ibid 70).

[20] cf Roger Cotterrell, *Sociological Jurisprudence* (Routledge 2018) 21.

[21] Heraclitus said that πάντα ῥεῖ (pánta rhei) 'everything flows'. The latter part seems to have been inspired by Plato (*Cratulys* 401d) who agrees with Heraclitus that τὰ ὄντα ἰέναι τε πάντα καὶ μένειν οὐδέν ('all things move, and nothing remains still'). Perseus, Digital Library, www.perseus.tufts.edu/hopper/.

is felt in the air as comparative law scholars crave recognition.[22] The amount of justificatory discourse is remarkable.

There is more to it. Comparatists have not even been sure whether comparative law is merely a method or an independent discipline.[23] It is no wonder that comparative law's desire to become an independent discipline has been described as a never-ending story.[24] The famous *Introduction to Legal Science* by Gustav Radbruch contains a quote with gravitas hinting that the idea of arrested development lingers on in the field as an academic ghost that cannot be expelled by frail comparatists:

> Sciences that concern themselves with their own methodology are sick sciences, the healthy person and the healthy science do not usually worry much about knowing themselves.[25]

Radbruch's disapproving diagnosis leaves plenty of room for critique but in comparative law it has enjoyed gravitas. For comparative law scholars, the original quotation is less potent as it was passed on and made famous by Konrad Zweigert and Hein Kötz, who strengthened its hand in their highly influential textbook on comparative law.[26] Be that as it may, today we should not give too much weight to Zweigert and Kötz's textbook. Comparatists have come a long way from the intellectual atmosphere of the late 1960s and early 1970s. However, because of the central role of Zweigert and Kötz's volume in comparative law it is useful to register how scholarly identity was built on the idea of being an 'unfinished discipline', an unhealthy discipline that worries about itself time and again. It is not a far-fetched interpretation that the idea of being unfinished has been a consequential factor for the self-understanding of comparative law scholars. Comparatists have long been in search of an audience.[27] The scholarly self-image of comparatists has been that of imperfection and the concurrent incentive has been to be free from this defect once and for all. The aura of imperfection loiters around theoretically-oriented comparative law literature to this day.

Now, as mentioned, there is no denying that comparative law has never been a unified field. However, it is another matter to argue that this state of affairs would have been solely harmful for comparative law as a field of legal scholarship.[28] This

[22] cf Peter de Cruz, *Comparative Law in a Changing World*, 3rd edn (Routledge 2008).

[23] See, eg, Michael Bogdan, *Komparativ rättskunskap* (Norstedts Juridik 2003) 21–25.

[24] Kischel (n 2) 27. As a result, comparatists are still seeking to make a systematic account of the field, see eg Valcke (n 2) 1.

[25] 'Wissenschaften, die sich mit ihrer eigenen Methodenlehre zu beschäftigen Anlaß haben, kranke Wissenschaften zu sein, der gesunde Mensch und die gesunde Wissenschaft pflegt nicht viel von sich selbst zu wissen', Gustav Radbruch, *Einführung in die Rechtswissenschaft*, 12th edn (KF Koehler 1969) 253.

[26] Konrad Zweigert & Hein Kötz, *Introduction to Comparative Law*, 3rd edn, tr T Weir (OUP 1998) 33.

[27] Basil Markesinis, 'Comparative Law. A Subject in Search of an Audience' (1990) 53 *MLR* 1–21.

[28] Recent scholarship builds on the assumption that comparative study of law need not indeed be unified as a field of legal study. See, eg, Simone Glanert, Alexandra Mercescu & Geoffrey Samuel, *Rethinking Comparative Law* (Edward Elgar 2021); Siems & Jap (n 19 above). See for further discussion Jaakko Husa, 'Comparative Law's Pyrrhic Victory?' (2024) 31 *Maastricht Journal of European and Comparative Law* 680–88.

book is based on an idea according to which controversies and scholarly conflicts have not merely been impediments for a more perfect comparative law to miraculously emerge sometime in the distant future, but they have, conversely, shaped the field and made it what it is today. Crucially, comparative study of law has taken shape through the controversies that shape the transformation of comparative law, both now and in the future.[29] The first outcome of these controversies is that today's comparative law can be described as *pluralistic*. In short, there is no ruling paradigm but, rather, diversity. The second outcome is that today many scholars tend to underline comparative law's nature as an inherently interdisciplinary endeavour.[30] In this sense, comparative law has indeed opened its doors as this is the genuine vocation of the comparatist.[31] For these reasons, referring to today's comparative law only as 'a pocket of legal studies' seems like an understatement.[32] Consequently, the gracious prediction from 2002 by Esin Örücü according to which the twenty-first century will be the age of comparative law may not be as hopeless as it may seem at first sight.[33] That said, it is not quite clear what the age of comparative law would actually mean. Hasty sceptics might say that comparative law has a bright future behind it and the awaited age of comparative law is already in the past. So, if we are to believe the sceptics, that ship has sailed long ago.

Avoiding the temptation of simplifying intellectual storytelling is imperative here. This author believes that it is important to do justice to the subtleties of comparative law endeavour. Portraying the story of modern comparative law is necessarily a balancing act. The caveat is that this story cannot be exhaustive given the scope of the field. One way of addressing comparative law as a form of legal scholarship is to depict it as a discipline of discordance. To that end, comparative law is a field of *contrarians*. 'Contrarian' refers to a person who tends to oppose or reject prevailing opinions or established practices. In essence, my view here is based on an assumption according to which comparative law has been an arena of dissenting academic entrepreneurs. Comparative law scholars have valued the opportunity to become their own authority as they have sought to escape the – real or imagined – iron grip of legal doctrine or, if you like, the mainstream. Soloism has, by and large, formed part of comparative law scholarship's intellectual fabric. This, in turn, has had an impact on a field that has been crafted by individuals who have appreciated and adamantly guarded the academic freedom to choose their own path. As a result, comparative law can be described as a jungle rather than a garden – as vibrant as it is confusing for someone who wishes to find a straight path.

[29] See eg Jaakko Husa, *A Research Agenda for Comparative Law* (Edward Elgar 2024).

[30] See Jaakko Husa, *Interdisciplinary Comparative Law* (Edward Elgar 2022). See also Siems (n 2 above) 9–11.

[31] Jacques Vanderlinden, *Comparer les droits* (E Story-Scientia 1995) ('le comparatiste a pour vocation d'ouvrir des portes', 423).

[32] Annelise Riles, 'Introduction' in Annelise Riles (ed), *Rethinking the Masters of Comparative Law* (Hart Publishing 2001) 1–18, 1.

[33] Esin Örücü, 'Unde Venit, Quo Tendit Comparative Law?' in Andrew Harding & Esin Örücü (eds), *Comparative Law in the 21st Century* (Kluwer 2002) 1–17 ('It is not fanciful to predict that the 21st century will be "the age of comparative law"').

On the negative side, the entrepreneurial spirit of the comparatists has always been a barrier to actually reaching the dreamed-of future: a unified field. It would be only too easy to perceive this merely as a form of scholarly stubbornness. In today's world, however, diversity may seem like a stroke of luck as the world of law around us can best be described as global legal pluralism.[34] As Mark Van Hoecke notes, today's comparative law (or, as he calls it, the 'new approach') 'is clearly characterised by pluralism – pluralism as to the kinds of legal systems compared (not just state law) and a methodological pluralism'.[35] In a similar vein, it is possible to make an intriguing observation here. Despite tendencies of unification and globalisation, comparative law has transformed into *a pluralistic field* of legal scholarship.[36] Besides, it is useful to bear in mind that globalisation of law is not a linear process with uncontradicted goals.[37] The fact that globalisation also brings about diversity should not cause eyebrows to rise among the ranks of comparatists. At the same time, it would be mistaken to assume that even modern comparatists would support any particular view on legal pluralism, but is more about accepting generally the idea of overlapping normativities and rejecting the idea of the state as the sole source of law. To that end, it would not be right to depict all comparatists as pluralists.

II. The Impact of Scholarly Collisions

The aim of this book is not to present a complete overview of all contested issues, but to illustrate the intellectual collisions that have shaped the field and are currently still ongoing among notable experts working in the area. The focus is on the years after the 1970s. In general terms – it is argued here – these collisions are *formative* as to their nature. Chapters discuss topics of debate such as whether the comparatist studies law in books or law in action, whether legal transplants are impossible, or whether comparative law is for academia or for practice. The quintessential idea is to provide an insider's view on comparative law's developmental collision points. Instead of lamenting the state of comparative law's professed feeble place in legal academia or to fantasise about the supposed great future of a unified discipline, this book chooses to highlight the collisions and to track their influence on the field. Admittedly, this is a tall order. To begin with, it is beneficial to grasp that scholarly conflicts may involve different kinds of ramifications for an academic field of study. There are both positive and negative impacts, although

[34] See Paul Shiff Berman, *Global Legal Pluralism* (CUP 2012) and Paul Schiff Berman (ed), *The Oxford Handbook of Global Legal Pluralism* (OUP 2020). See also Michael Palmer & Ling Zhou, 'Legal Pluralism' in Jan Smits et al (n 7) 490–501, 496–98.

[35] Mark Van Hoecke, 'Is There Now a Comparative Legal Scholarship?' (2017) 12 *JCL* 271–80, 280.

[36] However, relying on legal pluralism is not without problems if left undefined. See Catherine Valcke, 'Three Perils of Legal Pluralism' in Seán Patrick Donlan & Lukas Heckendorn Urscheler (eds), *Concepts of Law* (Ashgate 2014) 123–35.

[37] See Jaakko Husa, *Advanced Introduction to Law and Globalisation* (Edward Elgar 2018).

differentiating between them is not easy. Regardless, some signposts are possible to erect in the text that follows.

At least three kinds of potentially positive effects can be highlighted. First, collisions may help scholars to clarify important issues. These issues concern matters such as what it is that comparatists mean by 'law' and how it is possible to gain knowledge of law comparatively. Geoffrey Samuel captures this dimension by saying that comparative law scholarship has 'provoked a number of fundamental questions about methodology'.[38] Second, collisions also tend to sharpen scholarly minds in the sense that they increase the intellectual commitment of scholars as they passionately defend their views and criticise those of others. Sometimes this may seem something of an academic no-holds-barred fight, as – for example – some contributions to the debate on legal transplants seem to indicate.[39] Third, collisions may also encourage and inspire scholars to rethink and sharpen their views on contested issues. Although perhaps not too commonplace, scholars may also modify their views on the basis of debate. If a scholar unwaveringly explains and defends a theoretically coherent view, this may have an impact on the thinking of others, as Pierre Legrand's persistent appreciation of 'the different' seems to imply. Mainstream has not been successful in its initial attempt to leave Legrand's views unnoticed.[40]

Of course, negative effects of collisions can also be found. First, collisions create tensions if left unresolved. Tensions may come to the surface when one submits an article to a journal that chooses reviewers from an opposing scholarly faction. For instance, when taken by surprise on receiving scathing reviewer feedback and rejection, one may suspect that these tensions play a role. Second, it may be that especially younger or aspiring scholars choose to stay away from contested issues as they may feel that these are too controversial for them to get involved in. The underlying (legitimate) fear is easy to understand because the precariat is worried about their position in academia, and it may be wise to stay out of divisive debates as one never knows who will be sitting on the faculty search committee or on the board of a research funding institution. Third, collisions may create long-lasting divisions and even animosities between scholars and, in a worst case scenario, these will be inherited. In other words, senior scholars may transmit their convictions to their disciples, who will then continue the conflict in the next generation of scholars. Sometimes established senior scholars who have secured their institutional positions may function as totem poles around which faithful junior followers gather. For comparative law as a field of research, this sort of tribalisation has not been a boon. Scholarly bubbles have many features that may be considered negative.

[38] Geoffrey Samuel, 'Does One Need an Understanding of Methodology in Law Before One Can Understand Methodology in Comparative Law?' in Mark Van Hoecke (ed), *Methodologies of Legal Research* (Hart Publishing 2011) 177–208, 178.

[39] According to one description, 'Debates among comparatists appear sharp, almost combative', Leckey (n 14) 3. See also Giorgio Resta, 'Les luttes de Cloche en Droit Comparé' (2017) 62 *McGill Law Journal* 1153–99.

[40] See, eg, (2017) 65 *AJCL*, Issue suppl 1, Special Issue: 'What We Write About When We Write About Comparative Law: Pierre Legrand's Critique in Discussion'.

It is, I believe, crucial to understand that – as a field that generates and sustains scholarly collisions – comparative law today is not what it was before. Internet and now artificial intelligence (AI) have opened a Pandora's Box because, unlike in past decades, so much material and so many computer-generated possibilities and temptations are within easy reach.[41] Having said that, the value of comparative law today exceeds its modest role as a helping tool for the interpretation of legal texts.[42] If comparative law had obediently stayed within the narrow boundaries set by legal doctrine, then it would have remained a subsidiary practice of lesser intellectual value in an academic milieu that calls for a doctrinal focus on Western private law. Why this has been a problem is not difficult to grasp. The doctrinal mode of legal scholarship is based on 'the attempt to explain law solely through the internal evidence offered by judgments and statutes' and as such it never was well suited to the purposes of comparative law.[43] Regardless of this, legal doctrine's methodological and epistemic allure has been difficult to resist among the ranks of those who count themselves as comparatists. Consequently, it was once suggested by Max Rheinstein that one should try to forget what one has learned in one's own law when studying law comparatively.[44] This is, unfortunately, an extremely difficult if not impossible feat.

What we see today is a more extensive, more pluralistic and more interdisciplinary field than the comparatists of the 1970s and the 1980s could possibly have envisaged.[45] With that in mind, it is imperative to grasp that the change emanated from the collisions in which the transformation took – and is still taking – shape. Everything still flows, as Heraclitus put it. In this sense, the pluralistic comparative law of today was crafted and moulded by dissenting entrepreneurial legal scholars inspired by the contrarian academic spirit. This book is based on the assumption that the change has taken place during the last 50 years or so. To that end, there is no need to reach all the way back to the mythical naissance of the discipline emanating from the scholarly mist of the conference in Paris 1900.[46] In similar fashion, the time has come to stop discussion on the basis of an agenda set in the 1970s and 1980s. To be sure, this is one of the motivating factors behind this

[41] See, eg, Han-wei Ho, Patrick Chung-Chiua Huang & Yun-Chien Chang, 'Machine-Learning Methods' in Siems & Yap (eds) n 19 above, 177–207.

[42] None of this is to say that comparative law would not have at least potentially important practical uses too. See eg Mads Andenas, Duncan Fairgrieve & Francesco Quarta, 'Why and How Courts Use Comparative Law' in Luca Siliquini-Cinelli, Davide Gianti & Mauro Balesteri (eds), *The Grand Strategy of Comparative Law* (Routledge 2024) 67–85.

[43] Anthony Bradley, 'Law as a Parasitic Discipline' (1998) 25 *Journal of Law and Society* 71–84, 71.

[44] Max Rheinstein, 'Comparative Law' (1968) 22 *Arkansas Law Review* 415–25, 421.

[45] For example, the rise of decolonial comparative law, comparative law and geography, and comparative law and religion would have been difficult to predict in the past century. See Leyla Salaymeh & Ralf Michaels, 'Decolonial Comparative Law' (2022) 86 *Rabels Zeitschrift für ausländisches und internationales Privatrecht* 166–88; Matteo Nicolini, *Legal Geography* (Springer 2022); and Jaakko Husa, 'Comparative Law and Christianity' (2024) 44 *Oxford Journal of Legal Studies* 54–73.

[46] On the conference see Balázs Fekete, *Paradigms in Modern European Comparative Law* (Hart Publishing 2021) 67–81.

book: to be on the move instead of becoming stuck and backward-looking without accepting an overly linear view about a developing field.

III. Development of Comparative Law: *Linear v Winding*

Addressing comparative law through collisions makes sense because the very nature of comparative law scholarship has been conflictual either openly or implicitly. Scholars have been intellectually committed, which is why they passionately defend their views and criticise those of others.[47] One of the positive outcomes of this situation is that the field is dynamic even though also dispersed and somewhat tribalised.[48] To achieve this, for example, doctrinal comparatists have relied on so-called functionalism, whereas culturally oriented comparatists have placed their trust in hermeneutics. For these reasons, comparative law presents an ideal field to be described, analysed, and explained through scholarly conflicts. This approach is not unique as it is closely related to theoretical frameworks of dialectics, paradigm, and 'great debates'. Before embarking on the formative collisions of the field, it comes across as facilitative to explain how the present approach situates itself in relation to these three related frameworks to analyse the development of an academic field as a process that involves two relevant dimensions: conflict and - for want of a better word - development.[49]

In essence, scholarly collisions in comparative law are about contradictions between different assumptions and beliefs on what is law and how it is possible to gain knowledge of it. The idea of contradiction is elemental to the philosophy of Hegel (and Marx). According to this view, humane things are in a process of change and development so that the motion and change of things stems from contradictions which are inherent in all things. Scholarly (or rather scientific) knowledge is a process that involves continual conflict, interaction, and dialogue between different views. If this view is accepted, then accumulation of knowledge is a process based on contradiction.[50] Understood in this manner, dialectics is based on the idea of development that moves from less sophisticated views to more sophisticated ones. Dialectics is connected with the image of a process that concerns overcoming the contradiction between thesis and antithesis, doing so by means of synthesis. After some time, the process starts anew as synthesis becomes thesis. Later, the synthesis is contradicted so that the process repeats itself until some kind of perfection is reached.[51]

[47] For example, expressions such as 'sustained attack' and 'blasted' have been used to describe these debates, Leckey (n 14).

[48] cf Valcke (n 2) 6–7.

[49] See Geoffrey Samuel, 'Has Comparative Law Progressed?' in Luca Siliquini-Cinelli, Davide Gianti & Mauro Balestrieri (eds), *The Grand Strategy of Comparative Law* (Routledge 2024) 3–21.

[50] See Sean Sayers, 'Contradiction and Dialectic in the Development of Science' (1981) 45 *Science & Society* 409–36, 35–36.

[51] See, eg, Claudia Wirsing, 'Dialectics' in Michael N Forster & Kristin Gjesdal (eds), *The Oxford Handbook of German Philosophy in the Nineteenth Century* (OUP 2015) 641–78, 663–68.

If dialectics were to be applied to the development of comparative law as a field of study, then the idea of continual conflict would seem plausible. However, it is not quite clear if what has happened in comparative law's intellectual history can be described as a growth of knowledge because many of the matters that were being discussed over 100 years ago are still being discussed - and seemingly to no visible avail. No perfection (or synthesis) has been reached, that much is clear. There most certainly are contradictory processes between opposing sides but it seems implausible to claim that there would have been genuine development in the sense of scientific development through syntheses. In consequence, we need to look elsewhere. Perhaps the theory of paradigm may provide a more solid basis to discuss developments and/or changes in comparative law?

In a nutshell, Thomas Kuhn's original thesis argues that science develops through revolutions. Kuhn argued for an episodic model that contains periods of 'normal science' that are interrupted by periods of revolutionary science.[52] Revolutionary science grows from the discovery of anomalies that in the end lead to new paradigms.[53] Anomalies are a kind of violation of the 'paradigm-induced expectations that govern normal science'.[54] Paradigm in this theory is a universally recognised scientific achievement 'that for a time provides model problems and solutions to a community of practitioners.'[55] Here, 'practitioners' refers to the rank and file of scientists working in the field of the so-called hard sciences.

Kuhn's theory concerns scientific revolutions, but it is not quite clear how well, if at all, his ideas can be applied to law and legal disciplines. It has been suggested that asking if scientific revolutions have occurred in law is not even an appropriate question. Instead of applying Kuhn's theory directly to the study of law, it may work better if his thesis is modified - as Balàzs Fekete has done.[56] He recognises the problem with describing the development of comparative law based on linear terms that assumes the idea of an unbroken process of scholarly evolution.[57] Fekete's important insight is that - in order to recount the transformation of comparative law - one needs to abandon the dominance of descriptive linearity. He seeks to apply Kuhn's theory empathically so as to keep in mind 'inherent specificities of legal scholarship as a field of inquiry'.[58] This approach assuredly makes sense. But it is not problem-free.

Even though Kuhn abandoned the idea that science progresses smoothly, so that scientific knowledge builds on the successive contributions of generations of

[52] For a more detailed discussion see eg G Anand, EC Larson & JT Mahoney, 'Thomas Kuhn on Paradigms' (2020) 29 *Production and Operations Management* 1650–57.

[53] There are diverse ways to understand paradigm as Kuhn's book left room for interpretation. See Margaret Masterman, 'The Nature of Paradigm' in Imre Lakatos & Alan Musgrave (eds), *Criticism and the Growth of Knowledge* (CUP 1995) 59–89. Here the notion of paradigm is used mostly in its sociological meaning, see ibid 65. Fekete (n 46) refers to this by asking 'which Kuhn to apply' (19–20) for his study.

[54] Thomas S Kuhn, *Structure of Scientific Revolutions* (University of Chicago Press 1970) 52–53.

[55] ibid viii.

[56] Geoffrey Samuel, *Rethinking Historical Jurisprudence* (Edward Elgar 2022) 270.

[57] Fekete (n 46) 2–3.

[58] ibid 30.

scientists, he did not abandon the idea that science does progress, whether through revolutions or through smooth advancements. The case of comparative law is, I believe, more complicated and considerably more intriguing. Despite the fact that Fekete manages to narrate the story of the comparative law of the 1900s through the prism of a modified notion of paradigm, there is no denying that paradigm and the idea of scientific revolutions is more at home with hard sciences than with such a soft field as comparative law.[59] Softness does not mean that comparative law would be somehow of lesser value than hard sciences, but it does mean that comparative law is, as John Bell notes, creative and normative practice as interpretation occupies a central role in the enterprise of comparing laws and legal scholarship in general.[60] Accepting the idea of methodological pluralism does not mean that methods of non-interpretative fields could not be used in comparative study of law. Nevertheless, accepting that the beating heart of comparative study of law is closer to human sciences than to hard sciences has an impact on how we see the progress and growth of knowledge against the backdrop of comparative law. As Hans-Georg Gadamer says, 'the specific problem that the human sciences present to thought is that one has not rightly grasped their nature if one measures them by the yardstick of a progressive knowledge of regularity.'[61] This presents a difficulty for the present attempt to discuss the change of comparative law, because progressive regularity appears to be out of the question.

Despite the fact that both dialectics and paradigm provide apparently possible ways to frame the subject matter of this book, they are one-dimensional and somewhat naïve in terms of their belief in development through pattern-following stages moving forward as knowledge increases. To my mind, they are still too straightforward for a field such as comparative study of law. Even the very notion of 'development' is difficult to define in this context. As Samuel concludes discussion on scientific revolutions in legal scholarship: 'Lawyers today are still applying methods that are not dissimilar to those found in the *Digest* and in the medieval commentaries of Italian jurists.'[62] Accordingly, if we accept Samuel's clear-headed point, the notion of progress in comparative law needs to be taken with a pinch of salt.

When it comes to comparative law, there is a third option, that is, to address the divisive key issues through the somewhat pliable notion of a 'great debate'.

First, 'debate' would apparently be a more flexible way to conceptualise comparative law discussion than dialectics or revolutions . 'Debate' does not build on the idea of development. Second, many of the fundamental comparative law issues

[59] I have argued elsewhere that, in essence, comparative law belongs to humanities rather than sciences, Husa (n 2) 65–66. An alternative way is to tell comparative law apart from legal doctrine by underlining that it is closer to social science than to pure normative inquiry, Esin Örücü, 'Developing Comparative Law' in Esin Örücü & David Nelken (eds), *Comparative Law: A Handbook* (Hart Publishing 2007) 43–65, 48.

[60] John Bell, 'Legal Research and the Distinctiveness of Comparative Law' in Mark Van Hoecke (ed), *Methodologies of Legal Research* (Hart Publishing 2011) 155–76, 175.

[61] Hans-Georg Gadamer, *Truth and Method*, 2nd revised edn (Continuum 1994) 4.

[62] Samuel (n 56) 272.

appear to resist resolution. This is because – with some oversimplification – all comparatists seem to have done is question and criticise. To that end, comparative law scholarship has been particularly good at generating debates that run on and on. The contrast is striking between what dialectics and paradigm tell us, on the one hand and, on the other, the story of comparative law. For these reasons it might be possible to conceptualise the subject matter of this book as 'debates' instead of three-stage theses or paradigms facing anomalies. This approach is not unheard of. The books in the Great Debates in Law series ask what their central theme is or what it is that is being debated. In this sense the 'great debates' approach shares similarities with the approach chosen in this book. For example, the book on company law starts by asking the utterly *fundamental question* 'what is a company?' [63] In turn, the book on jurisprudence argues that major developments in the field have emerged from debates between important legal theorists.[64] Moreover – and much like many comparative law books – the volume on jurisprudence starts by addressing the question of the *nature* of jurisprudence.[65] This is typically the kind of question that comparative law scholars ask and have kept asking for decades. Perhaps ironically, the reader can see that this introductory chapter poses the same question, as this author seeks to provide at least some kind of answer to it in order to frame the analysis.

Instead of dialectics, paradigms, or great debates, this book frames disagreements as *scholarly collisions* crafted by legal scholars (academic as well as other legal experts and judges) who tend to be contrarian in terms of their academic mentality. This conceptualisation underlines that no linearity or straightforward development is conceived through the lens of scientific revolutions in comparative law; nor are there that many – though there are some – identifiable great debates. We are left with disagreements, which some can be seen as disputes, some as theses and antitheses, and some as 'great debates'. As a consequence, I choose to conceptualise these as 'collisions' as this seems to fit well in terms of addressing comparative law as a field because it captures its contrarian scholarly spirit.

Regardless of the above, there are no reasons to rule out the idea of comparative law's development. But that is not what is assumed here. Suffice to say that the issues in comparative law discussions are about questions entangled with the realities of human communities. Laws and legal systems are in constant interaction with their surrounding social environment, which in turn means that they keep evolving over time. In that sense, all forms of legal scholarship – not only comparative law – are in constant interaction with their societal environment. Accordingly, to conceive comparative law scholarship and discussion of comparatists as scholarly collisions makes sense: change creates collisions. Along these lines, 'collision' in this book refers to discussion among legal scholars in which they hold different opinions about comparative study of law. The concept of 'legal scholar' (or

[63] Lorraine Talbot, *Great Debates in Company Law* (Macmillan/Palgrave 2014) 1.
[64] Nicholas J McBride & Sandy Steel, *Great Debates in Jurisprudence*, 2nd edn (Macmillan/Palgrave 2018) xiii.
[65] ibid 1–29.

'jurist') in this context covers both legal academics and other legal experts, including judges, as holders of what can be labelled as *legal knowledge*, knowledge of law.[66] Nevertheless, this book's focus is on legal scholars, as broadly defined above, because they are the ones who have shaped the field more than practitioners. To be sure, this is not to belittle the role and importance of practitioners but merely to highlight the scholarly dimensions of collisions.

Importantly, the notion of 'scholarly collision' also includes situations where scholars have been talking past each other as they have refused to engage in direct debate. Many comparative law collisions lie below the surface, although some collisions have taken a more visible form of direct debate. However, the chosen approach comes with a caveat. Of course, it should go without saying that a single book cannot address all the potentially relevant issues of disagreement in comparative law. That would be simply too much of an uphill battle. It would be pointless to deny that some incompleteness is unavoidable. However, what *is* attainable is to identify important conflicts but without claiming to deal with all of the important collisions and strands of scholarship. In essence, I assume that an observant legal scholar who reads scholarly literature on comparative law swiftly realises that certain themes keep recurring, albeit in different forms and through different conceptual framings. Whether this book manages to address the most relevant collisions is a question that is ultimately left for readers to decide. Or, to be more precise, what is left out of this book and what is chosen for discussion is itself a potential subject for disagreement and contrarian reactions. In addition, the present author is, for better or for worse, a player in this field riddled with scholarly tensions;[67] which suggests, if nothing else, an essential feature about the very nature of comparative law as a field of legal scholarship. This is also why the title of this volume speaks of contrarians; they are scholars who almost instinctively assume a contrary position. This book seeks to tell that story; the story of contrarian legal scholars shaping the field through scholarly collisions.[68]

Despite the slightly gloomy view on the development of comparative law as expressed above, this book shows that some progress is possible. In all honesty, there would be no point in discussing collisions if there were not at least some possibility of progress, even though many of the issues would remain unsolved. But as noted by the authors of the Great Debates in Jurisprudence: 'Sometimes the lack of progress in a debate is justified, and we cannot have much hope that the debate will ever reach a successful conclusion'.[69] Despite this, it is important to understand that a field such as comparative law lives and changes in collisions

[66] See for more detailed discussion Christian Atias, 'Judges, Jurists, and Legal Knowledge' (1988) 74 *Archiv für Rechts- und Sozialphilosophie* 368–93.

[67] The path to comparative law of this author, see Jaakko Husa, 'Why I Became a Comparative Lawyer' (2025) 20 *JCL* 533–38.

[68] Or as Resta (n 39) 116 puts it: comparative law has indeed established itself as a 'dissident discipline'.

[69] ibid 270.

about the most basic questions.[70] Disagreements concern ontology, epistemology, and methodology. This, again, has to do with the fact that the idea of colliding views renounces the linear view of scholarly development. And yet, we can today consider the scholarship of the twentieth century 'to represent outdated views on comparative law, most notably as to its methodology'.[71] If nothing else, this at least hints that some kind of development is possible after all. Small steps forward, and some backwards, if nothing more.

IV. Structure of the Book

This chapter has clarified what comparative study of law is currently about and explained the chosen framework. Chapter two explains how the distinction between law in books and law in action has shaped and still shapes the field. Underlying tension goes between doctrinal and other kinds of approaches. One of the issues is the role of legal realism (broadly understood) in comparative law. Chapter three addresses the issue whether one should conceive comparative law as a field or as a discipline. This is because most controversies are based on differing views on the identity of comparative law. Chapter three deciphers views on this issue that centre around the separation between academic and practical purposes. Chapter four discusses the distinction between private law and public law. It shows how this divide shaped the field in the last century and how in this century it has lost much of its earlier potency. Chapter five is based on the observation according to which comparative law has at least two faces. One is theoretical scholarship centred around methodology and epistemology. The other is the more practically oriented comparison preferred by lawyers who self-identify more or less as pragmatists. Chapter five is built on the divide between those who do it and those who talk about it. Chapter six addresses the issue of cultural division between the West and the Rest against the backdrop of legal families/cultures/traditions. Much of the discussion in macro-comparative law stems from this cultural - often unspoken - division. Chapter six also discusses legal orientalism and decolonial comparative law as dimensions of cultural division.

Chapter seven highlights the difference between country experts and generalists. Collision is structured around those who identify as comparatists who stress the importance of the method and theoretical framework of macro-comparison whereas so-called country experts focus on studying a certain foreign country's legal system without a distinct comparative framework or avowed comparatist identity. Chapter eight dives into the long and winding debate on so-called functionalism, which has been one of the most persistent areas of open disagreement in comparative law. This discussion is still ongoing. Chapter nine is based on the fact

[70] And yet it is important to understand that if comparatists were to wait for perfect clarifications, they would not get into doing actual research at all. Bernhard Grossfeld, *The Strength and Weakness of Comparative Law* (Clarendon Press 1990) 8.

[71] Mark Van Hoecke, 'Foreword' in Fekete (n 46) v–viii, v.

that modern comparative law scholarship struggles to study law as part of a larger legal culture instead of a more narrowly understood legal system. Discussion builds on the longstanding debate surrounding legal transplants, which reveals underlying assumptions about law and its relationship to the surrounding society in the form of the so-called 'mirror theory'.

Chapter ten analyses the divide between individualisers and generalisers. Analysis rests on the fact that comparative law was traditionally a qualitative form of research but during recent decades this has met critique and challenges from quantitative forms of research relying on numbers. Analysis is framed through the old methodological debate known as the *Methodenstreit*. Chapter eleven addresses the role of critical scholarship in comparative law because in this century much of comparative law scholarship has, in one way or another, become critical as to its nature. Chapter eleven explains why this type of scholarship has been and still is in confrontation with other forms of comparative law scholarship. The last substantive chapter, Chapter twelve, discusses the impact of diminishing state sovereignty, which can be seen in the rise of transnational law and global law. Discussion centres around the debated question 'are we all comparatists now?' The concluding Chapter thirteen ponders what lies in the future of comparative law, briefly restates the major themes running through the book, revisiting key controversies against the backdrop of the future of comparative study of law and contrarianism.

2

Placing the Focus –Text, Action, Context

All fields of legal scholarship involve aspects that are taken for granted by the majority. Without these, academic disciplines could not function. In comparative law research, these aspects concern issues such as what is the object of comparison and how comparison should be made. Notwithstanding, where the precise focus of research should be placed is among the most-discussed and most-contested issues. Despite numerous disagreements, even the most critical minds need to accept at least some commonality with what they label as the mainstream that should otherwise be opposed at all times. One conceivable way to describe the implicitly accepted commonalities is to depict them as dogmas. In other words, these are beliefs about what to compare and are presumed by most scholars without further ado. Beliefs of this sort tend to be somewhat unconditionally and unquestionably accepted as true or at least so well established that questioning them would be bad form. Comparative law has its own sets of contested beliefs but at least one of them seems to have gained the position of a dogma. This established opinion concerns the study object of the comparatist, which typically takes the form of a self-professed creed. In other words, it occurs as a statement of shared beliefs of the scholarly community of comparatists. One of its most well-known formulations is familiar from the literature in the following form: 'law in books' and 'law in action'.

This dogma is based on a certain kind of academic creed of the scholarly comparatist, and it supposedly provides an answer to the key question as to where the comparatist should place the focus of their research. Should the focus be on black-letter law or should one spread the net wider and search beyond the traditional, formally emphasised understanding of the law? In other words, should one remain reluctant to include non-doctrinal views and interdisciplinary insights, or should one take a risk and attempt non-legal methodologies?[1] Essentially, the distinction between 'books' and 'action' is a credo that has become embedded in the

[1] This is a difficult question because becoming interdisciplinary is challenging for a legal scholar. See for a deeper analysis Jaakko Husa, *Interdisciplinary Comparative Law* (Edward Elgar 2022). See also Christoph Engel, 'Challenges in the Interdisciplinary Use of Comparative Law' (2021) 69 *AJCL* 777–97.

core of comparative law methodology and epistemology, though without necessarily being followed in actual research. In what follows, I shall argue that the distinction is, in terms of its origins, a contrarian reaction against legal doctrine's way of understanding law and conducting legal research. In addition, this chapter discusses how this dogma has been shaping the field, and how it has evolved in stages.

I. Creed and Reality – Books and Action

How to unpack the epistemic distinction that informs us how the comparatist should focus their research, is not an easy question. The concept of self-image may be of use here. Academic fields have self-images that encapsulate perhaps not how a specific field actually works but how a field is understood as it *ought* to work. Self-image of a field concerns how scholars by and large think their field should be.[2] In practice, self-image contains implicitly accepted dogmas of a field. Accordingly, an implied normativity is involved in terms of actual research practices; and the conceptions that scholars working in a particular field have of what it is that they should be doing are not identical. The self-image of a field comes close to a paradigm, but it lacks the certainties that paradigms are supposed to offer for scholars working in a field.[3] Self-image is blurred and allows more deviations than a paradigm as a way to conceptualise comparative law's idealistic understanding of itself and its object of study.

It seems possible to argue that, in the case of comparative law, some parts of its self-understanding are more generally accepted than others. For example, comparatists seem to agree that studying law comparatively means to study more than one legal system.[4] If the research concerns only one system, then it cannot be genuinely comparative.[5] Essentially, this means that at the front and centre of comparative law is the act of crossing the borders of legal systems (broadly understood) and

[2] The concept of self-image is familiar from psychology see, eg, Tara McMullen, 'Self-image' in Mark D Gellman & J Rick Turner (eds), *Encyclopedia of Behavioral Medicine* (Springer 2013) 1744–45.

[3] This has to do with so-called 'normal science' and what it provides for a field. See for more detailed discussion, John Watkins, 'Against "Normal" Science' in Imre Lakatos & Alan Musgrave (eds), *Criticism and Growth of Knowledge* (CUP 1970/1995) 25–37. For a more recent take, see Pablo Melogno, 'Normal Science' in K Brad Wray (ed), *Kuhn's The Structure of Scientific Revolutions at 60* (CUP 2024) 79–94.

[4] See, eg, Gilles Cuniberti, *Grands systèmes de droit contemporains*, 4th edn (LGDJ 2019) 21 'c'est à la comparaison des droits de diffèrents Etats'; Roberto Scarciglia, *Metodi e comparazione giuridica*, 2nd edn (Wolters-Kluwer 2018) 1 'metodo di confronto fra istituzioni e regole di paesi diversi'; Peter de Cruz, *Comparative Law in a Changing World*, 3rd edn (Routledge 2008) 3 'study of particular legal traditions'; Michael Bogdan, *Komparativ rättskunskap*, 2nd edn (Norstedts 2003), 18 'jämförande av olika rättssystem'; Alan Watson, *Legal Transplants*, 2nd edn (University of Georgia Press 1993) 6 'study of the relationship of one legal system and its rules with another'; Konrad Zweigert & Hein Kötz, *Einfürung in die Rechtsvergleichung* Vol 1, 2nd edn (JCB Mohr 1984) 4 'Rechtsvergleichung es mit dem Vergleichen verschiedener nationaler Rechtsordnungen'; Pierre Armanjon, Baron Boris Nolde & Martin Wolff, *Traité de droit compare*, Vol 1 (LGDJ 1950) 10 'compare les règles et les institutions des divers systémes juridiques'.

[5] Of course, in comparative legal history one can study one system comparatively in two periods of time. See, eg, Olivier Moréteau, Aniceto Masferrer & Kjell Å Modéer (eds), *Comparative Legal History* (Edward Elgar 2019). See also Jean-Louis Halpérin, 'Historic-Jurisprudential Methods' in Mathias

abandoning the relative security of one's own law – because studying foreign law is an epistemic and methodological obstacle to nationally trained jurists (academic as well as other legal experts and judges). In practice, virtually all comparative law theory centres around this quandary and discusses what techniques, risks, and possibilities are connected with abandoning the epistemic security of one's own law. At least two kinds of departures are pertinent here: departure from domestic law (substance) and from nationally oriented doctrinal study of law (method). For comparative law, both departures are of importance and consequence.

To be sure, the self-image of a field consists of several overlapping parts, and it is difficult to tell them apart successfully. Consequently, there is no need for hair-splitting here. One part of the self-image, a dogma if you prefer, of comparative law has been the demand to focus on law in action instead of law in books. This is where the unavoidable connection between legal theory and comparative study of law is revealed. Of course, comparative law is not legal theory but – as has been rightly pointed out – doing comparative law means that one has to have some theory of law.[6] Quite often, the theory of law that comparatists lean on remains implicit – unlike in legal theory, where scholars are expected to be explicit about their view on what is law. Legal theory is a wide field and the amount of scholarship is massive; thus, it would be inane here to dig deeper into it. In turn, comparative law has been interested selectively in a certain kind of theoretical thinking about law. The scholarly direction where inspiration and formative methodological ideas were drawn from during the past few decades is broadly understood: American legal realism.[7]

Now, American legal realism was a movement that held a diverse collection of ideas about law and the study of it; hence, it would not make sense to discuss it in detail for the purpose of this book.[8] That is because the way in which comparative law scholarship drew some ideas from American legal realism took place solely based on the specific needs of comparison, so that no attempt was made to take part directly in discussion of a legal theoretical nature.[9] It is safe to say that legal theory, or jurisprudence, is a field distinct from comparative law. Even though there undoubtedly are many points of contact, these fields do not share

Siems & Po Yen Jap (eds), *Cambridge Handbook of Comparative Law* (CUP 2024) 32–47 (discusses the relationship between comparative law and legal history).

[6] See Frederick Schauer, 'Legal Theory and Comparative Law' in Jan Smits, Jaakko Husa, Catherine Valcke & Madalena Narciso (eds), *Elgar Encyclopedia of Comparative Law* Vol. 2 (Edward Elgar 2023) 517–24.

[7] There are, of course, other schools of legal realism, too. See, eg, Heikki Pihlajamäki, 'Against Metaphysics in Law' (2004) 52 *AJCL* 469–87 (explores differences and the historical contexts of American and Scandinavian legal realism).

[8] For an overview see, eg, Frederick Schauer, 'American Legal Realism' in Mortimer Sellers & Stephan Kirste (eds), *Encyclopedia of the Philosophy of Law and Social Philosophy* (Springer 2019) 1–9.

[9] Legal realism had an impact on many later schools of thought in American legal scholarship, such as critical legal studies, and law & economics. See, eg, Edward White, 'From Realism to Critical Legal Studies' (1986) 40 *Southwestern Law Journal* 819–43; Carla Faralli, 'The Legacy of American Legal Realism' (2005) 48 *Scandinavian Studies in Law* 75–82; and Hanoch Dagan, 'The Real Legacy of American Legal Realism' (2018) 38 *Oxford Journal of Legal Studies* 123–46.

the same dogmas.[10] Consequently, in what follows the focus is firmly on comparative law and the question of *what* and *how* to study. It could be reasoned that the need to talk about method(s) is perhaps stronger in relation to comparative law than any other field of legal study. Methodological haze and the following bad conscience have always bedevilled comparative law scholarship. This is but one of the consequences caused by crossing the borders between different legal systems. As Mathias Siems puts it, legal scholars studying law comparatively may feel as if stranded on a foreign planet.[11] Domestic legal doctrine offers no shelter from alien elements for a legal scholar who ventures to cross the borders of law. Comparatists are – or at least they should be – acutely aware of this.

In many cases, it can be an onerous task to find the original source of legal theories. However, in the case of legal realism and comparative law this may not be so. The original formulation – 'books' and 'action' – comes from the famous American legal realist Roscoe Pound's article published in the early 1900s. The key argument of the article was understood to maintain that law in books can to a great extent differ from law in action. Essentially, Pound pointed out that judgments of the courts and what statutory law says do not always meet.[12] Pound was not alone in this way of thinking. He was part of an intellectual movement that we can label as sociological jurisprudence that highlighted the difference between statutory law and legal practice.[13] Another prominent legal realist, Karl Llewellyn, formulated the underlying idea provocatively by arguing that 'rules alone, mere forms of words, are worthless'.[14] Along these lines, Pound's sociological jurisprudence was supposed to pursue comparative study of law and pay attention 'more to the working of the law than to its abstract content'.[15] For comparative law, the message of sociological jurisprudence was tempting as it seemed methodologically helpful.[16]

Importantly, during the twentieth century the legal realist insights became part and parcel of the intellectual fabric of comparative law, at least in the form of a self-professed creed. To be sure, I am not claiming that comparatists would have followed the ideas of American legal realism devotedly.[17] For the self-professed creed, it is of less importance that Pound did not actually clearly distinguish between court decisions and statutory law. Not a surprise, then, that Pound's

[10] About the relation between legal theory and comparative law, see John Bell, 'Is Comparative Law Necessary for Legal Theory?' in Maksymilian Del Mar & Michael Lobban (eds), *Law in Theory and History* (Hart Publishing 2016) 127–45.

[11] Mathias Siems, *Comparative Law*, 3rd edn (CUP 2022) 1.

[12] Roscoe Pound, 'Law in Books and Law in Action' (1911) 44 *American Law Review* 12–36.

[13] The label comes from Pound himself, see Roscoe Pound, 'The Scope and Purpose of Sociological Jurisprudence I' (1911) 24 *Harvard Law Review* 591–619.

[14] Karl Llewellyn, *Bramble Bush: On Our Law and Its Study* (Oceana Publications 1930) 3.

[15] Pound (n 13) 489–516, 516.

[16] For example Rudolf Schlesinger took from American legal realism 'the attitude of looking at what really matters in law, beyond the rhetoric contained in the law in the books', Ugo Mattei, 'The Comparative Jurisprudence of Schlesinger and Sacco' in Annlise Riles (ed), *Rethinking the Masters of Comparative Law* (Hart Publishing 2001) 238–56, 255.

[17] It is more like some sort of methodological influences that were important not only to comparative law but also to the creation of legal anthropology. See Kaius Tuori, 'American Legal Realism and Anthropology' (2016) 42 *Law & Social Inquiry* 804–29.

article is invoked more on the basis of its catchy title than its actual content.[18] In other words, the title itself gained important status as an element of comparative law's self-image as a kind of dogma. This is also no surprise because Pound was not only a legal theorist but can be seen as one of the most distinguished comparative law scholars of the first half of the twentieth century.[19] Without a shadow of a doubt, Pound's work was known among contemporary comparatists.[20] Today, comparatists may not grasp this influence as it has become shrouded by layers of scholarship built on the rudimentary insights of sociological jurisprudence, now part of comparative law's established phraseology.

Distinguishing between legal reality and formal legal texts gradually became part of the *Stand der Lehre* of comparative law during the twentieth century.[21] Nevertheless, this distinction gained its strong foothold in comparative law scholarship after the 1960s as the field started to grow and became academically more ambitious than during the previous decades. It is possible to pinpoint the formative key moment – or a period at least – when law in action and law in books became transformed into an elemental dogma and an ingredient of comparative law's self-image. The dogma of law in action and law in books infiltrated comparative law scholarship's mainstream through so-called functionalism. Notwithstanding, timewise these two reached their zenith in different decades. Now, functionalism and the scholarly collisions that are involved with it will be discussed in more detail in chapter eight. Discussion here focuses on separating law in books from law in action as an underlying epistemic commitment.

Unfortunately, what we speak of when we speak of functional comparative law is far from clear. To cut a long story short and without venturing further in this chapter, functional comparative law gained a strong foothold, especially in European private law, as it became the central tool for common core studies.[22] The basic ideas came from Konrad Zweigert and Hein Kötz's influential textbook. Their methodological answer to the problem of crossing the borders of legal systems was as elegant as it was deceptively simple: One should study the different ways of resolving similar problems through law.[23] In essence, the comparatist was urged to identify foreign legal norms that are functionally equivalent to those rules, principles or institutions that have been taken into comparison from other systems.[24] Regardless of their shortcomings, Zweigert and Kötz brought method

[18] See Jean-Louis Halpérin, 'Law in Books and Law in Action' (2012) 64 *Maine Law Review* 46–76, 46.

[19] David S Clark, 'History of Comparative Law and Society' in David S Clark (ed), *Comparative Law and Society* (Edward Elgar 2012) 1–36, 22.

[20] See, eg, Arthur von Mehren, 'Roscoe Pound and Comparative Law' (1964) 13 *AJCL* 507–17.

[21] For example, in 1970 a German scholar writes in a leading German comparative law journal's issue dedicated to Konrad Zweigert's 60th birthday about the distinction between *Rechtswirklichkeit* (law in action) and its discrepancy with *Rechtstheorie* (law in books, literally 'legal theory'), citing Pound's article. See Andreas Heldrich, 'Sozialwissenschaftliche Aspekte der Rechtsvergleichung' (1970) 34 *Rabels Zeitschrift für Ausländisches und Internationales Privatrecht* 427–42, 428.

[22] Esin Örücü, 'Methodology of Comparative Law' in Jan Smits (ed), *Elgar Encyclopedia of Comparative Law*, 2nd edn (Edward Elgar 2012) 560, 563.

[23] cf Richard Hyland, *Gifts: A Study in Comparative Law* (OUP 2009) 9.

[24] Konrad Zweigert & Hein Kötz, *An Introduction to Comparative Law*, 3rd edn (OUP 1998) 35–36.

and methodology to the heart of comparative law theory.[25] In the late 1990s, the functional approach was depicted as 'the standard methodology, at least in Europe and the United States'.[26] But how does all this relate to the dogma of distinguishing between law in books and law in action?[27] On the surface, they do not seem like the same item. But, as is well known, appearances can be deceptive. That said, the underlying legal theoretical elements do, no doubt, overlap to an extent.

In essence, the core issue is the role of formal legal texts (namely, law in books) that is conceived as a kind of a surface level of law, containing only the formal language of law but which is not seen as sufficing because the comparatist is supposed to take into account the functions of legal institutions. Summarily, formalism does not suffice. In the end, it was in the functions of legal institutions and rules that the law was to be found but not from official (foreign) legal texts. In short, the comparatist was advised not to rely on law in books as the sole source of foreign law. The comparatist was supposed to concentrate on the functions of legal institutions and rules, not on the linguistic surface of foreign law.[28] The epistemic message conveyed was that of distrusting purely textual analysis of black-letter law. This is precisely why legal realist ideas were (and probably still are) of special interest to comparatists as they have offered an at least seemingly neat way to express and justify the need to go beyond textual analysis and abandon a purely doctrinal approach.

Relying on a rather simplified demarcation line between 'books' and 'action', functional comparative law sought to broaden the methodological horizon of doctrinal lawyers who dared cross the borders and study law comparatively. Curiously, though – and despite all advice – the research practice of functional comparative law has been focused on black-letter law. In other words, talking the talk does not mean that one would also walk the walk, a slogan that rings true in comparative law, too. This is curious because Zweigert and Kötz explicitly explained in the theoretical part of their volume that the solution to a problem of a legal nature may be provided 'by custom or social practice, and has never become specifically legal in form'.[29] Paradoxically, their methodological advice was not really followed by comparatists. This begs the question: how do functional comparative law and American legal realism coincide?

It has been noted that even though Pound himself was strictly speaking not about functions – as his interest lay in law in action instead of law in books – the

[25] This is, it seems, very much in line with the German tradition (concerning German-speaking countries) as law has been always an academic discipline there and methodology has been a core part of legal scholarship. See Reinhard Zimmermann, 'Legal Methodology in Germany' (2022) 26 *Edinburgh Law Review* 153–93.

[26] David J Gerber, 'System Dynamics: Toward a Language of Comparative Law?' (1998) 46 *AJCL* 719–37, 722. See also Mark Van Hoecke & Mark Warrington, 'Legal Cultures, Legal Paradigms and Legal Doctrine' (1998) 47 *ICLQ* 495–536, 495.

[27] However, Zweigert & Kötz (n 24) discuss law in books v law in action against the backdrop of American legal realism (247–49) without attaching the distinction directly to their account of the functional approach.

[28] I have discussed this in Jaakko Husa, 'Functional Method in Comparative Law' (2013) *2 European Property Law Journal* 4–21.

[29] Zweigert & Kötz (n 24) 35.

core ingredients of this thinking were central parts of what we call 'functionalist comparative law'.[30] The underlying theoretical dogma is the demarcation line drawn between text (books) and practice (action). Even though the vocabulary of today's comparative law has reimagined the distinction between these two, nonetheless it still forms a part of comparative law epistemology. A part of the confessed epistemic creed if nothing else; a core element in the scholarly vocabulary of comparative law scholarship. Nevertheless, the vocabulary may have changed as the field has modernised or even reinvented itself. Scholarship has, if not truly developed, moved on, driven by its own epistemic enigmas and disagreements that reflect more recent discussions.

II. Modern Incarnation – Text and Context

When I claim that the vocabulary has changed, then the question arises: what has it evolved into? No doubt, it would be an exaggeration to argue that law in books and law in action rhetoric would have left the stage of comparative law scholarship entirely. That said, against the backdrop of modern comparative law scholarship, one may be tempted to draw the conclusion that the influence of legal realism would have disappeared from comparative law. However, there is more to it than straightforward disappearance. This is no surprise, as in law and legal thinking deep-rooted concepts tend to persist – as, for example, the influence of Roman law on modern civilian legal systems clearly shows.[31] Without digging deeper, it is safe to say that much of Roman law's influence flowed from its concepts.[32] And the concepts that lawyers and legal scholars use have an impact on how we think about law.

All fields of study of law use and rely on established concepts. When a certain conceptualisation takes root in a field it will be difficult to get rid of it later – as, for instance, is indeed the case with legal transplants (see chapter nine). Additionally, dogmas, contained in established conceptualisations, may become part of the very fabric of a field. Distinguishing between 'books' and 'action' is one of those kinds of settled dogmas.[33] In a sense, this distinction has been more or less reincarnated in modern comparative law. For instance, among modern scholars Uwe Kischel discusses functional comparative law and connects it with legal realism against the backdrop of functional comparative law's attempt to seek the reality of foreign legal systems instead of the surface level of black-letter law:

[30] See Ralf Michaels, 'The Functional Method of Comparative Law' in Mathias Reimann & Reinhard Zimmermann (eds), *The Oxford Handbook of Comparative Law*, 2nd edn (OUP 2019) 345–89, 353.

[31] On Roman influence in general, see Hessel E Yntema, 'Roman Law and Its Influence on Western Civilization' (1949) 35 *Cornell Law Quarterly* 77–88.

[32] This idea can be stretched further to what Watson called 'nutshells', which include not only concepts but also the structure of Roman law. See Alan Watson, 'The Importance of "Nutshells"' (1994) 42 *AJCL* 1–23.

[33] It can be described as a 'basic legal concept' in comparative study of law, see Matteo Nicolini, '"Writing the Earth and Representing the World"' (2024) *19 JCL* 79–101, 80.

> The search for real solutions to real problems outside one's native legal system not only takes us beyond its limits and concepts, it also brings to light factors such as the difference between law in books and law in action; the influence of legal culture; understanding, significance, and scope of a foreign solution to a legal problem; and the possible importance of extra-legal factors which affect the solution to real problems or which offer such solutions in the first place.[34]

For the theme of this chapter, it is crucial to sense the spirit in which the above list of factors to take into account is offered. Like American realism, this is about going beyond the limits and concepts of one's native legal system. Importantly, this seems to go beyond Zweigert and Kötz's approach. The manner in which Kischel frames law in books and law in action signals a scholarly shift. Context(s) of law (or extra-legal solutions) move to the centre, seeking to break away from the succinct framing provided by Pound's article. Instead of language resembling that of American legal realism, comparative law of the twenty-first century has turned time and again to *legal culture*. Even though the concept of legal culture is vague, it became a fashionable part of comparative law scholarship in the early twenty-first century. One can argue with full credibility that it is a key notion in modern comparative law despite its undeniable vagueness.[35] Despite legal culture's substantive opaqueness, it appears like a unifying banner under which many modern comparatists apparently want to mobilise. Stressing the role of legal culture can be labelled as culturalism that seeks to oppose a previously dominant, more formalistic, view of comparative law.[36] The crux is on escape from normativism and an attempt to penetrate through the textual surface of law.

Be that as it may, the move from the language of legal realism is not a drastic change. In turning to legal culture, comparative law has been able to build on the existing self-image of the field. Accordingly, when describing modern comparative study of law, Siems has noted that 'research on legal culture goes beyond the "law in the books" in considering the "law in action"'.[37] As if these two conceptualisations would tacitly merge together. The key point, in my reading, is the common element: moving beyond what could be described as the doctrinal surface of the law. From the viewpoint of legal theory, this is about anti-formalism. Comparatists have repeatedly put this into words but using different vocabularies even though the animating spirit has been, more or less, the same: to go deeper, to pass beneath the surface of positive law, and formal sources of law. Or, to put it otherwise: to look beyond law in books.

Despite the fact that intellectual shift is a key factor, it is important to tread carefully as the transformation has been subtle and gradual in nature. It is not argued here that comparative law would have truly abandoned established theoretical dogma, but it is argued that modern comparative law seeks to surpass the

[34] Uwe Kischel, *Comparative Law* (OUP 2019) 8–9 (also cites Pound's 1910 article).
[35] See David Nelken, 'Legal Culture' in Smits et al (n 6) 336–43.
[36] See Balázs Fekete, *Paradigms in Modern European Comparative Law* (Hart Publishing 2021) 154–57.
[37] Siems (n 11) 175.

binary 'books' vs 'action' dogma. Along these lines, Catherine Valcke – who cites Pound's 1910 article – discusses the nature of law (or what it means for the comparatist) and – in a critical tone – law in books and law in action. In a footnote she says that William Ewald does not use Pound's distinction but distinguishes 'text-based' and 'context-based' accounts of law.[38] Here we can yet again detect the shift from the language of Anglo-American legal realism to a more up-to-date formulation as action/practice has morphed into the context of law or legal culture.

From my standpoint, the change is not radical, but it does indicate how comparatists instinctively seek to abandon previous conceptualisations by forging new ones. The urge to move forward from the earlier generation of comparatists seems like an innate quality of comparative law scholarship. In this sense, the move to context is *a contrarian move* – a breakaway in name even if nothing more for many. This is not to say that context would not go beyond 'action' but that the difference between them is not that significant in the comparative law scholarship of today. As Ewald puts this line of thinking '[n]ot law in books, but law in action is the proper object of study for the contextualist'.[39] In a way, legal realism and contextualism merge together in a layered manner. However, even scholars who recognise the importance of studying law in context do not necessarily use the notion of context to explain how and why they seek to look beyond black-letter law. For instance, Kischel discusses law in books and law in action but then adds a third contextual element: 'law in debate'. This means taking into account diverse opinions on specific legal questions.[40] Others, though, might argue that debates on law form part of the context of law.

Now, Pound's formulation drew a line between 'statutory' and 'real'. But what it is that 'context' seeks to achieve? Context, if nothing else, seems to draw the endeavour of comparative law closer to the methodologies of social scientific or cultural studies. The rise of context can be connected to what can be labelled as a post-modern critique of comparative law.[41] In general, this has to do with the persistent attempt to escape legal formalism and the methodological legacy of legal doctrine. Essentially, this critique is based on the idea that context goes beyond positive law and, hence, is difficult if not impossible to reach on the basis of a domestically pruned doctrinal legal approach.[42] Perhaps paradoxically, this is where functionalism's professed key idea and modern comparative law meet again. Furthermore, it is not difficult to grasp that some key ingredients of Pound's sociological jurisprudence are dressed in new clothes and smuggled back into comparative law theory as if they were a novelty. That being so, comparative law's functionalism – if understood as taking the context of formal law into

[38] Catherine Valcke, 'Comparative Law as Comparative Jurisprudence' (2004) 52 *AJCL* 713–40, 717 (note 25).

[39] William Ewald, 'The Jurisprudential Approach to Comparative Law' (1998) 46 *AJCL* 701–7, 702.

[40] Kischel (n 34) 186–88.

[41] See, eg, Anne Peters & Heiner Schwenke, 'Comparative Law Beyond Post-Modernism' (2000) 49 *ICLQ* 800–34 (explaining the post-modernist challenge to traditional comparative law).

[42] cf Vernon Valentine Palmer, 'From Lerotholi to Lando: Some Examples of Comparative Law Methodology' (2005) 53 *AJCL* 261–90, 64–65.

account – comes close to social scientific approach(es) to law. This also draws, at least in principle, legal sociology and comparative law closer to each other.[43] David Nelken sheds light on the issue:

> It is crucial, as taught by the Legal Realists long ago, to include studies of the 'law in action' if we want to try to explain or predict the actions of legal actors and others using the law. Only with such knowledge can we develop persuasive comparisons of law in the USA and Europe, or bring out the importance of infra-structural aspects of dispute resolution which can account for telling difference even within civil law jurisdictions.[44]

Bafflingly though – and as already pointed out above – what we call functional comparative law claimed to study social reality but has shied away from empirical methods used in social sciences (see chapter ten).[45] Where this leads comparative law scholarship is not clear. How can Nelken's persuasive comparisons take place? If comparatists have moved from action to context without genuinely resorting to a non-legal social science type of methodology, we need to ask: What then? It is possible to describe the change from action to context as a move that hints about the contrarian nature of comparative law scholarship. Yet the story does not end here. Along these lines, 'legal style' has also been proposed as a subject to be studied by comparatists.[46] In any case, scholarly shift gave room to the rise of 'the third way'. This may look like a Hegelian type of synthesis (see chapter one); but, regardless, it does open doors beyond the binary distinction upheld by the dogma of 'books' vs 'action' or 'context'.

III. Toolbox Theory – The Third Way?

It seems quite likely, though if not fully certain, that reading functionalism through the phraseological lenses of American realism is an indication of Anglo-American impact on legal scholarship in general, not only in comparative law.[47] If this holds water, then the shift to 'context' is a kind of contrarian move seeking to reconceptualise the anti-formalist dogma and at least offer novel wording for comparative law's epistemic creed and to liberate it from the discursive grip of the vocabulary of

[43] Discussion on the difference between comparative law and comparative legal studies reflects the same issue, see Michal Palmer, 'For Comparative Legal Studies' in Jaakko Husa (ed), *A Research Agenda for Comparative Law* (Edward Elgar 2024) 129–55.

[44] David Nelken, 'Comparative Law and Comparative Legal Studies' in Esin Örücü & David Nelken (eds), *Comparative Law: A Handbook* (Hart Publishing 2007) 3–42, 20 (Nelken cites Kagan and Blankenburg).

[45] cf Kischel (n 34) 17.

[46] See Catherine Valcke, 'Comparing Legal Styles' (2019) 15 *International Journal of Law in Context* 274–96 (suggests comparing reasoning styles).

[47] This has also taken place against the backdrop of EU law. See Anthony Arnull, 'The Americanization of EU Law Scholarship' in Antony Arnull, Piet Eeckhout & Takis Trimadis (eds), *Continuity and Change in EU Law* (OUP 2008) 415–31. See also Frans Van Waarden, 'Power to the Legal Professionals: Is There an Americanization of European law?' (2009) 3 *Regulation & Governance* 197–216. From the point of view of legal education, see Susan Bartie & David Sandomierski (eds), *American Legal Education Abroad: Critical Histories* (New York University Press 2021).

legal realism. From a broad scholarly point of view, this means abandoning strict ideas about what comparative law is and how comparatists should conduct their research.[48] Balázs Fekete speaks of the rise of methodological tolerance, which he analyses through the lenses of paradigm theory.[49] It seems to me that Fekete is on the right track even though I am not convinced of his chosen theoretical framework of paradigm, as was explained in chapter one.

Now, there is no single theory or school of thought that would take a stand against earlier dichotomies using clearly distinguishable epistemic arguments. Rather, it is about the way in which non-binary thinking has taken place in the methodology of modern comparative law in general.[50] 'Modern' in this context refers to post-2000 comparative law scholarship. Several noteworthy comparatists have, more or less, rebuilt their methodological self-image so that it is based on some kind of pluralism that embraces diversity and seeks to broaden both the epistemic and methodological boundaries of comparative law.[51] For example, scholars such as Geoffrey Samuel, Mathias Siems, Mark Van Hoecke, and this author all speak for a broad methodological scope that can be labelled the toolbox theory.[52] Even more traditional takes have started to conceive comparative law as a field that has relevant neighbouring disciplines.[53] In my view, all this seems to suggest that comparative law has sought to recede from legal doctrine's restrictive method by seeking more inclusive conceptualisations.

However, there is no need to go overboard when we describe the scholarly transformation. The shift from methodological narrowness to non-binary thinking and a more diverse understanding has not been swift. It has been taking place gradually. At first, it was understood that the one-method-one-vision type of approach coming from legal doctrine was essentially misguided.[54] On that kind of basis, it became possible to erect a new kind of self-image of pluralist comparative law that would not be based on any particular method but, as Van Hoecke puts it, on the idea according to which the comparatist wields a pluralist toolbox holding

[48] This is also noted by legal scholars who conceive comparative law in more practical terms: 'it may not have the coherence of an academic discipline that it had a generation ago', Mads Andenas, Duncan Fairgrieve & Francesco Quarta, 'Why and How Courts Use Comparative Law' in Luca Siliquini-Cinelli, Davide Gianti & Mauro Balestrieri (eds), *The Grand Strategy of Comparative Law* (Routledge 2024) 67–85, 79.

[49] Fekete (n 36) 157–63 (also speaks of 'the complex toolbox of comparatists' 163).

[50] See also H Patrick Glenn, *Legal Traditions of the World*,4th edn (OUP 2010) 368–72 (discusses bivalent and multivalent logic, favouring the latter).

[51] For a concise discussion on legal pluralism see, Michael Palmer & Ling Zhou, 'Legal Pluralism' in Smits et al (n 6) 490–500.

[52] See Geoffrey Samuel, *An Introduction to Comparative Law Theory and Method* (Hart Publishing 2014); Mark Van Hoecke, 'Methodology of Comparative Legal Research' (2015) *Law and Method* (DOI: 10.5553/REM/.000010); Siems (n 11); and Jaakko Husa, *Introduction to Comparative Law*, 2nd edn (Hart Publishing 2023).

[53] See, eg, Mathias Reimann, 'Comparative Law and Neighbouring Disciplines' in Mauro Bussani & Ugo Mattei (eds), *Cambridge Companion to Comparative Law* (CUP 2012) 13–34.

[54] See, eg, Jaakko Husa, Methodology of Comparative Law Today (2006) 58 *Revue internationale de droit comparé* 1096–1117.

methodological opportunities.[55] Along similar lines, in an encyclopaedia entry of 2023, Esin Örücü writes about methodologies not solely about methodology as she did in the 2012 edition. The move from singular to plural is noteworthy. She explains that comparative studies of law have different purposes and, hence, 'techniques used can differ according to those purposes.'[56] This is very much in line with modern comparative law theory in general.

A telling example of the toolbox theory is the *Cambridge Handbook of Comparative Law*, edited by Siems and Po Jen Yap.[57] The handbook provides not merely one chapter on the method or methods of comparative law, but offers nine full chapters on different methods: traditional, historical-jurisprudential, critical, cultural, linguistic, qualitative, economic, empirical, and machine-learning based.[58] The edited work is not, of course, exhaustive but it does show how methodological thinking in comparative law has moved from binary towards pluralistic. In similar fashion, Van Hoecke distinguishes functional, analytical, structural, historical, and law-in-context methods.[59] In turn, Samuel speaks of schemes of intelligibility; these are causal, functional, structural, hermeneutical, actional, and dialectical.[60] In practice, Samuel focuses on functional, structural, and hermeneutical. This author, for his part, discusses functional, structural, systemic, and critical.[61] Finally, Kischel discusses an array of methodological options, not merely one approach, in his massive textbook.[62]

It would seem that modern comparative law theory builds on the idea of a toolbox and goes beyond the distinction of books vs action or context. A further example broadening the toolbox even more, is Yenny Vega Cárdenas who discusses functional, structural, interdisciplinary, decolonial, and other approaches. Under these headings, Cárdenas analyses several alternative methodologies including all of those mentioned above and some more.[63] Along similar lines, Roberto Scarciglia writes about – and defends – methodological pluralism.[64] The overall situation seems to be diversity-embracing or at least moving towards that direction. Instead of a monolithic conception of comparative law, the 2020s has been witnessing the rise of a pluralistic field tolerating many methodologies.[65] As Fernanda Pirie puts it, comparatists need to leave behind traditional themes and topics in order to

[55] Mark Van Hoecke, 'Methodology of Comparative Legal Research' (2015) 5 *Law and Method* 1–35, 28

[56] See Örücü (n 22) and Örücü, 'Methodologies for Comparative Law' in Smits et al (n 6) 42–50, 48.

[57] Mathias Siems & Po Jen Yap (eds), *The Cambridge Handbook of Comparative Law* (CUP 2024). See also the helpful review essay of the Cambridge Handbook, Fernanda Pirie, 'Global Comparative Law?' (2024) *Oxford Journal of Legal Studies* 506–24.

[58] In *Comparative Law* (2022) Siems discusses traditional, postmodern, socio-legal, numerical, and empirical approaches.

[59] See Van Hoecke (n 55).

[60] Samuel (n 52) 81–84 (drawing from French epistemologist Jean-Michel Berthelot).

[61] Husa (n 1) 122 ff.

[62] Kischel (n 34) 87 ff.

[63] See Yenny Vega Cárdenas, *Methodology and Epistemology of Comparative Law* (LexisNexis 2024) chs 3–7.

[64] See Roberto Scarciglia, *Methods and Legal Comparison* (Edward Elgar 2023).

[65] About the pluralistic state of comparative law today, see Jaakko Husa, 'Comparative Law's Pyrrhic Victory?' (2023) 30 *Maastricht Journal of European and Comparative Law* 680–88.

'embrace context and to ask about change' of law.[66] All the above considered, it seems that the discursive grip of American legal realism has loosened as it has been replaced by other anti-formalist conceptualisations.

IV. Lessons Learned?

In sum, it seems plausible that law in action and law in books became popular in comparative law because it stood against a formally oriented way to study law. In this sense, it was born as a contrarian move against legal doctrine as it was understood by the comparatists that a doctrinal view was incompatible with the comparative approach. A breakaway from formalism was essential because doctrine is based on black-letter law taking form in treatises, monographs, articles in law journals, case commentaries, essays, and reviews of a legal nature.[67] Even though doctrine cannot be detected directly from legislation, preparatory materials of legislation, or judgments, doctrine does not normally venture outside formal law and because of that it is unwilling to take action, debates, or context into account in the manner that comparative study of law requires.[68] To that end, it is in the very nature of the textual-dogmatic approach not to embrace 'action' or 'context'. This is not to criticise legal doctrine as such, but to recognise that its quintessence lies elsewhere than that of comparative law.

In short, the purely textual doctrinal analysis of law was (and is) largely deemed unsuitable as an appropriate method for comparative law.[69] Comparative law stands in contradiction with the basic idea of a textual approach that requires focusing not on context but on black-letter law.[70] If one is to describe legal doctrine as the currency of law, then comparative law has actively sought to find a currency exchange kiosk because the currency of legal doctrine is domestic as to its nature but does not work when one crosses borders.[71] Maurice Adams and John Griffiths speak of casting the net wide as they underline that comparative study of law requires more than doctrinal analysis; it needs to go further.[72] I argue, in a similar vein, that comparative law simply cannot stop where doctrine stops.

[66] Pirie (n 57) 521.

[67] Yet doctrinal scholars do not have a common understanding of what is the method (or methods) of doctrinal scholarship. See Mark Van Hoecke, 'Legal Doctrine' in Mark Van Hoecke (ed), *Methodologies of Legal Research* (Hart Publishing 2011) 1–18.

[68] Cotterrell points out that legal doctrine is about legal expertise which is 'centred on communicable knowledge of legal doctrine (rules, principles, and concepts of law, and specifically legal ways of reasoning with these)', Roger Cotterrell, *Sociological Jurisprudence* (Routledge 2018) 21.

[69] One way of expressing this is to outline the whole field of comparative law as a critique of legal positivism, Alessandro Somma, *Introduzione al diritto comparato*, 3rd edn (Giappichelli 2025) 3–22.

[70] For those who support the textual approach 'the proper object of comparative study is not law in action, but law in books', Ewald (n 39) 703.

[71] Describing legal doctrine as 'currency of law' comes from Emerson Tiller & Frank Cross, 'What Is Legal Doctrine' (2006) 100 *Northwestern University Law Review* 517–34, 517.

[72] Maurice Adams & John Griffiths, 'Against "Comparative Method"' in Maurice Adams & Jacco Bomhoff (eds), *Practice and Theory in Comparative Law* (CUP 2012) 279–301.

This assumption has, in one form or another, been part of comparative law scholarship for more than 100 years. It may not have been on board from the 1900 Paris conference, but it did take shape in various forms during the following century as the idea grew stronger with the passage of time.

The diversification of comparative law with novel methodologies and breakaways from traditional comparative law is more or less building on the assumption that comparative law needs to go further than legal doctrine. In my view, the sense of being always on the move and never stopping is detectable under the surface of comparative law scholarship. The mentality of 'always on the move' explains why comparatists have lamented and keep lamenting the state of their field and why their eyes have always been fixed on a potentially rosy future. To that end, even in the 2020s scholars may speak of the 'maturity' of comparative law as if it would be both desirable and viable if only scholars would get it right.[73]

Looking beyond the limits erected by legal doctrine led to the expansion of comparative law's methodological scope. In this expansion, 'action' was a helpful concept as it departed from textual analysis of formal law. Sociological jurisprudence and especially Pound's rhetorically captivating title made it possible to encapsulate the methodological dogma of twentieth-century comparative law: the move beyond black-letter-law was understood as something that was needed and inevitable. Then again, it is not indisputable that the change from 'action' to 'context' took place because of a similar type of contrarian scholarly urge. Conversely, it looks more like fine-tuning of the self-professed epistemic creed. Arguably, it is not beyond the imagination to maintain that the change of dogma was not really needed in modern comparative law. Instead, perhaps, of a pressing need, comparatists' self-image changed from sociological jurisprudence toward social science and cultural studies and methodological pluralism as the toolbox of methods grew in size. The need to go beyond 'action' is recognised and taken seriously by many modern comparatists; that much is clear. How methodological pluralism is conceptualised by individual comparatists is a different matter altogether.

Is there a lesson to be learned? It could be argued that many comparatists of the 1900s understood law in action to mean roughly what modern comparatists understand as the meaning of 'context'. Of course, there are scholars who see that context means something more than what 'action' means. But this alone does not mean that the claim by comparatists in general of seeing action and context as meaning the same would be wholly redundant.[74] A notable example of such a scholar is Pierre Legrand, who for decades has been speaking for a culturally oriented comparative study of law.[75] It is blatantly clear that - for him - context means something more than merely law in action or a legalistic escape from

[73] See, eg, Luca Siliquini-Cinelli, 'Experience vs Knowledge in Comparative Law' (2021) 16 *International Journal of Law in Context* 443–58, 456.

[74] The comparative jurisprudential take argues that 'what we should be seeking to understand is not law in books nor law in action but law in minds', Ewald (n 39) 704.

[75] See, eg, Pierre Legrand, 'Jameses at Play: A Tractation on the Comparison of Laws' (2017) 65 *AJCL* Issue suppl 1, 1–132 (contrasts 'positivism' and 'culturalism' in favour of the latter).

the cage of legal formalism.[76] However, the general shift towards social sciences has not transformed comparative law into a social science even though it has persuaded comparative law conceptually further away from legal doctrine. What is more, the transformation fits well with the general aspiration of comparative law to be a serious scholarly undertaking.[77] In order to offer an answer to the call of scholarly earnestness, comparatists have assumed a contrarian stance in the face of legal doctrine's commitment to rely on textual analysis of black-letter law. Generations of legal scholars engaged in comparative study of law have in diverse ways pronounced 'no, this is not enough'. This gives rise to the question of what comparative law's identity is today.

[76] 'Socially-generated and shared context of meaning, which renders action intelligible to those involved and delineates the boundaries of relevance and irrelevance within a legal culture' in Pierre Legrand, 'Comparative Legal Studies and the Matter of Authenticity' (2006) 1 *JCL* 365–460, 375.

[77] cf Hyland (n 23) 63.

3

A Question of Identity – A Tool or Something More?

In the previous chapter, it was shown that comparative law scholarship assumed a contrarian stand against the textual approach derived implicitly from formalistic legal doctrine. The vocabulary in which this stand is expressed changed from legal realism to culturalism and appreciation of context in a broad sense. My above analysis was based on the idea that comparative law is an academic field of study, a discipline with its own identity but not a field of law like contract law or constitutional law. However, this view of comparative law has been contested by many. One of the scholarly collisions that has taken place has been between those who see comparison as a tool and those who see it as something considerably more. Despite this issue – tool or something more – having been discussed for decades, it persistently refuses to leave the comparative law stage. It does not merely linger on but re-emerges from time to time.[1] This means that it is of importance and thus may reveal something essential about comparative law. It is only fair to reveal my cards at this stage. I am one of those who see comparative law as something more than a mere tool. However, this does not mean that I would not recognise and appreciate the practical utility of comparative law.

What scholars writing about comparative law mean by *tool* is relatively easy to grasp as a tool is an instrument used for a particular kind of work. Whereas a carpenter's tools, for example, include saws, hammers and knives, a legal scholar may use comparative law as a tool to help them perform the primary functions of judging a case, interpreting law, or drafting legislation. According to this view, comparative law has a secondary function for legal scholarship and, more importantly, a primary function for the practice of law, judging, and legislating. What is meant by 'method' is far less clear. No doubt, 'tool' is easier to grasp as it means broadly the same as – narrowly understood – method.

[1] The collision between comparative law as a method and comparative law as a discipline is essentially one and the same collision. These can be conceived as 'idealist' (discipline) and 'realist' (method) views, see Matthias Reimann, 'Neighbouring Disciplines' in Mauro Bussani & Ugo Mattei (eds), *The Cambridge Companion to Comparative Law* (CUP 2012) 13–34, 15.

From the literature it becomes clear that even though comparative law scholars are frequently using the concept of method in a routine-like manner and even though many of them – this author included – write about methodology, different connotations are assumed by authors. Typically, authors present the different steps of how comparative research should be conducted.[2] In what follows, the concept of method is used in a broad sense, which means that it refers to particular ways in which study steps (research design, data collection and analysis, conclusion) are taken in a predetermined manner.[3] Understood in this way, method means more or less same as modus operandi: it means a particular way of doing something.[4] This is different from the way method is used in so-called exact sciences.[5] Requirements such as testability, replicability, falsifiability, and generalisability are challenging for legal scholarship in general and comparative law makes no exception in that sense.[6]

The flexible way to conceive method stands in comparison with how method is understood in cultural studies and humanities in general. Legal comparatists are not alone in this. In essence, the way in which comparatists tend to use the concept of method is flexible and comes close to what is meant by a rule of thumb. Distinctions between different ways to conceive method are discussed further in chapter ten. The elastic notion of method, as conceived by comparatists, refers to guidelines mostly based on research practice.[7] In essence, it provides simplified advice on how to do something without specifying the required steps in detail.[8] Notwithstanding, there are also more exact ways to define comparative method even though those ways are still a minority view.[9] In any case, this chapter is built on the idea of an elastic or flexible notion of comparative method which encompasses both broad and narrow understandings of it.

[2] See Jaakko Husa, 'Traditional Methods' in Mathias Siems & Po Jen Yap (eds), *The Cambridge Handbook of Comparative Law* (CUP 2024) 15–31, 18–21; cf Mathias Siems, *Comparative Law*, 3rd edn (CUP 2022) ch 2.

[3] For a more detailed discussion, see Jaakko Husa, 'Research Designs of Comparative Law' in Maurice Adams & Dirk Heirbaut (eds), *The Method and Culture of Comparative Law* (Hart Publishing 2014) 53–68.

[4] 'A method is a means of obtaining data – information classified into usable conceptual units – and a means of ordering and measuring data…how this comparison is to be carried out has no standard answer', Esin Örücü, 'Methodologies' in Jan Smits, Jaakko Husa, Catherine Valcke & Madalena Narciso (eds), *Elgar Encyclopedia of Comparative Law* Vol 2 (Edward Elgar 2023) 42–50, 43.

[5] As to what is meant by exact science, see Max Planck, 'The Meaning and Limits of Exact Science' (1949) 110 *Science* 319–27.

[6] For concise discussion on what is meant by science, see Samir Okasha, *Philosophy of Science* (OUP 2002) ch 1.

[7] I have distinguished between *scientia* and *prudentia*, arguing that comparative law is closer to prudentia, Jaakko Husa, *Introduction to Comparative Law*, 2nd edn (Hart Publishing 2023) 65–66.

[8] See, eg, Uwe Kischel, *Comparative Law* (OUP 2019) ch 3; Mathias Siems, *Comparative Law*, 3rd edn (CUP 2022) ch 2; and Husa (n 7) ch 6.

[9] For example this is true when comparatists speak of empirical or quantitative approaches. See, eg, Holger Spamann, 'Large-Sample, Quantitative Research Designs for Comparative Law?' (2009) 57 *AJCL* 797–810.

I. Comparative Law as a Tool

In the following sections, three diverse ways to conceive comparative law are discussed. The three areas are: comparative law as a tool, comparative law as a discipline or an autonomous field, and comparative law as something that exceeds but also contains these two conceptualisations. Even though the comparative approach is open to any field of law it is easy to see where, in two major areas of legal scholarship, the idea of conceiving comparative law as a helping tool comes from. These are international law - public and private - and European law. Of course, these fields are not exhaustive in terms of using comparative law as a tool.[10] This tells us something important about the nature of comparative law. Comparative law is like a Swiss army knife because of its versatility as a tool but this book deals only with some of those tools. However, the three fields mentioned above are areas where the significance of comparative law is recognised primarily as something that has a secondary function, whereas the key importance lies elsewhere. This section identifies the core components of views based on grasping comparative law as a tool, that is, a method in a narrow technical sense related to the formalistic view discussed in the preceding chapter. Moreover, these views are non-national in nature as they cross borders between legal families.[11]

A. Private International Law

To argue that comparative law plays a significant role in private international law (PIL) is certainly not a novel assumption.[12] Regardless, PIL is - like comparative law itself - a field that evades exact definition. For example, Ernst Rabel began his classic book on PIL by explaining how the notions of this field of law differ slightly in American, French, and German doctrine in terms of scope.[13] However, Rabel's choice of book title – *The Conflict of Laws* – explains how he understood the core of PIL as a field, which was the choice of law in a situation where a court case has connections to more than one jurisdiction. In essence, this is about *conflict* of laws. The ambiguity has not disappeared over the years as it is recognised that the notion of PIL is not clear, nor does it enjoy global recognition. Despite this, PIL as a field of law can be understood as covering matters that have to do with choice of law,

[10] One such field that is not discussed here is comparative law at the service of drafting legislation. See Nicola Lupo & Lucia Scaffardi (eds), *Comparative Law in Legislative Drafting* (Eleven 2014).

[11] This is different if one undertakes comparison within a close-knit legal family. 'In the absence of guidance from English authorities it is useful to inquire how other common law jurisdictions have addressed the same problem', Lord Mustill (*R v Kingston* [1995] 2 A 355). For a more detailed discussion, see Thomas Allen & Bruce Anderson, 'The Use of Comparative Law by Common Law Judges' (1994) 23 *Anglo-American Law Review* 435–59. See also Keith Stanton, 'Comparative Law in the House of Lords and Supreme Court' (2013) 42 *Common Law World Review* 269–96 (covers the period 1990–2013).

[12] Diego P Fernándes Arroyo, 'Private International Law and Comparative Law' (2009) 11 *Yearbook of Private International Law* 31–71, 31.

[13] Ernst Rabel, *The Conflict of Laws* (University of Michigan Press 1945) 1–2.

jurisdiction, and recognition of foreign judgments.[14] As a field of law, PIL is about legal relationships between cross-border private parties. This tentative definition suffices for present purposes as I am not making any claims on the substance of law because the emphasis lies elsewhere.

It has commonly been assumed that comparative law and PIL have a close linkage. For instance, Rabel saw the comparative method as holding a special place in private international law. This was because, in his view, courts necessarily come into contact with foreign institutions and this 'operation includes comparative research'.[15] Moreover, Rabel thought that interpreting foreign rules was 'necessarily of a comparative nature' and for that reason he argued that the role of comparison had always been recognised by 'thoughtful scholars'.[16] Of course, Rabel knew what he was talking about. The issue of legal comparison between laws is indeed difficult to avoid when the court needs to apply foreign law. In this basic sense, comparative law is understood as the bread and butter of PIL. Accordingly, it may seem only natural to regard private international law and comparative law as complementary simply because both are interested in different legal systems.[17] In essence, when a judge needs to choose the applicable law the 'choice is one made on the basis of comparative law' as Jürgen Basedow puts it.[18] Another scholar points out that private international law and comparative law are intricately connected in their objects and in their application. The same scholar also laments the fact that comparatists and PIL experts hardly pay attention to each other.[19] The unsatisfactory state of the use of comparative methodology in private international law has been recognised by others, too.[20] Even though it is not perhaps crystal clear how these fields are connected, nonetheless they are connected, at least that much is clear.[21]

Regardless of the unavoidable connection, certain key differences exist. First, comparative law is not a field of law but a field of legal scholarship, whereas PIL is both. Comparative law necessarily observes law from the outside whereas PIL's epistemic view is bound to its normative framework, which requires commitment to an internal view on law.[22] This difference has an impact on the nature of the two fields. Second, modern comparative law embraces pluralism but does

[14] Gisela Rühl, 'Private international law, foundations' in Jürgen Basedow, Giesela Rühl, Franco Ferrari & Pedro de Miguel Asensio (eds), *Encyclopedia of International Law* (Edward Elgar 2017) 1380–90.

[15] Rabel (n 13) 50.

[16] ibid 58.

[17] Horatia Muir Watt, 'Private International Law' in Smits et al (n 4) Vol 3 226–36, 226.

[18] Jürgen Basedow, 'Private international law, methods of' in Basedow et al (n 14) 1401–7, 1402.

[19] Ralf Michaels, 'Comparative law and private international law' in Basedow et al (n 14) 417–25, 424. See also Giesela Rühl, 'Who's Afraid of Comparative Law?' (2017) 25 *European Review of Private Law* 485–521, 489–90.

[20] See, eg, Arroyo (n 12) 33.

[21] For example, in continental European universities, it is still common to have a chair of private international and comparative law with the expectation that a suitable candidate would possess competence in both areas. I have been critical about putting private international and comparative law together, see Jaakko Husa, *Interdisciplinary Comparative Law* (Edward Elgar 2023) 54–56.

[22] It can also be noted that finding out about the content and applying foreign law does not as such require direct comparison; nevertheless, comparison is needed indirectly when foreign law and *lex fori* are contrasted. Michael Bogdan, *Komparativ rättskunskap*, 2nd edn (Norstedts 2003) 34–35.

not seek to resolve conflicts between legal systems as its focus lies elsewhere. Simply, modern comparative law seeks to combine external and internal views on law but without attachment to normative assumptions. As will be explained below, this issue is rather similar to that of public international law. Third, PIL as a field of law is a result-driven creature as it seeks to resolve judicial issues arising from conflicts of laws and choice of law. From there it follows that comparative law is necessarily a tool of PIL.[23] From the point of view of PIL, there is nothing wrong with this view as comparative law helps to resolve problems between conflicting laws.

Of course, the whole field of private international law has a similar kind of character; it is supposed to deal with resolving legal issues. Now, it can be a tool that some use very skilfully and others more routinely. Nevertheless, in the eyes of PIL, comparative law is by and large an instrument that serves the purposes of private international law. The interest of knowledge as between a comparatist and a judge is not the same despite the partial overlap.[24] A judge needs to know for the purposes of judging whereas a scholar wants to know for the purposes of gaining knowledge. Whereas a domestic judge is bound by the principle of territoriality (laws normally apply within a state), a comparatist is not bound by territoriality even though they need to be aware of formal law's territoriality.

A deeper issue is also at stake here as the fundamental nature of modern comparative law and essentials of private international law are built on different epistemic bases. Patrick Glenn pointed out that conflict of laws - which he saw as the heart of private international law - is fundamentally based on the idea of conflict between laws. In practice, this means that PIL forces foreign law into a procrustean bed as border-crossing activities are conceived in terms of conflict which, in turn, triggers a choice-of-law situation.[25] For Glenn, a national legal system is 'a kind of large, dumb animal which displaces all other legal animals within its territory, unless it leaves space for them because of their utility'.[26] In this sense, comparative law is a less conflictual form of legal knowledge as it seeks to understand laws but not to choose between them.

B. Public International Law, Human Rights

Public and private international law are both termed international but significant differences distinguish one from the other. In a nutshell, public international law governs the relationship between subjects of international law, such as states and

[23] See for a more detailed discussion on this, Husa (n 21) 206–13.

[24] Interest in knowledge refers to the idea according to which knowledge acquisition is guided by underlying interests. See Jürgen Habermas, 'Knowledge and Interests' in Gary Gutting (ed), *Continental Philosophy of Science* (Blackwell 2005) 310–21.

[25] H Patrick Glenn, 'Com-paring' in Esin Örücü & Andrew Harding (eds), *Comparative Law: A Handbook* (Hart Publishing 2007) 91–108, 97.

[26] H Patrick Glenn, 'Transnational Common Laws' (2005) *Fordham International Law Journal* 457–71, 460.

international organisations like the United Nations, whereas private international law addresses the private-law rights of natural or legal persons.[27] Whereas it is difficult to pinpoint the sources of PIL, it is easier to see that the sources of international law are outlined in Article 38 of the Statute of the International Court of Justice. These cover sources such as international custom, treaties, general principles of law, and judicial decisions.[28] Despite connections between public international law and comparative law they have been regarded as distinct fields – although this view may be less convincing than previously thought in the light of recent scholarly efforts.[29] In any case, we can note the clear similarities between cosmopolitan thinking and both private and public international law even though we may have lost awareness of this idea.[30]

What is clear is that public international law – as both a field of law and a form of scholarship – is so broad an area of law that it would not make sense to discuss it in detail. For this reason, what follows focuses on the relationship between comparative law and human rights as human rights is an important subfield of public international law that entails comparison.[31] Recently, a growing literature has been published in so-called comparative international law. This form of scholarship seeks to fuse international law's substance with comparative law methodologies.[32] Because comparative international law seeks to merge, in part, public international law and comparative law, it does not consider comparative law merely as a tool because its take is closer to modern comparative law. The vision of comparative law as a tool flows from elsewhere. In terms of international human rights law, perhaps the best institutional example is the European Court of Human Rights (ECtHR). Two further points can be made here. First, the ECtHR offers a good illustration as it can be regarded as among the world's most influential judicial institutions.[33] Second, the way the Court understands comparative law

[27] Despite their differences there is also overlap. See, eg, Harold Maier, 'Extraterritorial Jurisdiction at a Crossroads' (1982) 76 *AJIL* 280–320; Ralf Michaels, 'Public and Private International Law' (2008) 4 *Journal of Private International Law* 121–38; and Alex Mills, 'Connecting Public and Private International Law' in Verónica Ruiz Abou-Nigm, Kasey McCall-Smith, Duncan French (eds), *Linkages and Boundaries in Private and Public International Law* (Hart Publishing 2018) 13–32.

[28] See, eg, James Crawford, 'The sources of international law' in *Brownlie's Principles of Public International Law*, 9th edn (OUP 2019) 18–44.

[29] Mathias Forteau, 'Comparative International Law Within, Not Against, International Law' (2015) 109 *AJIL* 498–513.

[30] Martti Koskenniemi and Ville Kari, 'A More Elevated Patriotism' in Heikki Pihlajamäki, Markus Dubber, Mark Godfrey (eds), *The Oxford Handbook of European Legal History* (OUP 2018) 974–95.

[31] 'International human rights today comprise a distinct branch of international law, known variously as the international law of human rights or international human rights law', Thomas Buergenthal, 'Human Rights' in *Max Planck Encyclopedia of Public International Law* (2007) opil.ouplaw.com/display/10.1093/law:epil/9780199231690/law-9780199231690-e810.

[32] See Anthea Roberts, 'Comparative International Law?' (2011) 60 *ICLQ* 57–93. I discuss comparative international law in Husa (n 21) 178–82.

[33] 'The European Convention on Human Rights is the most effective human rights regime in the world', Helen Keller & Alec Stone Sweet, 'The Reception of the ECHR in National Legal Orders' in Helen Keller & Alec Stone Sweet (eds), *A Europe of Rights: The Impact of the ECHR on National Legal Systems* (OUP 2008) 3–28, 3.

well reflects the judiciary-focused view that conceives comparative law as a tool.[34] In short, it seems abundantly clear even at the outset that the Court's use of the comparative approach can be described as simplified.[35]

Typically, the ECtHR's narrow interest in comparative law arises from a need to discover if a convergence of legal views can be achieved in a situation where it uses so-called consensus interpretation.[36] This takes place against the backdrop of conceiving the Human Rights Convention as a living instrument. The idea is simply to see if a superficial comparative law survey would show that a sufficiently clear European consensus supports a new interpretation or filling a gap. Focus is on law in the formal sense. This kind of comparative survey is based on materials from comparative studies (produced by a party), the Superior Courts Network, or by the Court's Registry, international treaties, reports produced by international organisations, and EU law.[37] What this version of comparative law looks like is easy to answer: in essence it looks like a tick-the-box exercise that takes place only in special situations.[38]

There has been debate on the relationship between human rights interpretation and use of comparative methods. To generalise a great deal, the debate takes two major directions. First are judicially driven ideas underlining the role of comparative law as a tool. Second are academically driven ideas that conceive of comparative law as something more than a mere tool.[39] The movement – coined as human rights comparativism – seems, more or less, to share similar views of scholarly comparative law. Some comparatists have also defended comparative law as narrowly understood, in essence arguing that comparative law should be used by real-life lawyers.[40] This seems to suggest that scholarly comparative law should not drift too far away from lawyers' practical needs. No doubt, from the viewpoint of a practitioner or a judge, this makes sense.

Much of human rights comparativism seems captivated by the idea that comparative law needs to be understood narrowly, as a tool. In this it is, of course, not alone because this seems to be by and large a view shared among most public international law lawyers in general. This view is not accidental but connected to international law as a normative creature, that is, a field of law. There is a specific legal theoretical

[34] See, eg, Mónika Ambrus, 'Comparative Law Method in the Jurisprudence of the European Court of Human Rights in the Light of the Rule of Law' (2009) 2 *Erasmus Law Review* 353–71; Jaakko Husa, 'Judicial impartiality, decorative comparative law and the Human Rights Court' (2020) 27 *Maastricht Journal of European and Comparative Law* 387–96.

[35] See Filippo Viglione, 'Comparative Law at the European Court of Human Rights' in Matteo Fornasier & Maria Gabriella Stanzione (eds), *The European Convention on Human Rights and Its Impact on National Private Law* (Intersentia 2023) 285–304.

[36] For a concise discussion on courts and comparative law, see Mads Andenas, Duncan Fairgrieve & Francesco Quarta, 'Why and How Courts Use Comparative Law' in Luca Siliquini-Cinelli, Davide Gianti & Mauro Balestrieri (eds), *The Grand Strategy of Comparative Law* (Routledge 2024) 67–85.

[37] Janneke Gerards, 'European Court of Human Rights' in Smits et al Vol 2 (57–66) 64.

[38] See also Maija Dahlberg, '"The lack of such a common approach": comparative argumentation by the European Court of Human Rights' (2012–13) 23 *The Finnish yearbook of international law* 73–111.

[39] See Christopher McCrudden, 'Judicial Comparativism and Human Rights' in Esin Örücu & David Nelken (eds), *Comparative Law: A Handbook* (Hart Publishing 2007) 371–97, 372.

[40] See, eg, Basil Markesinis & Jörg Fedtke, *Engaging with Foreign Law* (Hart Publishing 2009).

idea that virtually compels the public international law view to regard comparative law in a restricted manner. From there it follows that international law scholars may worry about unnecessarily deep comparative law. One scholar expresses the worry of going too far beyond law and taking socio-political factors into account.[41] This would, according to this take, risk the very basis of international law as a body of legal rules. Even if one would support a broad flexible view of comparative law, this risk looks real if one takes the normative nature of public international law seriously.

Normativity – law as a binding set of rules – is the factor that drives public international law actors and scholars to conceive comparative law primarily as a tool. For international law as a field of law this view is legitimate. However, against the backdrop of modern comparative law scholarship the situation looks problematic. Nevertheless, this issue extends beyond international law and human rights, as indeed we can see in the case of European law.

C. European Law

The notion of European law refers here to EU law consisting of the founding Treaties and legal acts that European institutions adopt, which enables the EU to legally exercise its powers. The founding treaties are coined as primary legislation, whereas the other part – consisting of regulations, directives, decisions, recommendations and opinions – is called secondary legislation. However, in EU law circles it is typical to hold that EU law actually consists of all the rules of the EU legal order so that the Charter of Fundamental Rights and the general principles established by the Court of Justice of the European Union (ECJ) are considered as an elemental part of EU law.[42] A great deal of literature is available on comparative law and EU law, which would be futile to discuss at length here.[43] Instead, it is possible to focus on an article by Koen Lenaerts and Kathleen Gutman that discusses comparative method and the European Court of Justice.[44] The fact that at the time the paper was published Lenaerts was the president and Gutman legal secretary of the ECJ lends a certain gravitas to their take.

Lenaerts and Gutman make it clear that, when it comes to comparative law, the Court is mostly interested in the national norms of the Member States as their laws are internal to the EU legal order. This is different from how supreme courts function in other places but roughly similar to the approach of the ECtHR. Lenaerts and

[41] Alexander Orakhelashvili, 'The relevance of theory and history – the essence and origins of international law' in Alexander Orakhelashvili (ed), *Research Handbook on the Theory and History of International Law* (Edward Elgar 2013) 2–18, 4.

[42] This is how the EU itself defines the scope of EU law. eur-lex.europa.eu/EN/legal-content/glossary/eu-law.html.

[43] See, eg, Juha Raitio, 'European Union Law and Comparative Law' in Smits et al (n 4) Vol 2, 78–85 and Sir Francis Jacobs, 'Comparative Law and European Union Law' in Mathias Reimann & Reinhard Zimmermann (eds), *The Oxford Handbook of Comparative Law*, 2nd edn (OUP 2019) 524–66.

[44] Koen Lenaerts & Kathleen Gutman, 'The Comparative Law Method and the European Court of Justice' (2016) 64 *AJCL* 841–64.

Gutman make it clear that the importance of comparative method should not be underestimated. However, their view of method has a catch. What they mean by comparative method is 'the Union courts looking to the laws of the member states (or other jurisdictions as the case may be).'[45] Looking to the laws undoubtedly makes perfect sense for the purposes of judging. However, it leaves the context of law outside its scope as it also stays silent about the rich scholarly literature on comparative law.

Whereas in the case of international law the problem is conflicting legal orders, the ECJ, in turn, needs comparative law when an EU norm fails to offer a solution to the legal problem at hand. Looking at the laws of the Member States may show a common solution or point in a certain direction. It is also possible that comparative law shows divergences among the Member State laws, which may open the possibility for the Court to establish an autonomous interpretation of EU law.[46] In this case, goal-oriented comparative law reveals an opening for the Court to craft its own interpretation more freely.[47] Accordingly, Lenaerts and Gutman express a highly specific view of comparative law and its method: 'the comparative law method is an essential tool of the European Court of Justice that helps to make EU law operational in the legal orders of the member states.'[48] Crucially, they use the notion of 'tool' when they speak of comparative method. This choice of word is clearly not accidental.

Quite understandably, for the ECJ comparative law is not about law in action or the context of law but, rather, about judicial decision-making. As one would expect, the ECJ judges are not scholars who enjoy academic freedom.[49] Consequently, comparative law is conceived differently from the scholarly views that conceive comparative law more extensively and seek to underline its role as something that goes beyond a tool.[50] This view comes close to such fields as legal history and legal theory as it simultaneously distances itself from the view that depicts comparative law merely as an instrument.

II. More than a Tool

The above means-to-an-end types of visions of comparative law are seldom openly in conflict with more demanding takes on comparative law. These two conceptions exist simultaneously but because they vacate different corners of

[45] ibid 844.

[46] ibid 851.

[47] See for more detailed analysis, Michele Graziadei, 'The European Court of Justice at Work' (2020) 13 *Journal of Civil Law Studies* 1–32 (speaks for serious comparative study but also sees comparison as a tool).

[48] ibid 864.

[49] However, many judges and advocates general may have a background in legal academia; but as members of the court they are in the capacity of deciding cases. See Arjen Boin and Susanne Schmidth, 'The European Court of Justice' in Arjen Boin, Lauren Fahy & Paul 't Hart (eds), *Guardians of Public Value* (Palgrave Macmillan 2020) doi.org/10.1007/978-3-030-51701-4_6.

[50] This is not only about comparative law as academic lawyers and judges perform their functions quite differently altogether. See Richard Posner, 'The Role of the Judge in the Twenty-First Century' (2006) 86 *Boston University Law Review* 1049–68, 1054.

law and legal academia – practice oriented and theory oriented – they do not collide directly. As if pragmatist lawyers and theoreticians would not want to argue publicly and place comparative law (whatever one means by it) in a bad light. The collision between them may indeed be subtle; but this does not mean that it would not exist. The intellectual spirit or the driving force that animates these two is hidden under the surface and is thus hard to detect. On the surface, they seem to coexist quite happily. This gives the impression of active avoidance. Regardless, it is impossible not to detect the collision as each of these views paints quite different images of comparative law. No doubt the collision between these views is obvious to anyone who reads literature on comparative law scholarship and literature on international law or European law. The fear of too 'deep' comparative law felt by those who see comparative law as a tool clashes with the view of comparatists who, in turn, seek to 'deepen' comparative study of law. One such example can be found in a book chapter by Mark Van Hoecke.[51] It illustrates what 'more than a tool' may mean in the context of modern comparative law without distancing from the study of law as a part of the normative legal framework.

Van Hoecke addresses key epistemological and methodological issues on the basis of interpretation of contracts in English, French, and German law. No doubt, the substance is a classical theme in traditionally focused doctrinal Western private law comparison. Nevertheless, with Van Hoecke there is more to it than sticking to narrow doctrinalism.

He compares terminology, structure of law and textbooks on interpretation of contracts, and the underlying key conceptions of interpretation and contract. He then goes on to analyse Will Theory, the objective meaning of the text, and legitimate expectations. Against the backdrop of his analysis, he draws a conclusion concerning the methodology of comparative law: 'comparative law research may only be carried out meaningfully if it also includes the deeper level of underlying theories and conceptions'.[52] This goes against the ideas nurtured in the field of law-related views of comparative law. In a more practical sense, this means that the comparatist has to investigate not only law in a formal sense but also consider factors such as historical analyses, sociological studies, and political science. This, however, does not mean that the comparatist would not need to know about legal doctrine and court judgments.[53] It is more about what factors need to be considered *other than* law as narrowly understood. It seems clear that even though Van Hoecke does not use the notion of context while discussing methodology, what he means by 'deep level' incorporates context. Without a shadow of doubt, deep level comparative law means much more than grasping comparative law merely as a tool. Van Hoecke's deep level comparative law comes,

[51] Mark Van Hoecke, 'Deep Level Comparative Law' in Mark Van Hoecke (ed), *Epistemology and Methodology of Comparative Law* (Hart Publishing 2004) 165–95.
[52] ibid 191.
[53] ibid 191–92.

in my reading, close to what Catherine Valcke means by studying 'legal style'.[54] The idea is to respect law's normativity but at the same time place it in a broader context and beyond formalism.

It seems clear that the intellectual motivation is to go beyond the idea of comparison as a tool; to look deeper into law. Where does the need for 'depth' come from? The idea of studying law deeply is typical of those who identify themselves as comparatists, that is, specialists in comparative law. For scholars in the fields of international law and European law, the question of identity is different as they are bound to the epistemic and normative assumptions of their respective fields of law. It is easy to agree with Esin Örücü, who noticed that Van Hoecke's idea emerged from critique of mainstream's technical and legalistic view of law as the aim was to apply a more thorough approach. More generally, says Örücü, for twenty-first century comparative law scholarship '[d]epth is the crucial point of departure'.[55] This tells modern comparative law apart from the view that considers comparative law as a tool that serves primarily practical purposes. However, there are limits to how far this conclusion can be stretched. Importantly, modern comparative law does not renounce practical purposes, but it does venture beyond the borders of law as narrowly understood. This, in turn, tells it apart from the doctrinally focused goal-driven conception.

What explains the contrast between the two understandings is not that clear. It seems that the question of scholarly identity is of importance here. Comparative law specialists had, through the 1900s, a somewhat ambivalent relationship with the legal academy, as indeed Annelise Riles has pointed out. Sometimes, comparatists underlined their alienation from other legal scholars whereas at other times they stressed the importance of being a part of the mainstream legal academy.[56] Notwithstanding, comparative law scholars have been quick to remark that comparative law *also* has important practical value. Frankly, much of the scholarship has been about *justifying* the existence of comparative law to other lawyers and legal scholars.[57]

One could say that, throughout much of its intellectual history, comparative law has sat on the fence without really knowing on which side to fall: doctrine or theory, practice or academia. One of the key ideas in underlining the difference between comparatists and other legal scholars seems to be the idea of developing comparative law into a true science or at least a distinct or even autonomous field of knowledge within the legal academy. This is, I believe, an important observation. It can be argued that the objectives of comparative law started to change during the 1990s and one – but surely not the only one – of the objectives is scientific as to

[54] Catherine Valcke, 'Comparing Legal Styles' (2019) 15 *International Journal of Law in Context* 274–96 (suggests comparing styles of legal reasoning).

[55] Esin Örücü, 'Something Old, Something New in Comparative Law' (2015) 6 *Journal of International and Comparative Law* 323–36, 332.

[56] Annelise Riles, 'Introduction' in Annelise Riles (ed), *Rethinking the Masters of Comparative Law* (Hart Publishing 2001) 1–18, 6–9.

[57] This is not surprising as comparative law's contact to direct practical needs is more distant that that of legal doctrine.

its nature because it stresses the importance of gaining new knowledge, not only helping legal practice, judging, or policy goals.[58] The ambitious urge of post-1970s comparative law has been to gain academic gravitas and thus escape from under the shadow of legal doctrine and scholarly (normative) views tacitly assumed in fields of law. At the same time, it has been important to justify the existence of the field to other lawyers and legal scholars. Justifying has not been a great success but – as the case of Italy shows – comparative law may gain an important position in legal academia.[59]

However, it is prudent to proceed with caution here. Van Hoecke's vision in the above-mentioned paper is modern and does not clearly build on the idea of comparative law as a science or even as a distinct discipline. Nevertheless, it does not fall far from the intellectual endeavours – even as far back as the 1960s and 70s – of those who have sought to conceive comparative law as a scientific field worthy of being a legal discipline in itself. A prime example of the discipline stressing thinking is Léontin-Jean Constantinesco, who wrote a voluminous three-part treatise on comparative law which was published in the 1970s and early 1980s. His *Traité de Droit Comparé* reflects a kind of culmination point of legal comparativism seeking to be conceived as a fully developed science of comparative law.[60] In turn, Konrad Zweigert and Hein Kötz were not so heavily into 'science' except in the smaller theoretical part of their thick volume.[61] In essence, Constantinesco viewed comparative law as a science, not only as a method. This, more than anything else, tells us that his view differs from the narrow idea of comparative law as merely a tool or method. Along similar lines, the authoritative Italian scholar Rodolfo Sacco argued that the first and essential 'aim of comparative law as a science is better knowledge of legal rules and institutions.'[62] Sacco's choice of words ('as a science') is hardly a coincidence as it reflects his overall view of comparative law in general.[63]

It should go without saying that Constantinesco's view was not developed in a vacuum.[64] The general background can be found in mid-1900s thinking among comparative law specialists. One of the key facets of that thinking was to place more focus on methodology. The attempt to build comparative law into a true science (a distinct scholarly field) gained a foothold in French scholarship, whereas English scholarship seems to have been more inclined to regard comparative law

[58] See David J Gerber, 'System Dynamics: Toward a Language of Comparative Law' (1998) 46 *AJCL* 719–37, 724–6.

[59] Bianca Tedeschi, 'Italian Comparative' (2024) 18 *FIU Law Review* 797–820 ('In Italy, comparative law is not, today, a subject for few dreamers…it reaches a wide audience and is now mainstream', ibid 820).

[60] Léontin-Jean Constantinesco, *Traité de Droit Comparé*. Tome I. *Introduction au Droit Comparé* (Librairie Générale de Droit et de Jurisprudence 1973), Tome II. *La Méthode Comparative* (Librairie Générale de Droit et de Jurisprudence 1974), Tome III. *La Science des Droits Comparés* (Economica 1983).

[61] See Konrad Zweigert & Hein Kötz, *An Introduction to Comparative Law*, 3rd edn (OUP 1998) chs 1–3 (1–47).

[62] Rodolfo Sacco, 'Legal Formants' (1991) 39 *AJCL* 1–34, 5.

[63] See for more detailed discussion Michele Graziadei, 'Rodolfo Sacco's Theoretical Contribution to Comparative Law' (2024) 37 *International Journal for the Semiotics of Law* 1471–84.

[64] Simply looking at the footnotes of the three volumes makes this evident.

mainly as a method.[65] René David distinguished two ways of conceiving comparative law: as a method and as true science, an autonomic field of legal knowledge.[66] Nevertheless, underlining the importance of methodology and the attempt to build a precise method is not that far off from envisaging comparative law as a distinct field, a true science.[67] Crucially, both of these ideas are in conflict with the view according to which comparative law is merely a tool. In essence, both French and English conceptions paint comparative law as something more, whether in the form of more precise methodology or comparative law conceived as an autonomous discipline ('*discipline autonome*'). I am not sure that these overlapping dimensions are possible to tell apart as the intention looks rather alike: to elevate the comparative study of law in one way or another.

Curiously, though, Constantinesco built his extensive discussion of comparative law on the very question which asks whether comparative law is merely a method or a discipline in itself.[68] As mentioned above, the same division was also assumed by David. Volume III of Constantinesco's *Traité* reveals his take that relies on a comprehension of comparative law that takes both method and discipline visions into account in the form of 'science of comparative laws' ('*la science des droits comparés*'). The vision of comparative law as a science is, as already noted, common in French scholarship, whereas in English-speaking literature it is less common.[69] Indeed, the idea of comparative law as an autonomous field of legal knowledge has been explicitly refuted by those who underline its tool-like character.[70] Scholars with theoretical sensitivity have proposed more demanding ideas; for instance, Geoffrey Samuel, who suggested in the late 1990s that comparative law should 'consolidate itself as an independent subject with its own internal structure'.[71] The stimulus behind this sort of thinking, I suspect, is a desire to stop sitting on the fence and to jump down on the legal side of the fence – or tear down the fence – because even 'teaching comparative law as an autonomous subject perpetuates its image as an area separate from the rest of law.'[72] In a weaker form, this argument is presented to express suspicion of

[65] cf Balázs Fekete, *Paradigms in Modern European Comparative Law* (Hart Publishing 2021) 94–96.
[66] René David, *Les grands systémes de droit contemporains* (Dalloz 1982) 13.
[67] Kahn-Freund's inaugural lecture for the Oxford Chair of Comparative Law in 1965 is an example of this. For him, comparative law was a method, not a topic. Yet the point of the lecture was to discuss comparative law as a distinct discipline. Otto Kahn-Freund, 'Comparative Law as an Academic Subject' (1966) 82 *Law Quarterly Review* 40–61.
[68] See, eg, Constantinesco (n 60) 164.
[69] It is possible to trace this idea all the way to the Paris 1900 conference. See Édouard Lambert, 'Conception générale, définition, méthode et histoire du droit comparé' in Congrès International de Droit Comparé, tenu à Paris du 31 juillet au 4 août 1900. Procès-verbaux des séances et documents, vol I (Librairie Générale de droit et de Jurisprudence 1905) 26–61 (speaks of '*conception exclusivement scientifique du droit comparé*', ie 'exclusively scientific conception of comparative law').
[70] For example there has been a call to abolish comparative law as an autonomous subject in teaching of law. See Mathias Reimann, 'The End of Comparative Law as an Autonomous Subject' (1996) 11 *Tulane European and Civil Law Forum* 50–72.
[71] Geoffrey Samuel, 'Comparative Law and Jurisprudence' (1998) 47 *ICLQ* 817–36, 817.
[72] ibid 70.

making comparative law overly complex and sometimes even practically impossible because of the unavoidable complexity involved.[73]

Of course, developing comparative law as a distinct field or something that is extremely difficult and downright exclusive comes at a price. One of the ramifications may be that comparative law smacks of elitism in the eyes of practising lawyers and doctrinal legal scholars. For some, the urge to develop comparative law has meant an attempt to rebuild it as comparative legal studies by steering its focus away from the limiting doctrinal concept of law.[74] This would transform comparative law into comparative legal studies, which in turn would mean, of course, something more than changing only the name. This change, I suspect, would not mean escape from the epistemic prison of 'law' and, by extension, evasion of the boundaries set by 'legal science'.

A tentative answer to the problem of sitting on the fence has been provided by recent scholarship. This abandons binary opposition between the 'only-a-tool v more-than-a-tool' vision in comparative law. This kind of – though certainly not monolithic – way of thinking seems to argue that sitting on the fence is not really a problem, even though some balancing is needed. The binary setting appears to be melting away as novel flexible ways to think about comparative law and its identity have increasingly gained a foothold. Accordingly, some of the earlier contrarianism may be dwindling.

III. Walking a Tightrope – Purpose is Decisive

As to the need for balancing, it seems that comparative law is walking a tightrope concerning its identity. It appears to be in a situation that involves making a decision between two colliding plans of action. Either choice would be contrarian in relation to the other. As a kind of solution to this dilemma, modern comparative law scholarship has moved the focus away from the identity question. This, in turn, builds on an attempt to abandon the colliding binary setting between 'tool' and 'something more than a tool'. For someone who supports the merely-a-tool or more-than-a-tool vision, the more recent flexibility may seem lax or even a betrayal of the old ideals, yet it is what contemporary comparative law scholarship – at least indirectly – suggests: stop pondering whether comparative law is a distinct discipline or not.[75]

Binary views are relatively easy to grasp as they are built upon colliding foundations regarding different things as crucial. Flexible views are more challenging to pinpoint as they do not position themselves in a contrarian setting that involves

[73] See Mathias Siems, 'The End of Comparative Law' (2008) 2 *JCL* 133–50.

[74] See, eg, Michael Palmer, 'For Comparative Legal Studies' in Jaakko Husa (ed), *A Research Agenda for Comparative Law* (Edward Elgar 2024) 129–55.

[75] Discussion around the discipline or not an issue: see, eg, Samuel (n 71); and James Gordley, 'Is Comparative Law a Distinct Discipline?' (1998) 46 *AJCL* 607–15 (underlines the need for comparative lawyers to give other lawyers 'something they can use', ie the idea of being distinct is not encouraged).

a choice between two opposite views. Then again, it is important to grasp that flexible views are in dispute with the binary framing of the issue. This means relinquishing binary settings: practical vs theoretical or law vs legal studies. Against this background, it comes as a no surprise that even those who tend to underline the practical uses hold that comparative law is no longer an impractical academic discipline.[76] This seems to imply that distinctly scholarly comparative law would be impractical and thus useless for legal professionals. Without discussing this issue further, I think that it is safe to say that this seems like a simplification of a more subtle issue. I assume that the relationship between practice and theory is more nuanced than that.[77] Binarity, however, is not inherently a given but more likely constructed.

The focal point in all this is how comparative law is conceptualised. In other words, what kind of a conception one holds of comparative law as a result of forming an idea in one's mind. William Twining rightly says that confusion about this question has been rife. He rejects the binary setting and frames comparative law differently: 'In my view it is best conceived as an activity (like theorising) which takes many forms and has a wide potential application'.[78] From this kind of position follows a flexible or pluralist conception of comparative law or, as Twining puts it: 'Much of this broad area not only involves different lenses and audiences, but also difference of context, objectives, and methods'.[79] Now, surely it would be an exaggeration to claim that all present comparative law scholarship would be based on flexibility or pluralism. Clearly this is not the case, nor indeed is that argued here. Regardless, it is possible to argue that the latest layer of scholarship indicates that the notion of comparative law is understood increasingly in its widest sense, defusing previous binary constellations.

So, where are we with the collision between the notions of 'tool' and 'something more'? Answering this requires taking into account how comparative law scholarship has changed or is changing. What seems clear is that the previous certainties are no longer taken for granted. More importantly, the idea of one predominant method or identity for comparative study of law has – more or less – been abandoned.[80] These changes have not taken place merely on the basis of academic shift, but they reflect other developments such as globalisation and the decline of the Westphalian international law framework (see chapter twelve).[81] As a result, comparative law has grown in recent years because we live in a more complex and

[76] Andenas, Fairgrieve and Quarta (n 36) 79.

[77] See, eg, Luca Siliquini-Cinelli, 'Experience vs. Knowledge' (2020) 16 *International Journal of Law in Context* 443–58.

[78] Alexander Vereschagin, 'An Interview with William Twining' (2021) 16 *JCL* 445–57, 451.

[79] ibid 452.

[80] cf Mark Van Hoecke, 'Is There Now a Comparative Legal Scholarship' (2017) 12 *JCL* 271–80.

[81] Criticism of Westphalian ideas is an important part of so-called TWAIL scholarship. See, eg, James Thuo Gathii, 'The Agenda of Third World Approaches to International Law (TWAIL)' in Jeffrey Dunoff & Mark Pollack (eds), *International Legal Theory* (CUP 2022) 153–73.

interconnected world than before.[82] All this has given rise to comparative law's expanded areas of interest. From there, it follows that comparative law does not need to find the audience for which it was searching in the early 1990s.[83] It seems only natural that pluralist comparative law has audiences, not just one audience. A comparatist can speak in terms of their field of law: to legislators, to judges, to the general public, to legal theorists, to legal historians, to socio-legal scholars alongside speaking to the community of fellow comparatists. Moreover, it seems only natural that one speaks differently to different audiences.

Crucially, the transformations have shaped the manner in which comparative law is conceived today. Innovative ideas and novel approaches are discussed. Along similar lines, it seems that the very identity of comparative law is becoming altered. A changed intellectual atmosphere has brought about a way of thinking that rejects binary settings. In short, a growing portion of modern scholarly literature on comparative law no longer seeks to identify or defend a particular method or way of thinking. Instead, the *purpose of research* is underlined as a key factor when one chooses how to study law comparatively.[84] However, purposefulness is both a boon and a bane. A boon because it allows much freedom in choice of subjects and methods. A bane because expansion of the field means lost (alleged) coherence as an academic discipline.[85] It may be that Twining has a point when he argues that – instead of being a marginal subject for a small number of specialists – comparative law 'is increasingly more like a way of life'.[86] As a way of life, comparative law does not provide exact tools but a general mindset for seeking meaning in the study of law and being a legal scholar in today's world.

Twenty years ago, Örücü predicted that comparative law would reach its maturity during the current century.[87] I doubt Örücü's sanguine prediction, which seems unrealistically optimistic and unlikely as the field has become so pluralist and flexible that being a contrarian and adding new layers upon the old ones has become increasingly difficult. Assuming a contrarian view presupposes that there is something to disagree with. Today there are so many views and ideas about comparative law that contrarian legal scholars have to pick their fights more selectively than was the case during the previous century. Disagreeing with the mainstream is difficult unless we wish to fight a straw man of our own making. However, if contrarianism forms part of the way of life of the comparatist, then future disagreements will also be unavoidable. Perhaps in the absence of an indisputable mainstream, the comparatist may have to invent one if they choose to engage in contrarian debate.

[82] See, eg, Michele Graziadei, 'What Does Globalisation Mean for the Comparative Study of Law?' (2021) 16 *JCL* 511–36, 535.

[83] Basil Markesinis, 'Comparative Law – A Subject in Search of an Audience' (1990) 51 *MLR* 1–21.

[84] See, eg, Geoffrey Samuel, *An Introduction to Comparative Law Theory and Method* (Hart Publishing 2014); Uwe Kischel, *Comparative Law* (OUP 2019); Siems (n 8) and Husa (n 7).

[85] cf Andenas, Fairgrieve & Quarta (n 36) 67–68.

[86] William Twining, *Globalisation and Legal Scholarship* (Wolf 2009) 31.

[87] Esin Örücü, *The Enigma of Comparative Law* (Brill 2004) 7–8.

4

Private Law v Public Law and Beyond

The two previous chapters discussed where to place the focus of comparative law research and how to identify comparative law as a form of study of law. Discussion on the focus of comparative law concerned epistemological and methodological collisions. In turn, discussion on the identity of comparative law was about the collision between a goal-oriented practical view and a scholarly-oriented disciplinary view. However, a further point of collision is connected to both focus and identity issues. This collision concerns the substantive area of comparative law. In other words, what areas of law are considered suitable – or perhaps even natural – to be studied comparatively and what areas are deemed less suitable or less natural subjects. A longstanding but often merely implied dispute – especially in the twentieth century – was powered by comparative law's close connection to private law, which left public law (and other areas of law) in a minor role. It is easy to see that in the previous century the focus of comparative law research was firmly on private (civil) law.[1] However, in the twenty-first century of today the focus has been in a state of flux as the volume of comparative studies has grown and its scope has expanded.[2]

[1] Legal systems that belong to the civil law legal family/culture tend to distinguish between civil law and private law because the first mentioned does not necessarily include commercial law. Here the concepts of civil law and private law are used as synonyms as this text builds on the distinction between public law and civil/private law; hence, no need arises for a more elaborate demarcation. See, eg, Enrique AC Aztiria, 'Commercial Law and Private Law in Countries Having a Continental Legal System' (1959) 1 *Inter-American Law Review* 123–34; Jürgen Basedow, 'The State's Private Law and the Economy' (2008) 56 *AJCL* 703–21.

[2] See, eg, Michele Graziadei & Lionel Smith (eds), *Comparative Property Law* (Edward Elgar 2018); Peter Cane, Herwig Hofmann, Eric Ip & Peter Lindseth (eds), *The Oxford Handbook of Comparative Administrative Law* (Oxford University Law); Margaret Woo & Cornelis Hendrik van Rhee (eds), *Comparative Civil Procedure* (Edward Elgar 2025); James Gardner (ed), *Comparative Election Law* (Edward Elgar 2022); Ermanno Calzolaio, *Comparative Contract Law* (Routledge 2022); Emma Lees & Jorge Viñuales (eds), *The Oxford Handbook of Comparative Environmental Law* (OUP 2019); Shazia Choudhry & Jonathan Herring (eds), *The Cambridge Companion to Comparative Family Law* (CUP 2019); Francesco Palermo & Karl Kössler, *Comparative Federalism* (Hart Publishing 2019); Thomas Kadner-Graziano, *Comparative Tort Law* (Routledge 2018); Andreas Cahn & David Donald, *Comparative Company Law*, 2nd edn (CUP 2018); and Albin Eser, *Comparative Criminal Law* (Hart Publishing 2017).

In this chapter I will address and explain the collision between private law and public law and then proceed to illustrate how this collision has diminished in twenty-first century comparative law. Before addressing these issues, it is first beneficial to define briefly what these areas of law are about. In other words, what the colliding elements are in terms of their nature. It would be unnecessary here to dwell too much on this issue as so much ink has been spilled on the division between these two main areas of law which are recognised, in one way or another, in all modern legal systems.[3] In any case, erecting signposts for the following discussion is useful as it sheds light on what the collision has been about. Of course, the distinction between private and public law is a feature that is also reflected in the organisation of the judiciary. The separation of administrative courts – dealing with public law issues – from the ordinary civil and criminal courts is a typical feature of systems that belong to the family of civil law.[4] That dimension of the distinction is not discussed here as this chapter focuses on the significance of the distinction for comparative law scholarship in general.[5]

Now, we can resort to different ways to define and understand the main branches of law.[6] The classical – and classic – definition is to be found from Ulpian, an influential Roman jurist, who divided law into two areas: public law and private law.[7] According to this definition, public law concerned the administration of the Roman government, whereas private law concerned the interests of individuals.[8] For Ulpian, in essence, this was also the way to divide branches of legal study.[9] This is to say that the roots of the distinction go deep in Western law and legal thinking. In the world of modern law there are, of course, significant differences between legal systems but, at heart, the classical Roman definition gives the basic guideline on what these areas of law contain. In a nutshell, private law mainly concerns

[3] However, the distinction between these areas of law seems to be in a state of flux. See, eg, Michel Rosenfeld, 'Rethinking the Boundaries Between Public Law and Private Law for the Twenty First Century' (2013) 11 *International Journal of Constitutional Law* 125–28; Mark Freeland & Jean-Bernard Auby (eds), *The Public Law/Private Law Divide* (Hart Publishing 2006).

[4] For further discussion, see JWF Allison, *A Continental Distinction in the Common Law* (Clarendon Press 1996).

[5] For example in France, see John Bell and François Lichère, *Contemporary French Administrative Law* (CUP 2022) 128–53.

[6] See, eg, Jacques Chevallier, 'À quoi sert la distinction droit public/droit privé ?' in Antoine Bailleux (ed), *Distinction (droit) public / (droit) privé* (Presses universitaires Saint-Louis Bruxelles, 2022) 9–25; Bernardo Sordi, *Diritto pubblico e diritto private* (il Mulino 2020); and Thomas W Merrill, 'Private and Public Law' in Andrew S Gold et al (eds), *The Oxford Handbook of the New Private Law* (OUP 2020) 575–92.

[7] More about Ulpian (Latin: Gnaeus Domitius Annius Ulpianus), see Tony Honoré, *Ulpian* (Clarendon Press 1982). It should be noted that Honorés book caused debate and his interpretation of Ulpian's thinking has not been fully accepted. However, the book provides useful background info on Ulpian and his thinking.

[8] It needs to be kept in mind that the concept of public law is notoriously difficult even though it is recognised by Roman law, Andrew Harding, 'Comparative Public Law' in Andrew Harding & Esin Örücü (eds), *Comparative Law in the 21st Century* (Kluwer 2002) 250–66, 256.

[9] Original quote: 'Huius studii duae sunt positiones, publicum et privatum. Publicum ius est quod ad statum rei Romanae spectat, privatum quod ad singulorum utilitatem: sunt enim quaedam publice utilia, quaedam privatim', Digesta 1,1,1,2. See Erida Pejo & Esmeralda Kolaneci, 'The Role of Roman Law in the Formation of the State and Modern Law' (2024) 45 *Statute Law Review* doi.org/10.1093/slr/hmae027.

circumstances relating to legal relationships between individuals. This means that private law (or civil law/*ius civile*) covers such areas of law as property, trust (or equivalent legal arrangements), contract, and tort (or non-contractual liability).[10] Public law, when defined generically in the style of Ulpian, is based on the straightforward idea that public bodies - for example, central and local government - have to obey the law because it governs their organisation and conduct. Typically, this means that such modern areas as constitutional law and administrative law are counted as belonging to public law.[11] Of course, the way common law and civil law legal families understand these fields is not identical, but they cover roughly similar types of issues.[12]

Even though this is a rudimentary way to divide areas of law, it helps to point out what has also been the central substantive area of comparative law research. It is also beneficial to keep in mind that the distinction is not without its problems.[13] Regardless, there is no shadow of a doubt that much of twentieth century comparative law scholarship was built around private law. On top of that, the comparative law of the twentieth century was by and large comparative private law. This is an important observation because the twentieth century was the formative century of comparative law as a specialised field. As discussed in chapter three, much of this is explained by the close connection between private international law and comparative law. Nevertheless, the link between private law - as an area of law - and comparative study of law has been more profound in the sense of the substantive area of comparative study. Notwithstanding, it would be a simplification to argue that comparative law's focus has been on private law only because of the influence of private international law. But the situation is more nuanced than that, as will be shown in the following text.

I. Private Law as the Centre and Foundation

In reading comparative law scholarship of the twentieth century, one detects underlying ideas that show why the focus is on private law, not on public law. Reasons for this circle around epistemic suspicion and lawyerly doubt. Such great names of the early twentieth century as Raymond Saleilles and Édouard Lambert

[10] In Germany Reinhard Zimmermann, *The New German Law of Obligations: Historical and Comparative Perspectives* (OUP 2005) ch 1; in common law Kit Barker, 'Introduction' in Kit Barker (ed), *Private Law: Key Encounters with Public Law* (CUP 2013) 3–42.

[11] See Rolf-Peter Magen, *Staatsrecht: Eine Einführung* (Springer 1985) 3–4; Lisa Webley & Harriet Samuels, *Complete Public Law*, 5th edn (OUP 2021) ch 1; and Jacques Ziller, 'Public Law' in Jan Smits, Jaakko Husa, Catherine Valcke & Madalena Narciso (eds), *Elgar Encyclopedia of Comparative Law* Vol 3 (Edward Elgar 2023) 260–64.

[12] 'Sometimes in conversation with our continental friends we sense a potential confusion', Carol Harlow, '"Public" and "Private Law"' (1980) 43 *MLR* 241–65, 241.

[13] It has been argued that the distinction is multifunctional and context-dependent. See Gerdy Jurgens and Frank van Ommeren, 'The Public-Private Divide in English and Dutch Law' (2012) 71 *Cambridge Law Journal* 172–99.

were interested in private law.[14] They were the leading figures and as such not without influence. For instance, in the early 1930s in his introduction to comparative study of law, Mario Sarfatti wrote about different political currents and said that – despite certain border-crossing – 'imitation' institutions of public law tend to be of national origin showing divergence, whereas in private law a certain uniformity stretches over different territories.[15] This tells us about the idea according to which private law fits for comparative study whereas public law has too many differences in order to be studied comparatively. In other words, alleged similarities between the private law of different legal systems were a justification, whereas public law was excluded. Sarfatti, an expert in private law with a special interest in English private law, was certainly not alone in that line of thinking.[16]

Another illustration of suspicion and exclusion can be found from the massive and influential three-volume book by Pierre Arminjon, Boris Nolde and Martin Wolff published in the early 1950s.[17] They said that, in principle, comparative study of law can be divided in a manner equivalent to national fields of law. This would mean including – besides private law – public law and criminal law. Despite their apparent openness towards public law, they continued to explain that their study is about comparative study of the sources of law in the different private law systems of the modern world.[18] This approach differs from that of Sarfatti because it first explains that comparative law study can in principle focus on public, private, or criminal law. After that, however, they go on to focus on private law but without explaining explicitly why they do so. It is left for the reader to assume that even though they admit that comparative study of law can – in principle – focus on any area of law, their choice of focus flows from their personal specialisation in something other than public law. A quick glance at their backgrounds seems to confirm and, to an extent, explain this.

Arminjon wrote about Egyptian and Ottoman law but also about international private law.[19] Boris Nolde was originally a Russian historian and later a legal scholar who wrote about international private law.[20] Martin Wolff, in turn, was an expert in private law (property) and international private law.[21] Against this

[14] See Christophe Jamin, 'Saleilles and Lambert's Old Dream Revisited' (2002) 50 *AJCL* 701–18.

[15] Mario Sarfatti, *Introduzione allo studio del diritto comparato* (Giappichelli 1933) 46. The book was translated and published in Spanish later. See Mario Sarfatti, *Introducción al estudio del derecho comparado* (Imprenta Universitaria 1945).

[16] Web source *Intellectuals Displaced from Fascist Italy* tells the story of Sarfatti, labelled 'a travelling jurist', www.intellettualinfuga.com/en/Sarfatti/Mario/245.

[17] Pierre Arminjon, Boris Nolde, and Martin Wolff, *Traité de droit comparé*, Tome I (LGDJ 1950), Tome II (LGDJ 1950), Tome III (LGDJ 1951).

[18] 'Cette étude sera complétée par l'étude comparée des sources de droit dans les différents systèmes de droit privé du monde moderne', Tome I (1950) 41.

[19] See, eg, Pierre Arminjon, *De la nationalité dans l'Empire ottoman spécialement en Egypte* (Pedone 1901) and *Nature, objet et portée des règles de droit international privé* (Tenin 1920).

[20] See, eg, Boris Nolde, 'Les Étapes historiques de la codification législative du droit international privé' (1927) 22 *Revue de droit international privé* 361–74 and 'La codification du droit international privé' (1936) 55 *Recueil des cours de l'académie de droit international de La Haye* 299–432.

[21] See, eg, Martin Wolff, *Das Sachenrecht* (Elwert 1910) and *Private International Law* (Clarendon Press 1950) in which he says very little about comparative law. See also 'Wolff, Martin' in Michael Stolleis (ed), *Juristen: ein Biographisches Lexikon* (CH Beck 2001) 676–77.

backdrop, it is only to be expected that they focused on private law even though they do not express their suspicion towards public law as openly as – a couple of decades later – Alan Watson in his highly influential volume on legal transplants in the early 1970s.[22] Watson underlined the similarity of legal systems in the area of private law but was sceptical about public law. This is only natural as his theory of legal transplants was altogether based on the impact of Roman law.[23] Importantly, in Western legal scholarship – comparative law included – Roman law's influence has been on private law.[24] The favourite areas of comparative law have been property, contract, and tort.

A particularly noteworthy step in the path of what one might label the comparative law mainstream was taken in an influential introductory book on comparative law by German scholars Konrad Zweigert and Hein Kötz. This was first published as two volumes in the late 1960s[25] and was later translated into several other languages as *Introduction to Comparative Law*.[26] Interestingly enough, the German editions have a longer title called 'Introduction to Comparative law in the Field of Private Law.' The first English translation (by Tony Weir) appeared in 1977, also in two volumes but without the specification 'Private Law' (*Privatrecht*).[27] The latest English one-volume edition is from 1998 but its theoretical parts remained practically unchanged.[28] The book's first part concentrates on theoretical issues (General Considerations) and macro-comparative law (The Legal Families of the World).[29] The second part discusses central areas of narrowly understood private law: contract, unjustified enrichment, and tort.[30]

This widely spread and still commonly cited book leaves public law aside completely. Curiously, no explanation is given that explicitly states why this is done. The book's index does not even mention public law.[31] This does not come as a surprise when the background of the authors is taken into account.[32] What is important is that this volume paired comparative law scholarship on theory and method together with private law, making these two look like a natural pair a

[22] Alan Watson, *Legal Transplants: An Approach to Comparative Law*, 2nd edn (University of Georgia Press 1993).

[23] ibid 7–9.

[24] See, eg, Paul du Plessis, 'Roman Law and Comparative Law' in Smits et al (n 11) 341–49.

[25] Konrad Zweigert and Hein Kötz, *Einführung in die Rechtsvergleichung auf dem Gebiete des Privatrechts*, Vols 1-2 (Mohr Siebeck 1969).

[26] See, eg, *Introduzione Al Diritto Comparato* I and II (Giuffrè 1992, 1998) tr Barbara Pozzo & Estella Cigna; *Introducción al derecho comparado* (OUP 2002) tr Arturo Aparicio Vázquez; and 比较法总论 [Bǐjiào fǎ zǒng lùn] (Legal Publishing House 2004) tr Pan Handian, Mi Jian, Gao Hongjun, He Weifang.

[27] *An Introduction to Comparative Law*, Vols 1–2 (North Holland 1977).

[28] *An Introduction to Comparative Law*, 3rd edn (OUP 1998).

[29] ibid 1–319.

[30] ibid 323–708.

[31] ibid 709–14.

[32] Of Zweigert see, eg, brief description on the web page of the Max Planck Institute for Comparative and International Private Law: www.mpipriv.de/konrad-zweigert-scholarship. Also Kötz has published extensively, mostly in the areas of contract law and comparative law. See, eg, *Europäisches Vertragsrecht*, 2nd edn (Mohr Siebeck 2015), which has been translated into several languages (English, French, Italian, Japanese, Chinese).

match made in heaven, if you will. Now, of course it can be observed that they did not invent the connection but because their volume gained such a central position it became more influential than other volumes. Those who wrote about comparative law theory and methodology along the path trodden by Zweigert and Kötz did not question the bond that appeared as 'business as usual'. Public law had no role as it was tacitly assumed that comparative law was about private law. This 'normality' became a kind of silent epistemic assumption or tacit knowledge not put into words or otherwise communicated but still shared by the majority; an invisible paradigm, one might say.

Tacitly focusing on private law even though being aware of comparative law's potentially broader scope reigned supreme - and not only in central European scholarship. Ramifications are to be found in many places. For example, Michael Bogdan, with a Czech and Swedish background, published his textbook on comparative law in the mid-1990s.[33] The book deals with issues that concern methodology and theory and then describes the most important legal systems of the world.[34] As Bogdan's specialty is private international law, it comes as no surprise that the focus is firmly on private law even though he also acknowledges the impact of a country's political system on the legal system.[35] Mind you, the political system is not an object of study as such but a factor that is taken into account when the comparatist seeks to explain their findings in the field(s) of private law.

In similar fashion, Peter de Cruz's textbook on comparative law does not exclude public law but it is easy for the reader to see where the focus lies.[36] Cruz, a law professor in the UK, does not pair comparative law with private international law and in this sense paints a picture of comparative law as an independent field of legal scholarship.[37] Nevertheless, Cruz also discusses the distinction between civil law (private law) and public law, which implies that he - like the mainstream in general - was and is aware of the potentially broader scope of comparative law.[38] Regardless, when it comes to addressing substantive laws Cruz focuses on statutory interpretation, obligations, corporate and commercial law, sale of goods, and labour law.[39] Against the backdrop of these two 1990s textbooks the overall view is that there are no compelling reasons to leave public law out or to focus only on private law. But at the same time, in practice, the actual focus is on private law (broadly understood).

In some cases, though, the private law base is more difficult to detect. French comparatist René David's influential book on legal families, which saw its first

[33] Michael Bogdan, *Comparative Law* (Kluwer 1994).

[34] ibid Part 1 17–98 and Part 2 101–228.

[35] ibid 72–73.

[36] Peter de Cruz, *Comparative Law in a Changing World*, 3rd edn (Routledge 2008).

[37] ibid 'private international law is much more selective than comparative law, to the extent that the "choice of law rules" are very narrow', at 9.

[38] ibid 46–47.

[39] ibid chs 9–13 (273–492)

edition in the early 1960s, illustrates this difficulty.[40] In essence, David's classification of great legal families was built on macro-concepts based on private law. However, a substantial portion of the book was dedicated to Socialist law as David could not rely only on private law because public law played such an elemental role in the socialist legal systems. Yet he pointed out that even socialist laws were based largely on the tradition of learned Roman (private) law.[41] Importantly, David's volume was and remains somewhat indifferent in its relation to the distinction between private law and public law.[42] Unlike Zweigert and Kötz, David focused not on specific private law issues but addressed more general features such as historical evolution, structure of the law, and sources of law.[43] Similarly to the other great comparatists of the past century, David's academic profile, beyond comparative law, lay in private law and in particular in unification of private law. For instance, he worked on many projects undertaken by the International Institute for the Unification of Private Law (UNIDROIT). David also had a role in the United Nations Commission on International Trade Law (UNICITRAL). Moreover, he was one of the authors of the Ethiopian Civil Code (1960).[44]

Before moving to the next section, we need to state that, of course, focus on private law had an impact on macro-comparative law and the classifications of legal systems that the comparatists drew up. As Roberto Scarciglia notes, the macro-classifications 'were drawn up without considering the public law perspective, which would undoubtedly have resulted in a different classification of systems into legal families.'[45] This is yet another indication of the innate private law focus not discussed here.

II. Bringing in Public Law, a Contrarian Move?

As noted in the preceding section, one area of comparative law where the precedence of private law is particularly evident is macro-comparative law. Whereas micro-comparison focuses on individual legal rules, judgments, or legal institutions,

[40] The book has numerous editions, and has been translated into several languages. The first edition of David's *Les grands systèmes de droit contemporains* (Dalloz 1964) was published in the mid-1960s. The 12th edition, with Camille Jauffret-Spinosi and Marie Goré, was published in 2016, 26 years after David's passing.

[41] The second English edition, *Major Legal Systems in the World Today* with John C Brierley (Stevens & Sons 1978, 21), notes that Romano-Germanic law evolved as 'essentially private law'. The scholarly tradition of 'great contemporary legal systems' is continued in France, see eg Gilles Cuniberti, *Les grands systèmes de droit contemporain*, 4th edn (LGDJ 2019).

[42] This is not uncommon in French-speaking comparative law scholarship. See, eg, Jacques Vanderlinden, *Comparer les droits* (E. Story-Scientia 1995).

[43] 'la formation historique du système', 'structure des droits', and 'sources du droit'.

[44] See for a more detailed picture from his autobiography, René David, *Les avatars d'un comparatiste* (Paris 1982). See also Jorge Esquirol, 'René David: At the Head of the Legal Family' in Annlise Riles (ed), *Rethinking the Masters of Comparative Law* (Hart Publishing 2001) 212–35 ('Throughout his life, David was involved in one way or another with projects of legal unification', ibid 229).

[45] Roberto Scarciglia, *Methods and Legal Comparison* (Edward Elgar 2023) 72.

macro-comparison takes place between whole legal systems.[46] The classic groupings of legal families, such as those by Arminjon, Nolde and Wolff, and Zweigert and Kötz, were epistemically based on private law. Making this point today is, nevertheless, vulnerable to criticism because legal families seem to be a thing of the past. Accordingly, one can doubt the future of legal families, but it would be incorrect to assume that macro-comparative law scholarship based on private law is dead and gone.[47] Even in this century, some scholarship has been based on the epistemic urge to discuss legal families or make other kinds of macro-constructs serving the same essentially taxonomic goals as legal families.[48] For example, a fresh attempt has been made to group the world's legal systems (as a family tree) based on systematic coding of the contents of private laws.[49] Because macro-comparative law will be discussed in chapter six, there is no need to dwell on that topic here. More importantly for the present discussion, to make a general observation, private law's dominance is not limited to macro-comparative law even though its impact is easier to detect in micro-comparative law.

For the reasons addressed above, it was long implicitly held natural that comparative law was focused on private law. But – as Jacques Ziller points out – this seems strange against the backdrop of such pioneer comparatists as Aristotle and Montesquieu. Accordingly, arguing that comparative public law is a young discipline seems to make no sense but yet comparative law scholarship has been mostly self-limited by its private law focus.[50] One needs to tread carefully here because it is important to note that even though the mainstream scholarship on comparative law has been private law-oriented, this does not mean that there would not have been attempts to develop comparative public law.[51] The epistemic difficulty I am referring to here is that public law long resided in the shadows of predominant comparative law scholarship by leading scholars such as Zweigert and Kötz, who had a private law background and were interested in unification of private laws.[52] Similar public law-related ideas came much later, as indeed the appearance

[46] See, eg, Zweigert and Kötz (1998) 4–5. In a critical tone, Geoffrey Samuel, *An Introduction to the Comparative Law Theory and Method* (Hart Publishing 2014) 50–53 ('dichotomy must be treated with caution', ibid 50).

[47] I discuss this at length elsewhere, see Jaakko Husa, 'The Future of Legal Families, *Oxford Handbook Topics in Law* (online edn, *Oxford Academic*) doi.org/10.1093/oxfordhb/9780199935352.013.26.

[48] Esin Örücü, 'Family Trees for Legal Systems' in Mark Van Hoecke (ed), *Epistemology and Methodology of Comparative Law* (Hart Publishing 2004) 359–75. See also Ugo Mattei, 'Legal Metaverse and Comparative Taxonomy' (2023) 71 *AJCL* 900–29 (revisits Mattei's article on legal taxonomy published in the *AJCL* in 1997).

[49] Yun-chien Chang, Nuno Garoupa, Martin Wells, 'Drawing the Legal Family Tree' (2021) 13 *Journal of Legal Analysis* 231–82.

[50] Ziller (n 11) 260.

[51] An excellent example of an attempt to develop comparative public law is Ludwik Erlich, 'Comparative Public Law and the Fundamentals of Its Study' (1921) 21 *Columbia Law Review* 623–46. The article focuses on practical uses of comparative law in the area of public law ('Why should not the science of man in society, and of public law, which is the basis of social organization, be utilized by lawyers and legislators', ibid 625).

[52] The 'reason why comparative law has been for long considered as a matter for private law is probably linked to the history of contemporary comparative law, which has been very much dominated by the Paris Congress of 1901. As a consequence of this meeting, which seems to have been dominated by lawyers who were in search of some kind of a *jus commune* in the fields of private law', Ziller (n 11) 261.

of so-called global constitutionalism shows.[53] Public law-related harmonisation ideas seem to have grown independently from private comparative law.

Describing this more or less subtle situation is an attempt plagued with uncertainty, I must admit. It implies that there would have been a shared delusion that proper scientific comparative study of law was supposed to mean study of private law. Saying the quiet part out loud seems to be in order despite the uncertainties involved.

Interestingly, the relationship of public international law to comparative law is different from the relationship of private international law to comparative law. There is no close connection although some attempts have been made to bind comparative law and public international law more closely, but these are not part of the mainstream as they remained the voice of the minority. The outnumbered voice existed but had no real impact. For instance, in the late 1970s and early 1980s William Butler made a pioneering attempt to draw these fields closer together but his ideas did not gain traction among public international law scholars or among comparatists.[54] More recently, though, Anthea Roberts with her colleagues have sought to develop comparative (public) international law as a remedy to the epistemic problems of public international law scholarship.[55] This novel form of scholarship seems to have no meaningful connection to the present discussion on private law's epistemic dominance in the field of comparative law. It may carry more weight in public international law or global law scholarship, though.[56] It would seem that non-nationally focused legal scholarship takes place in separate compartments.

Moreover, although there have been contacts between comparative private law and public international law, nevertheless these contacts seem to have had no significance in terms of the development of comparative law as a field. For example, at one point in his career the highly influential international law scholar Hersch Lauterpacht tried to develop international law on the basis of comparative private law.[57] Early in his career, Lauterpacht used private law-based ideas as kind of a foundation of international law.[58] In addition, Ernst Rabel – the father of

[53] There is a growing literature on global constitutional law. A flagship journal of this form of scholarship is *Global Constitutionalism* (since 2012). 'The journal publishes cutting-edge peer-reviewed work which refers to and advances global constitutionalism as an interdisciplinary field', www.cambridge.org/core/journals/global-constitutionalism/information/about-this-journal. I have presented critical thoughts on these ideas, see Jaakko Husa, 'Global Constitutionalism' (2017) 46 *Hong Kong Law Journal* 73–88.

[54] See William E Butler, 'International Law and the Comparative Method' (1977) 30 *Current Legal Problems* 105–21 and William E Butler, 'Comparative Approaches to International Law' (1985) *Recueil des Cours de l'Académie de Droit International* 9–90.

[55] See Anthea Roberts, Paul B Stephan, Pierre-Hugues Verdier & Mila Versteeg (eds), *Comparative International Law* (OUP 2018).

[56] See, eg, Mathias Siems and Robert Schütze (eds), *Comparative International Law* (Hart Publishing 2026).

[57] See Hersch Lauterpacht, *Private Law Sources and Analogies of International Law* (Longmans, Green 1927).

[58] See Ralf Michaels, 'Private Lawyer in Disguise?' (2013) 27 *Temple International and Comparative Law Journal* 499–521, 502–04.

functional comparative law – justified the need for comparative law on the basis of the need for German lawyers to understand and interpret the Versailles treaty, which itself was a creation of international law, so that German jurists needed to have an understanding of non-German law in order to properly understand international law.[59] At this phase, legal comparativism and international law were rubbing shoulders in a somewhat cosmopolitan spirit.

Against this kind of backdrop, it is no wonder that – when comparative public law started to step out of the shadow of private comparative law – it did so by stating its contrarian position in relation to private law-oriented comparative law. Comparative public law hoped to make its existence known by painting a contrarian image of itself. To simplify a great deal, comparative public law scholars stated that 'We exist, we are different'. As a consequence, it may have been the case that, in doing so, scholars hoping to move the focus more to public law painted a picture of comparative law that is arguably more of a straw man than an accurate picture. The difficulty in addressing this issue is that often the collision between private law and public law needs to be read between the lines because comparative law scholars with a private law background do not openly state that comparative study of public law would be out of the question – indeed, quite the opposite. Much among the contrarian views of comparative public law scholars appears to be directed against what tends to be quietly assumed in general comparative law scholarship; hence, it is not necessarily openly claimed that comparative public law exists as an opposition to comparative private law. To be sure, it would have been difficult to claim to be a serious comparatist and to openly maintain that public law is beyond the boundaries. None the less, silence speaks volumes…

Taking into account the influence of Zweigert and Kötz's volume, it makes sense to start from there. For them it was important to distinguish between law that can be compared and law that is less suitable for comparative study. In essence, this is about drawing an ontological and epistemic demarcation line between law and politics.[60] In their view, not all areas of private law are considered as 'unpolitical' or not influenced by 'moral views and values'. Accordingly, they casually ruled out such areas of private law as family law and law of succession.[61] Their epistemic suspicion extends well beyond public law. The bottom line is, the indirect message – which is of course open to many sorts of critiques – that comparative study of law should stay out of areas that are political or connected to moral views and values. These areas may be 'law' but not purely law enough in order to be studied comparatively by a legal scholar. Even though they do not rule out public law, it is easy to grasp the

[59] See Ernst Rabel, 'Experiences of a Comparatist' (1986) 50 *Rabels Zeitschrift für ausländisches und internationales Privatrecht* 282–311 ('Germany, you see, had learned by the war experiences what it means not to have proper knowledge of the outer world, not the least part of which proved to be foreign law', ibid 297).

[60] This is an age-old issue in the field of legal theory/philosophy; for that reason, it makes no sense to discuss it further here. See for a concise discussion, Larry Alexander, 'Law and Politics: What Is Their Relation?' (2018) 41 *Harvard Journal of Law & Public Policy* 355–63.

[61] See Zweigert & Kötz (n 46) 40. See also Balázs Fekete, *Paradigms in Modern European Comparative Law* (Hart Publishing 2021) 126.

under-the-surface message: public law is not *really* suitable for comparative study of law. In other words, the subtle message was: let the cobbler stick to his last. Susan Millns characterises this view aptly:

> it is dangerous, if not impossible, to compare public law rules, as this branch of the legal system is too intimately linked to the state and the moral particularities of each country[62]

Without claiming that Millns' characterisation is wrong – in fact, I agree with her – it can be said that this part of her paper lacks references. That said, I do not doubt what she argues because she accurately summarises the mood of mainstream comparative law. What she writes just a few lines after the quoted text is telling. She rightly points out that among public lawyers there is an increasing awareness of the usefulness of comparative studies. Instead of going straight to justifying comparative study of public law she provides a list of contrarian arguments as to why comparative public law makes sense. These arguments are presented against what can only be described as a private law-based comparative law mainstream.[63] It does not end here, either, as a few pages later Millns notes that the comparatist needs to be aware of the pitfalls of comparative research and 'this applies particularly to the domain of public law'.[64] I find it difficult not to think that this awareness is also needed when it comes to comparative study of private law. Somehow, it would appear, the epistemic grip of private law seems to rule from the shadows. Then again, underlining the uniqueness of comparative public law also requires some stress on the difference between public law and private law. In my view, this appears like a contrarian stance, resulting in shadow boxing. It is not clear to me why the comparatist should think that private law is purely legal and without connection to societal contexts and morality.

An earlier illustration of constructing the identity of comparative public law in a contrarian manner against the private law-focused mainstream can be found from François Venter's book on comparative constitutional law, published in 2000.[65] Before moving to constitutional comparison, Venter lays the groundwork by discussing general issues of comparative law and its methodology against the backdrop of public law. Even though he does not build on the distinction between public and private law, he does outline comparative study of constitutional law against the backdrop of private law. Venter notes that, historically speaking, most of the theoretical scholarship on comparative law 'was developed in the context of private law'.[66] Then, relying on earlier work by Tim Koopmans, he identifies problems against the backdrop of private law. These problems are primarily the kind of problems that one does not (allegedly) face in comparative private law. First, there

[62] Susan Millns, 'Making the Case for European Comparative Legal Studies in Public Law' in Maurice Adams & Dirk Heirbaut (eds), *The Method and Culture of Comparative Law* (Hart Publishing 2014) 283–300, 288.

[63] ibid 288–91.

[64] ibid 295.

[65] François Venter, *Constitutional Comparison* (Juta/Kluwer 2000).

[66] ibid 19.

are no systematic classifications of concepts in public law. Second, factors such as historical differences and political culture 'have more extensive effects on public law'. Third, public law 'tends to be tinted in stronger national tones than private law'.[67] All this may be perfectly true but it also shows the might of private law's epistemic grip as it shapes the arguments of public law comparatists.

Along similar lines, John Bell, who discusses comparative public law in the early 2000s, says that public law has so many institutional features that it is significantly different from private comparative law research.[68] He continues and states that in public law 'the core function of law is distinctive from private law'.[69] Without arguing against Venter or Bell, it can nonetheless be said that the picture they paint of comparative public law takes shape within private law-crafted frames. What I mean is that their 'opponent' shapes the arguments merely by existing.

However, it is important to see that there are also attempts to define, build, and identify comparative public law as distinct from private law without building on a palpable contrarian foundation. For example, Ran Hirschl discusses comparative law in many places in his seminal book on comparative constitutional law.[70] He criticises the theory and methodology of earlier scholarship in drawing on political science, but does so without building explicitly on the assumed epistemic difference between public law and private law.[71] Even though Hirschl could perhaps discuss comparative law scholarship in more detail, it can be seen that when building modern comparative constitutional law he is aware of theoretical comparative law scholarship resting on the foundation of private law.[72] In a sense, this is what Andrew Harding suggested in the early 2000s when he urged comparative public lawyers to join in the general comparative law conversation.[73] Regardless, it would seem that comparative public law's most dynamic area, namely constitutional law, has been much more interested in constitutional comparison than joining general comparative law discussion.[74] The reluctance of comparative public law scholars may be explained by their assumption that public law in general has become global

[67] ibid 20.

[68] John Bell, 'Comparing Public Law' in Andrew Harding and Esin Örücü (eds), *Comparative Law in the 21st Century* (Kluwer 2002) 235–47.

[69] ibid 236.

[70] Ran Hirschl, *Comparative Matters: The Renaissance of Comparative Constitutional Law* (OUP 2014).

[71] For example when Hirschl discusses macro-comparative law (citing Zweigert & Kötz) he does not refer to the influence of private law but keeps the criticism on a more general methodological level, ibid 196–98 and 233.

[72] Voices from the private law community have also welcomed the gist of Hirschl's argument. See Anna Di Robilant, 'Big Questions Comparative Law' (2016) 96 *Boston University Law Review* 1325–45 ('My hope is that Hirschl's call for "big questions" comparative law will be heard by comparative private law scholars, and that Hirschl's book will begin a new conversation in comparative law', ibid 1345).

[73] Harding (n 8) 254–56.

[74] See, eg, Rosalind Dixon & Tom Ginsburg, 'Introduction' in Rosalind Dixon & Tom Ginsburg (eds), *Comparative Constitutional Law* (Edward Elgar 2011) 1–15; Michel Rosenfeld & András Sajó, 'Introduction' in Michel Rosenfeld & András Sajó (eds), *The Oxford Handbook of Comparative Constitutional Law* (OUP 2012) 1–22; Xenophon Contiades & Alkmene Fotiadou, 'Introduction' in Xenophon Contiades & Alkmene Fotiadou (eds), *Routledge Handbook of Comparative Constitutional Change* (Routledge 2020) 1–21.

and that this, in turn, means an 'increasingly integrated field of global public law', as Tom Ginsburg puts it.[75] This integrated field – if we assume that it exists – seems rather distant from private law and its tacit epistemic and methodological assumptions lie elsewhere. Then again, the idea of global law is not distant from the classic dream of private law comparatists: unification of laws. Public law comparatists seem almost to end up with the classic ideals of comparative private law suggesting that what goes around comes around.

III. Fading Demarcation?

As has become clear from chapters two and three above, comparative law's intellectual outlook has changed – or at least is about to do so. One dimension in which this can be seen is the disappearance of at least a blurring of demarcation lines that were held as so important in the past. As American constitutional comparatist Mark Tushnet has pointed out: comparative law was previously characterised by various boundaries such as subject matter-related, disciplinary, and geographical but now '[a]ll of those boundaries have become blurred over the past generation, though they will never disappear completely.'[76] One indication of this blurring can be seen in contemporary scholarship on comparative law that seems unexpectedly little interested in building the identity of comparative law in a contrarian manner, that is, painting a picture of the mainstream that needs to be opposed in order to justify more space for previously less practised comparative public law. Accordingly, modern theoretical scholarship in comparative law is less reliant on the contrarian position of public comparative law in its relation to comparative private law. Along similar lines, comparative public law scholarship has grown remarkably and the same applies to fields that do not follow the private-public distinction. Environmental law, labour law, and consumer law can be mentioned as examples.[77]

Some theoretically oriented modern comparatists have assumed a subtle contrarian stance: for instance, Esin Örücü and David Nelken, who jointly edited a comparative law handbook published in 2007. Their contrarianism is, however, implicit as it takes the form of leaving out rather than arguing against. In the preface they note that:

> Traditional topics of private law, such as contracts, obligations, unjustified enrichment and tort (delict) are deliberately omitted as these have been amply covered in comparative law textbooks.[78]

[75] Tom Ginsburg, 'The State of the Field' in David S Law (ed), *Constitutionalism in Context* (CUP 2022) 23–40, 30.

[76] Mark Tushnet, 'The Boundaries of Comparative Law' (2017) 13 *European Constitutional Law Review* 3–22. And yet Tushnet takes the trouble to point out his having 'far less familiarity with scholarship in comparative private law', ibid 22 fn 21.

[77] Michele Graziadei, 'What Does Globalisation Mean for the Comparative Study of Law?' (2021) 16 *JCL* 511–36, 332–3.

[78] Esin Örücü & David Nelken, 'Preface' in Esin Örücü and David Nelken (eds), *Comparative Law: A Handbook* (Hart Publishing 2007) v–vi, v.

Along similar lines, a contemporary scholar can assume a less conflictual stance and may simply say that the 'scope of comparative law encompasses study of all branches of law and all types of legal rule.'[79] Furthermore, this inclusivity is based on a view that takes globalisation into account as it is held that the distinction between private law and public law is unable adequately to capture the complexity of the new globalised environment of law.[80] Globalisation of law, regardless of what one thinks about it, is one of the factors that have rendered the sharp distinction between fields of law less relevant.[81] Muddying the waters of legal systematics does not make comparative law irrelevant, though; indeed, on the contrary. It seems, I dare say, that comparative law will remain as an essential tool in terms of coping with today's challenges of legal research.[82] Yet this new kind of comparative law will most likely not look the same as it did in the past century, as I will argue later in chapter twelve against the backdrop of globalisation.

Along similar lines, theoretical scholarship on comparative law seems quite indifferent as to the distinction between private law comparison and public law comparison. One example is Geoffrey Samuel's textbook on theory and methodology, which is general in nature.[83] In essence, it is not difficult to detect that Samuel's background is in private law because most of the examples he uses do not come from public law. However, the approaches discussed by Samuel are such that they could also be applied in the comparative study of public law.[84] The same pertains to Mathias Siems' important volume on comparative law.[85] Siems is aware of the distinction and its potential meaning for comparative study of law, but his scholarship does not build on the distinction and, moreover, the distinction does not seem to play a significant role.[86] Regardless, Siems chooses examples and discussion points rather from the areas of private and commercial law than from public law.[87] There is nothing wrong with this as such even though it may indicate, so to speak, that a leopard never changes its spots.[88]

Modern comparatist Siems's quite understandable preference is, I believe, symptomatic and applies to theoretical comparative law scholarship more generally. To be sure, it does not take much time and effort for this assumption to

[79] George Mousorakis, *Comparative Law and Legal Traditions* (Springer 2019) 2.

[80] ibid 44.

[81] See for more detailed discussion, Jaakko Husa, *Advanced Introduction to Globalisation and Law* (Edward Elgar 2018).

[82] cf Graziadei (n 77) 13.

[83] Geoffrey Samuel, *An Introduction to Comparative Law Theory and Method* (Hart Publishing 2014).

[84] Samuel, following epistemologist Jean-Michel Berthelot, speaks of 'schemes of intelligibility'. Importantly, these schemes seem neutral as to what kind of law the comparatist studies.

[85] Mathias Siems, *Comparative Law*, 3rd edn (CUP 2022).

[86] ibid 105, 'a more general comment starts with the observation that, from early on, private law has often spread across borders (e.g., received Roman law), whereas the development of public law has been more dependent on national borders. Thus, it has been suggested that classifying legal systems in public law may be less meaningful than in private law'.

[87] For example 'private law' has 97 hits in the book whereas 'public law' has only 17 hits in word search.

[88] Siems's substantive law specialisation lies in the areas of private, corporate, and financial law. See, eg, Siems, *Convergence in Shareholder Law* (CUP 2007); and Siems & David Cabrelli (eds), *Comparative Company Law* (CUP 2013).

be confirmed; those who write about comparative law theory and methodology instinctively do not choose their examples from the field of public law. From there, it follows that comparatists pick their examples and illustrations mostly from private law, so that it is much more common to stumble upon contracts, property, or obligations, articles of civil codes, and the like than it is to find examples from administrative or constitutional law when it comes to general comparative law texts. Interestingly, even those who write about mixed jurisdictions follow the mainstream's private law focus and leave public law virtually aside.[89] Similar phenomena are also to be seen in legal history, as a Romanist writing about the methodologies of legal history and comparative law shows by focusing on private law because it provides common points with legal history.[90] Again, I am making an observation but not criticising features that are explained by the intellectual history of legal scholarship.

However, the fact that the modern comparative law of the twenty-first century recognises a blurring of the fields of law does not mean that comparatists would have become blind to their existence. For example, in his massive textbook Uwe Kischel writes that in 'contrast to private law, public law is particularly ideological.'[91] In earlier scholarship, following Zweigert and Kötz, this would have meant that public law would have been deemed unsuitable for comparative study. For Kischel, this kind of simplified conclusion would be mistaken. Instead of ruling comparative public law out from the domain of proper comparative law, he turns the tables when he discusses political values in public law and beyond. Importantly – and this is in line with recent theoretical comparative law scholarship in general – he notes that private law 'is not generally apolitical and value neutral.'[92] As examples, he mentions family law and inheritance law. These, in his view, are 'particularly likely to be driven by value judgments.'[93] My own views are very much in line with these ideas as I have pointed out elsewhere that general issues of comparative law are essentially similar in all areas of law.[94] Assuming that private law – or even its core areas – would be apolitical is too blunt as it disregards much of the context(s) of law. A comparatist coming from a non-Western legal culture quickly notices how Christianity has had an impact on many areas of law: for instance, family law.[95] Moreover, it would be a mistake to think that law would be purely legal because, as

[89] See, eg, Vernon Valentine Palmer, 'A Description and Comparative Overview' in Vernon Valentine Palmer (ed), *Mixed Jurisdictions Worldwide*, 2nd edn (CUP 2012) 19–92.

[90] Laurens Winkel, 'The Method of Comparative Law Reconsidered in the Light of Legal Epistemology and the Reception of Roman Law' in Seán Patrick Donlan & Jane Mair (eds), *Comparative Law* (Routledge 2020) 158–70, 164.

[91] Uwe Kischel, *Comparative Law* (OUP 2019) 36. Originally the book was published in German: *Rechtsvergleichung* (CH Beck 2015), English translation by Andrew Hammel.

[92] ibid 37.

[93] ibid 38. This is clearly different from Zweigert & Kötz.

[94] See Jaakko Husa, *Introduction to Comparative Law*, 2nd edn (Hart Publishing 2023) 13–18.

[95] See, eg, John Witte & Gary Hauk (eds), *Christianity and Family Law* (CUP 2017). The issue from the point of view of comparative law, see Jaakko Husa, 'Comparative Law and Christianity' (2024) 44 *Oxford Journal of Legal Studies* 54–73.

Brian Tamanaha puts it, law 'swims in the social sea with everything else'.[96] Instead of arguing for the uniqueness of public law, the comparatists of today underline that all comparative study of law needs to be aware of the law's context in general.

Overall, it would seem that even though discussion and scholarship on what fields of law one should study was based on the opposition of public law in its relation to private law, today's situation is different. The flexibility and pluralism of this day and age have left much of the old collision-based scholarship behind. Regardless, it is useful to be mindful because comparative law is not a monolith – and has never been – and what I argue here needs to be taken with a pinch of salt because there are many ways to study law comparatively and the earlier scholarly layers still exist, as indeed comparative law literature gives reason to believe. Someone who reads that literature finds out that comparative law as a field is not a neatly organised garden but more like a vibrant jungle with many paths crossing each other.[97] As the imagined twentieth century formal garden of comparative law has been transformed into a jungle, it has become increasingly meaningless to uphold contrarian lines of separation between fields of law.

Contemporary comparative law seeks increasingly to study law in context regardless of whether it is public or private. Importantly, this idea grows out of previous colliding layers of scholarship. Yet, it has to be said, the transformation of comparative law is still in motion as previous forms of scholarship are still with us whether we like it or not. After all, comparative law – like any form of legal scholarship – does not appear out of nowhere because we stand on the shoulders of giants, whether we consider them giants or not. Accordingly, even if the comparative public law scholar would not address comparative private law, nevertheless the latter exists as the foundation of comparative study of law. In turn, even if the private law comparatist of today would leave public law out, even so a rapidly growing body of comparative public law is out there. Only time will tell how long this evasive contrarianism takes place.

[96] Brian Z Tamanaha, 'The Primacy of Society and the Failures of Law and Development' (2011) 44 *Cornell International Law Journal* 209–47, 247.

[97] For more about this argument, see Jaakko Husa, 'Introduction' in Jaakko Husa (ed), *A Research Agenda for Comparative Law* (Edward Elgar 2024) 1–14.

5

Talking About It vs Doing It

While reading published works in the field of comparative law, it is not difficult to notice that there are different genres.[1] Books and articles published under the banner of comparative law can be very different indeed in many respects. Linguistic differences are easiest to spot.[2] Of course, it is more than obvious that, even though English has virtually taken over, there is still a lot of comparative law literature in national languages. The spectrum of languages is wide and shows no signs of shrinking. To be sure, comparative law is far from being a monoglot field even though English is the common language among those who publish scholarly texts in comparative law.[3] What is more, there are also theoretical divisions, more difficult to perceive, many of which are discussed in this book. These may concern issues on methodologies, fields of law, geographical focus of research, or schools of thought. One of the dividing differences that is general as to its nature is the distinction between types of scholars and scholarship. In broad terms, this division concerns the difference between theoretical scholars and scholars – or comparative lawyers – who see themselves as just doing comparative law research without becoming entangled with deeper (and thus difficult) theoretical issues.[4]

It may seem that the division addressed in this chapter – theory vs practice – perhaps comes disturbingly close to the competing views on the nature of comparative law, as discussed in chapter three, namely: is comparative law only a tool or something more? However, the collision addressed in chapter three and the collision here are not identical. Whereas the question 'tool or something more?' focuses on the identity of comparative law as a field, the juxtaposition between

[1] See, eg, Luca Siliquini-Cinelli, 'Experience vs. Knowledge in Comparative Law' (2020) 16 *International Journal of Law in Context* 443–58 (discusses Pierre Legrand's, James Gordley's, and James Whitman's comparative law methodologies).

[2] One indication of the growing significance of language for comparative study of law is the new field of comparative legal linguistics. See Heikki Mattila, *Comparative Legal Linguistics*, 2nd edn (Routledge 2013).

[3] This fact also makes English the language in which the mainstream exists even though rich traditions of comparative law/legal studies exist in many non-English speaking countries.

[4] Catherine Valcke, 'comparative law groundworkers tend to show little or no interest in theory, and comparative law theorists conversely display little if any appetite for doing the groundwork' in 'Why I Became a Comparative Lawyer' (2025) 20 *JCL* 151–59, 158.

'talking about it vs doing it' concerns the identity of the individual scholar and their personal choice of genre or style of doing scholarship. Even though comparatists are bound by the legal materials they study, their personality and views colour the way they understand and interpret the materials.[5] This – among other things – has to do with what can be labelled the comparative law theory vs practice-focused comparative law juxtaposition.[6] In more simple terms, this is about the distinction between the lawyer and the scholar.[7] My aim here is to venture beyond this dichotomy and shed light on the possibility of defusing the collision by showing that in today's world the contrarian dichotomy is more or less artificial or, in a way, misguided. This is not tantamount to suggesting that the collision would have been more reasonable in the past, though.

It is, no doubt, difficult to tell these forms of scholarship apart in a manner that would leave no room for criticism or different interpretations. Certainly, it would be futile to assume that the following discussion is not open to critique or contrarian arguments. This, however, does not mean that one should not seek to inspect the distinction between talkers and doers. Something can be done in order to distinguish these forms of scholarship even if we acknowledge the unavoidable imperfection of the attempt. Where to start the analysis? The bottom line is that it would be difficult to undertake sanitised comparative law scholarship without any theoretical dimensions as it would be equally difficult – if not impossible – to undertake purely theoretical comparative law scholarship without any connections to law as a normative phenomenon that is closely connected to the legal professions.[8] Accordingly, it would not make sense to provide evidence to a parliamentary committee in the same manner as one writes a theoretical paper for a specialised law journal. Much depends on who comparative law is meant for, or who are its clients.[9]

Having said that, it seems possible to assume that a difference exists between theoretical genre(s) and less theoretical genre(s). Drawing this distinction means assuming that reading about something, discussing something, writing about something, and thinking about something are not the same thing as actually doing it. In the world of comparative law this would mean drawing the distinction between *theory* and *practice*.[10] In this chapter I will first investigate the difference and then set the scene for elucidating this issue. Instead of reviewing a great number

[5] cf Esin Örücü, *The Enigma of Comparative Law* (Martinus Nijhoff 2004) 163. Örücü also mentions differing emotional attitudes and philosophies of life.

[6] The distinction is well explained in Catherine Valcke, *Comparing Law* (CUP 2019) 'the groundwork typically is…largely a-theoretical whereas the theoretical scholarship comes across as strictly theoretical, i.e., detached from any field work', ibid 7.

[7] On this see, eg, Michael Madison, 'The Lawyer as Legal Scholar' (2004) 65 *University of Pittsburgh Law Review* 63–81 (review essay by Eugene Volokh, *Academic Legal Writing* 2003).

[8] cf Valcke (n 6) 9.

[9] See also Alessandro Somma, *Introduzione al diritto comparato*, 3rd edn (Giappichelli 2025) 68–73.

[10] By no means does the difference concern only study of law. In fact, the difference has been a part of Western thinking for a very long time. See, eg, James Allen, 'Practical and Theoretical Knowledge in Aristotle' in Devin Henry & Karen Margarethe Nielsen (eds), *Bridging the Gap Between Aristotle's Science and Ethics* (CUP 2015) 49–70.

of publications, I seek to provide a reasonably thick description of the division by illuminating a few important – what I consider mainstream – publications. The simple aim is to cut through the thicket of voluminous literature by highlighting examples I consider relevant and telling. My belief is that this approach will shed sufficient light on the issue of this chapter even though the chosen approach limits the conclusions drawn. In the last section I seek to unpack the juxtaposition between talking and doing.[11] My argument here builds on the intuition that, in essence, the juxtaposition may prove to be at least an artificial one – and perhaps even downright mistaken.

I. Talkers – Explicating the Assumptions

'Talker' refers here to a theoretical scholar, a theorist of comparative law. Against the backdrop of comparative law, again in its broadest sense, it seems a tall order to provide a general definition of what one means by a theorist. In principle, it is safe to say that a comparative law theorist refers to a scholar who is concerned with the theoretical aspects of comparative law. By and large – but by no means always – this boils down to identifying oneself as a comparatist or an academic comparative lawyer. However, in the case of comparative law theorists it needs to be pointed out that they are not like legal theorists per se, albeit differences are sometimes lines drawn on water. Yet there is not much theoretical discussion on classic legal theoretical issues – and even if there is, it does not follow the conventions of legal theory as an academic subject.[12] Whereas legal theorists tend to discuss at length eminent scholars – such as Hans Kelsen, HLA Hart, Ronald Dworkin, or Joseph Raz – comparatists are less prone to do so. Comparatists do not confine themselves to issues that stay within the limits of legal theory as an academic subject.[13] Instead, comparative law theorists typically specialise in methods of studying law comparatively and cite legal theorists only in passing.

In other words, comparative law theorists are scholars who discuss, construct, and criticise steps taken to conduct comparative study of law. In practice, comparative law theorists are specialists in methods and methodologies employed in comparative law. We need to look behind the facade of theoretically oriented scholarship in comparative law in order to get a grip on what comparative law theorists are about. The problem is that this is easier said than done. Nevertheless,

[11] Valcke (n 6) at 7 makes exactly same observation; some comparatists are theorists who 'talk about it' whereas others are more like field workers who do it. So, 'Few are both'.

[12] See, eg, William Ewald's massive article 'Comparative Jurisprudence (I): What Was It Like to Try a Rat?' (1995) *University of Pennsylvania Law Review* 1889–2149. This paper goes deep into questions that are essentially philosophical: 'the central claim is this: if comparative law is appropriately combined with legal philosophy the result is a substantially new discipline, "comparative jurisprudence"', ibid 1891.

[13] It has been noted that 'while legal theory is concerned with the general definition of law in terms of principal function, comparative law looks at the function of law within specific legal traditions and the way these functions are performed', Geoffrey Samuel, 'Comparative Law and Jurisprudence' (1998) 47 *ICLQ* 817–36, 823.

it seems to me that a special way of thinking - *Anschauung* - animates those who work with the methodology of comparative law. Their thinking grows from an urge to explain to themselves and to other legal (doctrinal) scholars what comparative law is about and what it is that comparatists (or comparative lawyers) do.[14] This means also, by extension, that they discuss what is law. How is this not legal theory, one may ask. If their game is not legal theory or legal philosophy, then what is it actually?

We are, alas, quite unlikely to be able to pinpoint what comparative law theory and comparative law theorists are about in an exhaustive manner. Scholarly diversity in research focuses and approaches is simply too vast to provide even an approximately reliable definition. For example, studying indigenous or religious normativities and studying property law in civilian legal systems require different kinds of methodologies. Accordingly, it would seem feasible to say that comparative law theorists tend to be interested in comparative law itself. In other words, they venture to conceive what their discipline is and how they see their own role as comparatists. Of course, one may wonder why there is seemingly an inescapable need to explain (and justify) the existence of comparative law scholarship. Comparatists complain about their discipline but at the same time they constantly renew the implicit project of justifying the existence of their field.[15] Esin Örücü described this as the enigma of comparative law; something that remains a riddle or mystery.[16] It is this very enigma that animates theoretical comparative law scholars to pursue their work in order to unravel it by making it truly understood. This is very different from what one may label as ordinary legal scholarship because doctrinal scholars seldom question the justification or nature of their branch of scholarship.[17] The situation is not easy to put into words but Örücü has described this insightfully:

> I have been researching and teaching comparative law for over twenty-five years and one of the questions addressed to me which has always astonished me, is the second question after the question, 'What is your specialism?' has been answered. The answer: 'I am a comparative lawyer', invariably gives rise to variants of a second question: 'What do you compare?', 'What is your substantive area of law?' or better still 'Yes, but what is your specialism?' One could of course repeat the first answer or try something like 'I am a generalist', or 'I am a methodologist'. This usually brings a rather blank look and an 'Ah!'[18]

[14] 'Most comparatists take it for granted that their field of research and study qualifies as an academic discipline, even if it may still be incoherent, of a "piecemeal nature," and in need of theoretical-methodological overhauling', Günter Frankenberg, *Comparative Law as Critique* (Edward Elgar 2019) 9.

[15] Vivian Grosswald Curran speaks of comparative law's 'existential angst', 'Comparative Law and the Legal Origins Thesis' (2009) 57 *AJCL*, 863–76, 863. See also Frankenberg (n 14) 3–4.

[16] See Örücü (n 5).

[17] Sometimes comparatists address stark criticism against doctrinal study of law. See Geoffrey Samuel, 'Can Doctrinal Legal Scholarship Be Defended?' (2022) 4 *Amicus Curiae* 43–70. An alternative approach would be to argue that comparative law is in fact an ordinary form of legal scholarship, see Stephen A Smith, 'Comparative Law as Ordinary Legal Scholarship' (2010) 5 *JCL* 331–56.

[18] Örücü (n 5) 3.

This witty excerpt makes it clear what the differences are between field-of-law focused (doctrinal) legal scholars and someone who is interested in the theory and methodology of comparative law but without being a legal theorist or legal philosopher.[19] Indeed, as noted by Oleksiy Kresin, theoretical comparative law was not born as a derivative from legal philosophy and legal theory, which is why it is not their faithful servant.[20] From there it also follows that the need arises to explain (and justify) comparative law as a form of *legal* scholarship. Characteristically, theoretical comparative law scholarship tends to have a critical nature in one way or another. Theoretical scholarship in comparative law is by nature contrarian and its key focus leans towards methodology-related issues that are addressed in a critical tone. This kind of – and still continuing – form of scholarship came into existence in the mid-1980s when the seminal contribution by Günter Frankenberg was published. He called for a re-think of comparative law.[21] It is safe to say that Frankenberg's contrarian article has strongly influenced later development in the field. In my view it is an important milestone. Moreover, it contains critical ideas still relevant today (see chapter eleven).[22]

Frankenberg's original attack, which he has later refined and further developed, was aimed at so-called functionalist mainstream comparative law.[23] He labelled functionalists as 'legocentrics' who were, according to his analysis, unable to see anything outside formal legal texts and institutions.[24] The key focus of the critique was based on the idea according to which theory and methodology of comparative law was in terrible shape, hence in need of serious re-thinking. The fundamentally critical spirit of this kind of scholarship depicted alleged mainstream comparative law as superficial and unsystematic, which is why it was also prone to error.[25] Having greater than mainstream's scholarly ambitions seems to be mostly motivated by an honest interest in improving comparative law in intellectual terms, and also to help the field to gain its long-desired academic recognition.[26] At the same time, though, this kind of specialised theoretical scholarship has become more burdensome for practically oriented scholars and lawyers who prefer rather to do than to complicate and talk. For instance, Pierre Legrand's theoretical scholarship is in nature so far from what practical lawyers or pragmatically oriented

[19] This is not quite the same as distinguishing between a comparatist and a comparative lawyer, as Örücü herself also speaks of both. See Esin Örücü, 'Methodologies for Comparative Law' in Jan Smits, Jaakko Husa, Catherine Valcke & Madalena Narciso (eds), *Elgar Encyclopedia of Comparative Law* Vol 3 (Edward Elgar 2023) 42–50.

[20] Oleksiy V Kresin, 'World Picture of Comparative Law' (2024) 19 *JCL* 3–55, 55.

[21] Günter Frankenberg, 'Critical Comparisons: Re-thinking Comparative Law' (1985) 26 *Harvard International Law Journal* (1985) 411–55.

[22] Balázs Fekete, *Paradigms in Modern European Comparative Law* (Hart Publishing 2021) says that 'Frankenberg's insights are still valid', ibid 156.

[23] In his 2019 book (*Comparative Law as Critique*), Frankenberg explains that he wants 'to lay out and submit to critical scrutiny dominant styles and practices' of comparative law, ibid 16.

[24] Frankenberg (n 21) 438.

[25] Ewald (n 12) 1891.

[26] Mathias Reimann, 'The Progress and Failure of Comparative Law in the Second Half of the Twentieth Century' (2002) 50 *AJCL* 671–700.

comparative lawyers do that it seems to go unnoticed by doctrinally-minded comparatists, whereas in the field of comparative law theory his oeuvre would be virtually impossible to fully ignore even if one would disagree.

Legrand's ambitious call to culturalise comparative study of law is very different from the doctrinally flavoured mainstream, which is less interested in the primary and fundamental difference between laws of different legal cultures.[27] Whereas mainstreamers are interested in homogenisation of laws and what could be labelled 'singularity', Legrand adamantly opposes these views as 'primordial resistance to the totalizers.'[28] In my reading, Legrand is a parade example of an important comparative law scholar who focuses on talking about it. Unlike those scholars who consider themselves 'doers', Legrand builds on general philosophy. Accordingly, philosophers such as Martin Heidegger and – especially – Jacques Derrida are frequently cited even though Legrand does not seem to follow any particular philosophy faithfully. No doubt, placing a heavy accent on *foreignness* is not what more practically minded comparatists would do.[29] Positivistic comparatists, instead, would focus on 'statutes, cases, parliamentary debates, and doctrinal works.'[30] Then again, this does not mean that less theoretical comparatists could not regard Legrand's contrarian work as both stimulating and inspiring.[31] This issue also concerns one's scholarly style.

Because the theoretical literature on comparative law – 'talking about it' – is highly voluminous, it would not make sense to try to review it all here. What is important is to note the theoretical nature of this contrarian form(s) of scholarship. As Robert Leckey rightly notes in a paper published in 2017, '[t]he last quarter of the twentieth century witnessed a sustained attack on the purported mainstream of comparative law'.[32] In my reading, this intellectually stimulating critical scholarship is in essence a rich collection of contrarian literature consisting of talking rather than doing. This scholarship has built an erudite wall against what one might describe as positivist-minded legal reformers and pragmatic commonality-seeking comparative lawyers who conceive comparative law in a less ambitious way and choose to do it rather than talk about it. Crucially, those who talk about scholarly comparative law underline the need for the comparatist to open up and explain their theoretical assumptions about law and comparing it.[33] This is different from those who perceive themselves mainly as doers who leave their assumptions unopened.

[27] See, eg, Pierre Legrand, 'The Guile and The Guise: Apropos of Comparative Law as We Know It' (2021) 16 *Asian Journal of Comparative Law* 155–81 ('comparative law demands spontaneous attunement to differences across laws – or so one would readily expect. But comparatists are enthralled to universals, equivalences, and commonalities, often disingenuously so', ibid 155).

[28] ibid 180.

[29] See, eg, Pierre Legrand, *Negative Comparative Law* (CUP 2022) 276–79.

[30] Örücü (n 19) 47.

[31] cf Balázs Fekete's review essay of Legrand's book, 'The Power of Negative' (2023) 18 *JCL* 379–90, 389.

[32] Robert Leckey, 'Review of Comparative Law' (2017) 26 *Social & Legal Studies* 3–24, 3.

[33] Theorists take definitional problems very seriously. See, eg, Geoffrey Samuel, *An Introduction to Comparative Law Theory and Method* (Hart Publishing 2014) 8–15.

II. Doers – Assumptions Unexplained

I dare say that for a lawyer - even for a comparative lawyer - theoretical and critical literature or 'talking about it' may be difficult to follow or to understand as it seems distanced from what legal professionals do in their line of work. This is because theoretical and critical literature dissolves into non-legal fields such as anthropology or general study of culture.[34] If this is taken into account, it is not surprising that the majority of comparatists seek actively to avoid contrarian theoretical scholarship and choose instead an implied contrarian stance against those who focus on 'talking' instead of 'doing'. In short, if a comparative lawyer studies differences between tort law in civilian and common law, then learned discussion on Derrida or epistemology of comparison may quite understandably feel like an unnecessary detour or a lecture from the above.[35] It may feel more natural to focus on legislation, case law, and legal doctrine. Part of the alleged pragmatism in comparative law seems basically to mean avoidance of translation issues in the sense that there is no discussion about translation challenges even though today it is increasingly understood that comparative study of law requires translation.[36] Translation seems to be a non-issue for the tool-focused anti-theoretical view of comparative law.

As there are many ways of talking about comparative law theoretically and critically, so there are also many ways of being 'a pragmatic comparatist' and to nurture a reserved attitude towards talking about it. Differences between these two comparative law camps are not overly difficult to detect. Sometimes the reservation is put into words but it is more common to read this attitude between the lines. An example of the first mentioned is Michael Bogdan, who reviewed my book on interdisciplinary comparative law. He notes, quite rightly, that 'most of the book consists not of research about the phenomenon of law but rather of research about research or, at times, research about research about research'.[37] The criticism is, in essence, that there is too much talk and too little doing. Bogdan opens his thinking on the issue:

> This reviewer must confess that this kind of theoretical approach to comparative legal work is not his cup of tea. While I appreciate macro-level studies of the general problems of comparative law, I prefer pragmatic comparative work dealing with actual law.[38]

This way of disclosing one's non-theoretical preferred thinking is quite rare as it is more common to express the reserved attitude in more subtle ways. Nevertheless,

[34] cf Leckey (n 32) 11.

[35] About the claimed importance of Derrida, see Pierre Legrand, 'Siting Foreign Law: How Derrida Can Help' (2011) 21 *Duke Journal of Comparative & International Law* 595–630. As to the epistemology of comparative law, see Geoffrey Samuel, 'Epistemology of Comparative Law' in Smits et al (n 19), Vol 2 (Edward Elgar 2023) 27–35.

[36] See for discussion on comparative law and translation, Jan Engberg, 'Comparative Law for Legal Translation' (2020) 33 *International Journal for the Semiotics of Law* 263–82; Przemysław Kusik, 'Comparative Law in the Eyes of Translation Scholars' (2024) 64 *Hermes* 111–24.

[37] Michael Bogdan, 'Book Review of Jaakko Husa, Interdisciplinary Comparative Law (Edward Elgar 2022)' (2023) 87 *Rabels Zeitschrift für ausländisches und internationales Privatrecht* 217–19, 218.

[38] ibid 218.

Bogdan well illustrates the 'doing it' attitude as he openly prefers pragmatic work dealing with what he calls 'actual law', thus neatly capturing how 'doers' conceive the field. Now, I do not criticise Bogdan's preferences here, but I think he neatly expresses the differences between comparative law camps that I am discussing in this chapter. It is my intuition that even though many would not open their thinking like Bogdan, he is not alone with his preferences.

Along rather similar lines, for example, Tony Weir once even suggested that there is no need for theory in the study of law.[39] Without going deeper into Weir's view, we can see that both camps identify as comparatists (or comparative lawyers) but they do not share the same understanding of what it means. Accordingly, comparative law genres end up being different as there is no paradigm in modern comparative law. Theorists and pragmatists reside in different camps.

Reading comparative law scholarship that either avoids - or is very curt about - the underlying theoretical assumptions brings to mind a quote from Ralph Waldo Emerson who said that '[i]n skating over thin ice, our safety is in our speed'.[40] This is not a harsh critique of this kind of scholarship as, in the end, speed is what ensures that one gets over the ice. In honesty, this is understandable as this is also how scholars get their articles and books written and published. To be sure, much of comparative law scholarship appears to be about dealing with 'actual law'. However, one needs to tread carefully here as the fact that research does not engage with comparative law theory or methodology does not mean that the research would be atheoretical. Leaving theoretical assumptions implicit and unexplained or being unaware of their existence does not mean that they would not exist.[41] Silence may speak volumes when it comes to this issue although, unfortunately, it is not quite clear what it says. Let me attempt to tease out what the silent part is about with the help of illustrative examples.

One noteworthy example is a comparative study of precedents, published in the late 1990s.[42] This volume is filled with contributions by eminent legal scholars from different countries. The introduction, penned by the editors, is virtually silent about the comparative method(s) used in the book. They say, nevertheless, that '[s]o far, we have said nothing about the already sizeable literature of comparative law and legal theory of relevance to our study'. The editors continue by stating that 'we have individually and collectively consulted much of the existing literature while doing the current project'. Moreover, they admit not making 'any effort to cite all of these, and a comprehensive compendium of references to the existing comparative

[39] Tony Weir, 'Contracts in Rome and England' (1992) 66 *Tulane Law Review* 1615–48: 'Like history itself, we are not opposed to casuistry. It is possible for us, like Hamlet, to tell a hawk from a handsaw, and to do so without a complete theory of aerial predators or an exhaustive inventory of the carpenter's toolbox; furthermore, we can effect such telling without having a theory of telling, though the current fad of epistemology might lead one to doubt that (given a theory of doubting)', 1616.

[40] Ralph Waldo Emerson, *Essays* (James Munroe & Company 1841) 194 (in the essay 'Prudence').

[41] It has been noted that an anti-theoretical or common-sense view 'is no less a statement of theory', Samuel (n 13) 826. Accordingly, alleged pragmatism is also a theoretical stance.

[42] D Neil MacCormick and Robert S Summers (eds), *Interpreting Precedents: A Comparative Study* (Ashgate 1997).

and theoretical literature on precedent is not to be found here'.[43] However, the appendix reveals the final version of common questions the contributors were expected to answer.[44] Curiously – at least for a comparatist – methodology is demoted in the shape of an appendix having, at best, secondary relevance. This kind of belittling way of dealing with comparative methodology does not appear favourable in the eyes of the 'talkers', that much is clear. To me, it does look like an attempt to sweep methodological issues on comparison under the carpet in the spirit of 'doing it'. This may be, nevertheless, like throwing the baby out with the bathwater as comparison is an act that is based on certain assumptions.

I have no doubts concerning the scholarly quality of the book as to precedents – indeed, quite the contrary. However, from the viewpoint of comparative law scholarship, how methodology is treated in the book does look peculiar. In essence, the editors say that there is relevant literature, and they are aware of its existence. Regardless, they are unwilling to explain how the volume's approach is based on comparative law scholarship. Instead, the editors chose to be silent and leave it to readers to sort out – presumably on the basis of the appendix and individual chapters – what methodology is being used. The tacit message conveyed is that they choose to do it rather than talk about doing it.

Interestingly, the volume on precedents has a predecessor, published seven years earlier and edited by the same scholars. The earlier book is a comparative study on statutory interpretation.[45] Unlike the later book, this volume tackles the comparative method more openly. The editors briefly explain the comparative element as a part of the chapter on method and methodology. However, this short text does not explain the comparative method used as it focuses on justifying the use of comparison. The book also contains a separate chapter of some 50 pages explaining significant similarities and differences between arguments, patterns of justification, modes of settling conflicts between arguments, structure and styles of arguments.[46] From the point of view of comparative law scholarship, it is remarkable that not a single scholarly work in the field of comparative law is cited or even mentioned.[47] None of this is meant to criticise the scholarly quality of these volumes on interpretation of precedents and statutory law. Instead, I highlight a certain latent attitude towards theoretical scholarship on comparative law. In fact, these two books clearly show a will to do comparative study of law but not to talk about doing it. This approach recalls what Otto Von Bismarck allegedly said about laws, likening them to sausage-making in that laws inspire respect only if we do not know how they are made.

Another, more recent, example is Maartje de Visser's book on constitutional review in Europe, published in the mid-2010s. She analyses how constitutions limit

[43] Quoted excerpts ibid 14.
[44] ibid 551–61.
[45] D Neil MacCormick and Robert S Summers (eds), *Interpreting Statutes: A Comparative Study* (Dartmouth 1991) 24.
[46] ibid 261–510.
[47] In many chapters of the book use of comparative law arguments by the courts is mentioned.

state powers and protect basic rights.[48] The focus of the study is on how constitutional review – which both limits and protects – is organised. In practice, de Visser analyses comparatively 11 European systems, how they organise constitutional review, and how the legal order of the European Union influences national models of review. In essence, the book identifies what one can label as a European constitutional tradition against the comparative backdrop of constitutional review. This volume is clearly excellent scholarship in the field of comparative (constitutional) law. However, de Visser chooses to remain virtually silent about the comparative method she uses in the book. Yet she makes it clear that the book is essentially a comparative study of law as she defends the choice of countries to be 'large enough to make meaningful comparisons and tease out similarities and differences.'[49] Again, I have no doubts about the quality of the book. Instead, I make the observation that she chooses to do it rather than to talk about doing it.[50]

A more recent example is an interesting book on the law of loyalty by Lionel Smith, Oxford's Professor of Comparative Law.[51] Smith, who identifies as a comparative lawyer, seeks to find unity across borders between legal systems and fields of law. In doing so, he crosses the borders between common law and civil law and between private law and public law.[52] Noteworthily, even though he seeks and speaks for the unity of law, he is not blind to diversity. He argues convincingly that a kind of a conceptual unity marks the treatment of all the situations in which a person is empowered to carry out a mission to act for other-regarding purposes. Yet he does not argue that the law would be the same in both common law and civil law. Nor does he argue that the same legal norms apply to all actors everywhere. Instead, he argues that common justifying principles are useful when one seeks to grasp why border-crossing commonalities exist at all. Notwithstanding, he shows that the diversity of contexts illustrates that differences do exist and that those differences are based on certain reasons. The outcome of the study takes the form of justificatory principles.[53] These are not legal rules operating directly on facts, but higher-level ideas that explain and justify legal rules.

Again, I have no doubt about the scholarly quality. The methodological dimension raises questions, however. He describes his methodology as 'interpretative methodology'. This means an attempt to examine a body of law and to provide the best account of intelligible connections between the features he is interested in. This approach is, as to its nature, reflexive in terms of examining how the law allows one to articulate an intelligible order. When this order is understood and articulated it can be used to assess the law.[54] This makes perfect sense, but it does not say anything about the applied comparative approach.

[48] Maartje de Visser, *Constitutional Review in Europe: A Comparative Analysis* (Hart Publishing 2014).
[49] ibid 6.
[50] Method is dealt with in brief footnotes on three pages, ibid 6–9.
[51] Lionel Smith, *The Law of Loyalty* (OUP 2023).
[52] ibid preface.
[53] 'A justificatory principle is not a legal rule that operates directly on facts that have occurred; it is a higher-level idea that explains and justifies one or more legal rules', ibid 431.
[54] See ibid s III(A).

In essence, Smith's interesting study is theoretically ambitious legal scholarship. However, it remains a mystery why he does not open the comparative approach used in the study. The reader is left in the dark on the issues that concern Smith's methodological choices and how the study fits in the existing comparative law scholarship. I venture to speculate and claim that two viable explanations are possible. First, perhaps he is not aware of the rich theoretical scholarship on comparative law and comparative law methodology. Second, he is aware of that kind of scholarship but chooses not to engage but focuses on the substance instead. The second explanation seems more likely as Smith explains that '[l]ike all comparative lawyers, I am a legal positivist as legal positivists understand that term'.[55] Against the backdrop of modern comparative law scholarship, this is a bold statement in the sense that describing all comparative lawyers as legal positivists seems dubious.[56] A reading of comparatists – Frankenberg, Legrand, Örücü, William Ewald, Uwe Kischel, Geoffrey Samuel, Mark Van Hoecke, Mathias Siems, Ugo Mattei, Michele Graziadei, Ralf Michaels, Catherine Valcke, Pier Giuseppe Monateri, or this author – suggests that identifying oneself as a legal positivist appears quite an unpopular if not downright contrarian stance among comparatists.[57] A book on precedent whose author claimed to be a positivist comparatist would have made sense in the past but in the 2020s it seems to be aiming to wilfully avoid theoretical comparative law even when explicitly identifying as a comparative lawyer. In my reading, the message in between the lines says that 'doing it' is what counts but 'talking about it' is not necessary. Again, this is a possible choice and fits within the academic freedom of a legal scholar. No doubt it is a choice that sits well in the mainstream's idea of the lawyerly basic method, namely doctrine.

Before moving on to discuss the possibility of overcoming the dichotomy between 'talking' and 'doing', one further point remains to be made about the avoidance of opening and/or explicitly addressing comparative methodology. As has become clear, contemporary comparative law needs to look beyond law as narrowly understood. While doing so, the issue of interdisciplinarity surfaces. Interestingly, the dichotomy known from comparative law scholarship seems to be reflected in closely related fields. For instance, the new emerging field of comparative legal history circles around the comparative approach to legal history but so far seems unexpectedly reluctant to enter into discussion on comparative methodology.[58] As pointed out by Dirk Heirbaut in his thick volume on the history

[55] ibid 12. On the other hand, using a very different tone though, Smith is not alone in thinking that comparatists are legal positivists. Pierre Legrand argues 'that orthodox comparativists largely share an approach to the law that can legitimately be designated as 'positivism' or 'legal positivism', Legrand (n 35) 598.

[56] Frankenberg (n 14) at 6 argues, rather convincingly, that 'Mainstream comparative law embraced the formalist notion of legal validity entertained by legal positivism as well as its unlikely ally, the anti-formalist style. This combination betrays the impossibility of what positivists are desperately trying to do: to neutralize, albeit analytically, all extralegal incursions – notably politics, ethics, culture and the economy – on law-making and law-deciding'.

[57] This is how I read the scholarship of these comparatists, regardless of how they may define themselves.

[58] See for more detailed discussion, Jaakko Husa, 'Seeking a Disciplinary Identity' (2020) 8 *Comparative Legal History* 173–93 (review essay of *Comparative Legal History* 2019).

of codifications, 'comparative legal history just follows the established pattern for legal historians, who are more interested in unearthing details than developing methods and constructing theories'.[59] Accordingly, we can see that the distinction between talking and doing stretches beyond comparative law as narrowly understood. This shows that the distinction is vigorous, but the question remains; is it really an insurmountable obstacle? Surely the distinction between doers and talkers is blunt whereas the reality is fuzzier.

III. The Futility of Juxtaposition?

Taking into account the nature of comparative law (broadly understood) it seems that scholarly work requires both dimensions, namely theoretical and practical. As Max Rheinstein noted in the late 1960s, comparative law can be a field of practical utility, yet full of intellectual challenge.[60] In all honesty, the distinction addressed here looks a lot like the collision between contextualists and doctrinalists, addressed above in chapter two. However, despite overlap these are not fully identical distinctions. Whereas distinctly theoretical forms of scholarship distance themselves from the practical work of lawyers, manifestly practical forms of scholarship virtually deny or belittle any theoretical difficulties involved. Theorists, for their part, feel the urge to explain and justify comparativism in an explicit manner and criticise comparative law scholarship that they deem theoretically insufficient. In contrast, self-proclaimed pragmatists tend to keep their comparativism at least partially unexplained and seemingly feel no urge to justify or to further explain their methodology, in this respect reminiscent of doing doctrinal study of law where there is no need to explain methodology. Therein lies the problem if we are interested in a balanced approach. As far as I can tell, it is not desirable that comparatists drift into loyalties to their methodological views as the diversity of law and pluralism in comparative law itself seem incompatible with extremes. Practical wisdom is to be found in the words of Vernon Valentine Palmer: the '[m]essage from Mount Olympus must not be that comparative law is always forbidding and difficult'.[61] This sort of message would be self-defeating and harmful for the endeavour to encourage lawyers to study law across borders.

Now, as I pointed out at the beginning of this chapter, it would be difficult to undertake sanitised comparative law without theoretical dimensions as it would be equally difficult to undertake purely theoretical comparative law scholarship without connections to the legal professions. As Frederick Schauer notes, 'It is impossible to do comparative law without having a theory of law'.[62] Then again, this does not mean that comparatists are, or should become, legal theoreticians.

[59] Dirk Heirbaut, *Redefining Codification* (OUP 2025) 359.
[60] Max Rheinstein, 'Comparative Law' (1968) 22 *Arkansas Law Review* 415–25, 424.
[61] Vernon Valentine Palmer, 'From Lerotholi to Lando' (2005) 53 *AJCL* 261–90, 290.
[62] Frederick Schauer, 'Legal Theory and Comparative Law' in Smits et al (n 19), Vol 2, 517–24, 517; cf Valcke (n 6) 9.

In my view it does not even mean that comparative law and legal theory would be mutually dependent enterprises.[63] A reading of the illustrative methodology-allergic scholarship discussed above clarifies that those volumes are based on certain understandings of law that come close to legal positivism understood as a preference for a doctrinal approach.[64] For modern comparative law scholarship, this is a problem because, by and large, it favours contextualising law and is ready to accommodate competing and overlapping methodologies. Is there a way out of the cul-de-sac caused by colliding ideas about what it means to be a comparatist or a comparative lawyer? I have no solution to this, but perhaps this collision is not as drastic as I painted it above. This may be the case, as it seems attainable to find a tolerable mean or medium. In fact, this kind of scholarship already exists.

It seems possible to combine talking about it and doing it. An interesting and important contribution of this kind of balanced comparativism can be found in Richard Hyland's book on gifts.[65] This is an example of a study that addresses, and analyses, intricate doctrinal issues but also explains and carefully discusses the comparative approach and the methodological choices. Crucially, Hyland both talks about and does comparative law between the covers of his ambitious volume.[66] This does not, however, mean that he would not be a contrarian, as indeed his discussion on method and criticism of so-called functional comparative law indicates.[67] Hyland shows that major Western legal systems seem to have significant doctrinal problems when gift-giving is conceived in terms of law. The volume shows how general characterisations and conceptual frameworks typical of private law systems suffer from serious issues in their conceptual and theoretical frameworks in terms of gifts.[68]

In essence, Hyland asks: where do gifts fit in the private law puzzle? Importantly, he is acutely aware of the relationship between law and society and he appreciates the crucial role which customary norms play without formal legal recognition in terms of making gifts which 'perhaps more than any other field governed by the private law, is already structured by customary norms before it becomes a legal institution'.[69] Hyland discusses comparative methodology at length as he uses elements of theoretical comparative law debate while meticulously explaining his own understanding of methodology as he applies a comparative approach. The chapter on methodology discusses and evaluates the comparative approach in a chapter of more than 60 pages.[70]

[63] This is, however, how Schauer sees the relationship, ibid 519–20.

[64] This is not to say that the above-discussed books would be doctrinal in a narrow sense.

[65] Richard Hyland, *Gifts: A Study in Comparative Law* (OUP 2009).

[66] For Hyland, the critical question for comparative law 'is how to establish the perspective from which different legal systems should be compared', ibid 64.

[67] Hyland understands functionalism as 'purposivism', which refers to a kind of comparative law that 'investigates how the institutions created by the various legal systems fulfil their articulated purposes', ibid 96.

[68] See also my review essay of the book, Jaakko Husa, 'Gift: The Piece That Does Not Fit the Legal Puzzle' (2009) 16 *Maastricht Journal of European and Comparative Law* 341–59.

[69] Hyland (n 65) 8.

[70] ibid 63–126.

Another example of a balanced approach is Mitchel de S.-O.-l'E. Lasser's book on judicial deliberations, published in 2004.[71] He compares how and why the European Court of Justice, the French Cour de cassation, and the United States Supreme Court provide different approaches to producing judicial accountability and control, judicial debate and deliberation, and judicial legitimacy. The focus of comparison on judicial argumentation is based on the distinction between civil law (France) and common law (the US) and goes on to use this comparison as the basis for investigating the judicial argumentation used by the European Court of Justice. The methodological question is essentially comparative: 'what facet(s) of these courts should one study, and why?'[72]

Lasser compares the different approaches and ends up critically addressing settled comparative law ideas about the difference between French civil law and American common law judicial decision-making. In his comparison, the European Court of Justice is revealed as combining both civilian and common law elements in its judicial work. The study is openly comparative as it 'seeks to offer a major reassessment of comparative law theory and practice'.[73] Importantly, Lasser does not stay silent about comparative law methodology, and he explains the project against the backdrop of theoretical comparative law scholarship.[74] In short, the book on judicial deliberations does what Hyland's study of gifts does, too; it both talks about it and does it.

Let us consider these two studies that I chose as illustrative works showing what balanced comparative study of law may look like. It seems that even though these studies are exemplary, they could not work as models as there is no easy way of having to think out one's comparative approach. This is simply because both studies carefully *tailor* their comparative method against the backdrop of theoretical comparative law scholarship and the purpose of their research. There is a lesson here. Others, too, need to tailor their methods according to what it is they are studying and what it is they want to achieve with their studies. It is also important to see that – even though both of these studies discuss comparative law theory – what they argue is, again, tailored to fit the needs of their particular projects. This differs from general comparative law theory in which the message is more demanding and sometimes even normative. This is due to the specific nature of theoretical comparative law scholarship. So, after reviewing modern comparative law, Leckey observes that many comparatists 'urge their fellows to abandon some varieties of comparative law and to unite around particular approaches'.[75] This is not what Hyland or

[71] Mitchel de S.-O.-l'E. Lasser, *Judicial Deliberations: A Comparative Analysis of Transparency and Legitimacy* (OUP 2004).

[72] ibid 10.

[73] ibid 5.

[74] The whole introductory chapter (2–23) is essentially based on explaining the project against the backdrop of comparative law scholarship. In the footnotes a great deal of comparative law literature is cited and further discussed. So, familiar comparative law scholars such as Ugo Mattei, Horatia Muir Watt, Pierre Legrand, William Ewald, and John Bell are cited.

[75] Leckey (n 32) 3.

Lasser do and this, I believe, conveys an important message to all those who engage in or with comparative law or aspire to do so.

A concluding remark to this chapter needs to be made on the significance of the purpose of each comparative law study. It seems undeniable that serving the needs of law reform or unification of law is bound to be different from unearthing relationships between systems or seeking to understand law as part of the surrounding legal culture and societal fabric. Accordingly, it is important to grasp the reality of different types of comparative law scholarship. Traditional or positivistic private law comparison between common law and civil law may indeed work with less theoretical and methodological framing than comparing indigenous, historic, or traditional systems.[76] In any case, it seems believable that the inborn tendency not to explicate one's method and theoretical assumptions about law flows from the doctrinal tradition where typically there is no need to explicate one's method.

None of what I have said above about the strands of comparative law scholarship should be taken as rebuffing them. In the end, the takeaway concerns conceiving how comparatists and/or comparative lawyers tend to build their scholarly identities in a manner that is explicitly or implicitly contrarian as to its nature. The takeaway, if there is any, may be that contrarianism can also take place between the lines in the form of leaving things out or simply avoiding to cite disliked scholars but without telling why. Some might say that this is perfectly normal and belongs to the poetic licence of each comparatist. Of course, those who stress the importance of research ethics may hold a different view.[77]

[76] cf Fernanda Pirie, 'Global Comparative Law?' (2025) 45 *Oxford Journal of Legal Studies* 506–24.

[77] About ethical issues in legal research in general, see Mario Serio, Rosalba Potenzano, Giancarlo Geraci, Rosario Petruso & Nicoletta Patti, 'Ethics in Legal Research' in Lorella Congiunti, Francesco Lo Piccolo, Antonio Russo & Mario Serio (eds), *Ethics in Research* (Springer 2023) 11–34.

6

The West and the Rest

One of the most persistent internal collisions or juxtapositions in the field of comparative law is an area of research labelled as macro-comparative law. Its ramifications stretch to micro-comparative law, but the main theatre of scholarly collision has been on the macro-level. This has to do with comparative law's ardent attempt to gain an epistemic grasp of the world's legal systems and create taxonomies.[1] There is no need to discuss the volumes of literature in detail here.[2] In the literature, nevertheless, one can see a myriad of classifications and groupings of the world's legal systems.[3] As Mark Van Hoecke points out, in the macro-comparative law of the twentieth century scholars tried to construct a world map of 'legal families' following the ideals of the exact sciences.[4] This form of scholarship, peculiar in the eyes of the non-comparatists, has produced a great number of comparative law books and articles; indeed, it is still being written.[5] This scholarship has altered surprisingly little over the years even though conceptual frameworks may have changed.

Essentially, this form of legal scholarship is a distinctly scholarly form of comparative law. Theoretical comparative law of this sort discusses and analyses topics such as common law, civil law, mixed law, and Islamic law. These constructions are typically called 'legal families', albeit there is no consensus on what a 'legal family' actually is. Other competing and overlapping

[1] See for more detailed discussion, Jaakko Husa, 'The Future of Legal Families' in *Oxford Handbook Topics in Law* (Oxford Academic 2016), doi.org/10.1093/oxfordhb/9780199935352.013.26.

[2] See, eg, Balàzs Fekete, *Paradigms in Modern European Comparative Law* (Hart Publishing 2021) 99–116.

[3] See, eg, Åke Malmström, 'The System of Legal Systems' (1969) 13 *Scandinavian Studies in Law* 127–49.

[4] Mark Van Hoecke, 'Macro Comparison' in Jan Smits, Jaakko Husa, Catherine Valcke & Madalena Narciso (eds), *Elgar Encyclopedia of Comparative Law*, Vol 3 (Edward Elgar 2023) 3–9, 3.

[5] See, eg, Helmut Heiss, 'Hierarchische Rechtskreiseinteilung' (2001) 100 *Zeitschrift für Vergleichende Rechtswissenschaft* 396–424; Esin Örücü, 'Family Trees for Legal Systems' in Mark Van Hoecke (ed), *Epistemology and Methodology of Comparative Law* (Hart Publishing 2004) 359–75; Paolo Carozza, Mary Ann Glendon & Colin Picker, *Comparative Legal Traditions in a Nutshell*, 3rd edn (Thomson/West 2008); H Patrick Glenn, *Legal Traditions of the World*, 4th edn (OUP 2010); Raymond Legeais, *Grands systèmes de droit contemporains*, 3rd edn (LexisNexis 2016); and Gilles Cuniberti, *Grands systèmes de droit contemporains*, 4th edn (LGDJ 2019).

conceptualisations are to be found, such as 'legal culture' or 'legal tradition' but in this chapter the focus is on the legal family approach.[6] Regardless, it is my assumption that, as macro-concepts, all these are virtually the same as to their overall features. 'Legal family', in essence, is a conceptual tool of the comparative lawyer far less popular among sociologists or legal theoreticians.[7] It has also been used in law and economics scholarship.[8] In my view, comparatists who write about macro-comparative law are those who one can safely label as theoretical comparatists. Characteristically, these kinds of scholars identify as comparatists. Comparative lawyers with a more pragmatist mindset - real or imagined - seldom, if ever, engage in this sort of scholarship even though they use macro-concepts time and again. Indeed, it would be burdensome to find a comparative law paper that would completely manage to avoid at least mentioning common law or civil law. These concepts are deeply rooted in comparative law discourse but also frequently used by other legal scholars as part of their established professional vocabulary.

Despite the constant nature of macro-comparative law's generalising constructs, some change has been taking place. Before the collapse of the socialist states, the key contrarian distinction was drawn between socialist law and bourgeois law.[9] The distinction formed an important part of post-World War II scholarship. After the downfall of socialism in Central and Eastern Europe, socialist law lost its position as a key construction used in macro-comparative law.[10] This does not mean that today's comparatists would stay silent about socialist law but it does mean that the status of socialist law has diminished significantly.[11] Or, as William Butler puts it, socialist law is 'now a ghost in the world of comparative law'.[12] It is no longer part of mainstream scholarship,

[6] See for further discussion, H Patrick Glenn, 'Comparative Legal Families and Comparative Legal Traditions', in Mathias Reimann & Reinhard Zimmermann (eds), *The Oxford Handbook of Comparative Law*, 2nd edn (OUP 2019) 423–41; Jaakko Husa, 'Macro-Comparative Law – Reloaded' (2018) 131 *Tidsskrift for rettsvitenskap* 410–47.

[7] See, eg, Jaakko Husa, 'Classification of Legal Families Today' (2004) 57 *Revue internationale de droit comparé* 11–38; Maria Pargendler, 'The Rise and Decline of Legal Families' (2012) 60 *AJCL* 1043–74.

[8] See Nuno Garoupa & Maria Pargendler, 'A Law and Economics Perspective on Legal Families' (2014) 7 *European Journal of Legal Studies* 33–55.

[9] Of the collapse see, eg, Valerie Bunce, *Subversive Institutions: The Design and the Destruction of Socialism and the State* (CUP 1999) 1–19.

[10] The family of socialist laws played an important part in several editions of René David's *Les grands systèmes de droit contemporains*, but these were cleared away in the editions published after the collapse of socialist states' socialist law. A similar occurrence happened in Konrad Zweigert & Hein Kötz's *An Introduction to Comparative Law*; the two-book 1987 edition contained socialist law but the 1998 edition omits socialist law completely even though Zweigert & Kötz considered it a legal family. In the 2nd edition they anticipated this by saying that '[t]oday, however, the very existence of a socialist legal family is seriously in question' (297).

[11] See, eg, Peter de Cruz, *Comparative Law in a Changing World*, 3rd edn (Routledge 2007) which deals with socialist law in 30 pages in a book that contains well over 500 pages. René David & John Brierley's *Major Legal Systems in the World Today*, 2nd edn (Stevens & Sons 1978) dedicated almost 150 pages to socialist law. Both of these books concentrate on Soviet/Russian law.

[12] William Butler, 'Comparative Law and Socialist Legal Systems' in Mattias Dahlberg (ed), *Law and Society* (Justus 2019) 75–104.

despite still making occasional appearances in the literature. Consequently, modern volumes on macro-comparative law hardly mention it anymore as it is considered water under the bridge.[13] This, however, does not mean that socialist law would be meaningless in today's world or in comparative law.[14] The fact that it is rarely discussed does not mean that even significant parts of it would not persist in pockets where it is endemic.

The existing legal systems of countries such as the People's Republic of China, the Socialist Republic of Vietnam, and the Republic of Cuba prove that socialist law still exists even though not in the same seemingly vibrant form as it did before.[15] Crucially, it would be a mistake to assume that socialist law would have completely lost its legal cultural influence in the former socialist countries.[16] It still lingers like a ghost, invisible but still wielding influence. In any case, it is evident that the overall significance of socialist law as a macro-comparative construction in the field of comparative law is remarkably more modest than it was in the twentieth century. Regardless, the juxtaposition between Western law and non-Western law – that was also internally woven into the macro-comparative law of the twentieth century – still exists: it has been reinvented. In a certain sense it would appear that Asian law/legal systems and Islamic law have taken the place of the Other in the eyes of comparatists.[17] Similar questions and suspicions of a contrarian nature which the comparatist held about Soviet law are now alive and thriving regarding legal systems that are not Western. This is no surprise if we take into account that forming the legal 'self' and the 'Other' has been an important dimension of comparative law's identity in general.[18]

Another change in macro-comparative law worthy of mention has been the rise of so called mixed legal systems. From the beginning of the twenty-first century a new kind of legal family has emerged in the form of mixed legal systems. Of course, these systems have long existed, but they have not been taken seriously before the present century in terms of mainstream comparative law. Mixed legal systems have more scholarly weight than previously. These are systems that contain elements of law and legal culture from more than one legal family:[19] the legal systems of Scotland, South Africa, Louisiana, and Quebec are typical examples. These systems

[13] See, eg, George Mousorakis, *Comparative Law and Legal Traditions* (Springer 2019).

[14] See Ngoc Son Bui, *Legal Reform in the Contemporary Socialist World* (OUP 2024) ch 1. Bui argues, in essence, that socialist law should be 'relocated to the main place in comparative law', ibid 5. Bui's book discusses the systems of China, Vietnam, Laos, North Korea, and Cuba.

[15] See, eg, Bui Ngoc Son, 'The Law of China and Vietnam in Comparative Law' (2017) 41 *Fordham International Law Journal* 135–205 and María Elena Cobas Cobiella, 'The Influence of the Spanish Legal System and Socialist Legal Systems on Cuban Civil Law' (2024) *Florida International University Law Review* 735–53.

[16] See, eg, Rafał Mańko, 'Survival of the Socialist Legal Tradition?' (2013) 4 *Comparative Law Review* 1–28 ('The Socialist Legal Family may well be dead and buried, but the same cannot be said of the Socialist Legal Tradition', ibid 27).

[17] The Other refers to constructing and identifying of the Self and the Other in a way that builds on unequal opposition by ascribing inferiority or alienness to the other group. See, eg, Lajos L Brons, 'Othering, an analysis' (2015) 6 *Transcience, a Journal of Global Studies* 69–90.

[18] See also David Bonilla Maldonado, *Legal Barbarians* (CUP 2023) 29–45.

[19] About the concept, see Jaakko Husa, *Introduction to Comparative Law* (Hart Publishing 2023) 224–26.

have a mixed nature in particular in terms of their private laws whose contents are derived partly from the civil law legal family and partly from the common law legal family.[20] Furthermore, the idea that systems would be 'pure' can be criticised as no more than a myth because all systems are mixed to some extent.[21]

Mixed legal system(s) as a macro-construct elevated to the status of a legal family can be seen as a relatively recent development. A key scholar in this area, Vernon Valentine Palmer, has argued that mixed jurisdictions constitute a new legal family of their own. In essence, he defends the idea of a third legal family as a new legal family alongside common law and civil law. Mixed law as a macro-construct makes sense, according to Palmer, because it provides better insights into law on a global level.[22] It abandons the idea of 'pure' legal systems and builds on being mixed. Against a backdrop of the virtually vanished socialist law it seems that mixed law as a new legal family is one of those contenders that seeks to fill the empty space that socialist law left in macro-comparative law scholarship. However, a thick volume edited by Palmer shows that mixed legal systems are mostly about mixes where Western law enjoys a strong foothold. Systems that are included in the volume are South Africa, Scotland, Louisiana, Quebec, Puerto Rico, The Philippines, Botswana, Malta, and Israel.[23] Asia is left out completely even though there are systems that mix different elements from civil law and common law with local, regional, and in some cases religious ingredients.[24] However, in practice it is not always clear what is a mixed legal system.[25] For instance, one could argue that even though Singapore's legal system is clearly based on common law it has also elements that make it more or less a kind of a mixture.[26]

This chapter first discusses and explains the 'othering' practice of macro-comparative law against a backdrop of scholarly work in comparative law. Then it proceeds to address countermoves to the binary distinction between the West and the Rest by discussing non-Western oriented macro-comparative law, legal orientalism, and decolonial comparative law. Finally, this chapter considers the significance and relevance of the juxtaposition and its potential future in comparative law.

[20] These are systems typically on the move as they can be described as 'entrenched', 'endangered', or 'blended'. See Sue Farran & Esin Örücü (eds), *A Study of Mixed Legal Systems* (Routledge 2014).

[21] Vernon Valentine Palmer, 'Legal Systems…and the Myth of Pure Laws' (2007) 67 *Louisiana Law Review* 1205–18.

[22] Vernon Valentine Palmer, 'Introduction to The Mixed Jurisdictions' in Vernon Valentine Palmer (ed), *Mixed Jurisdictions Worldwide*, 2nd edn (CUP 2012) 3–18.

[23] ibid Part II 'The Comparative Evidence'.

[24] eg the legal system of Indonesia would fit very well in the definition of a mixed legal system. See, eg, Lita Tyesta Addy Listya Wardhani, Muhammad Dzikirullah H Noho & Aga Natalis, 'The Adoption of Various Legal Systems in Indonesia: An Effort to Initiate the Prismatic Mixed Legal Systems' (2022) 8 *Cogent Social Sciences* doi:10.1080/23311886.2022.2104710.

[25] See also Esin Örücü, 'What is a Mixed Legal System' (2008) 3 *JCL* 34–52.

[26] See, eg, Kevin YL Tan, 'Singapore' in Ann Black and Gary Bell (eds), *Law and Legal Institutions of Asia* (CUP 2011) 330–71.

I. The West and the Rest

Describing today's situation in comparative law requires a perception of the underlying factors in terms of the West and the Rest and othering practices of comparative law. Again, much needs to be read between the lines. Moreover, we need to say something about earlier scholarship even though the focus here is on more recent comparative law. In these times, it seems that a growing number of scholars are ready to admit that what can be labelled as the Global North dominates comparative law in the sense that 'the discipline is heavily dependent on Western scholars, methodologies, and assumptions of Western superiority' as Roger Merino puts it.[27] This is a broad statement, and it generalises too much. Regardless, for the most part it seems a justified claim, even if not completely free of problems. In fairness, all generalisations leave details in the shadows and lead easily into stereotypes.[28] This is, in any case, the innate sin of macro-comparative law, which is not discussed here as the analysis takes place through the framework of scholarly collisions.

What we mean by the West is not necessarily crystal clear. When scholars discuss what the West is, certain qualities tend to be assumed as essential. This list is hardly surprising. Christianity, capitalism, and the rule of law are commonly mentioned in this context.[29] These qualities are attached to cultural Occidentalism, which is the opposite of Orientalism.[30] According to Niall Ferguson, the West created 'killer applications' that enabled Europe and North America to gain global dominance, which the rule of law helped by providing predictability and stability.[31] Roots of the juxtaposition also run deep in the fabric of comparative law scholarship and legal thinking in the West.[32] A quick glance at the past is needed here.

Historically speaking, Montesquieu was probably the first to regard the Western world as a cultural sphere living by government of laws, unlike the rest of the world. Some of the underlying ideas appear emblematic and have far-reaching ramifications. There seems to be an inherent ranking order at the core of this kind of thinking. When it comes to law, the idea that 'the rule of law' was invented in Europe goes back all the way to Antiquity, extending to Aeschylus and Herodotus setting the tone for modern accounts of the allegedly distinctive

[27] Roger Merino, 'Decolonial Theory and Comparative Law' in Mathias Siems & Po Jen Yap (eds), *The Cambridge Handbook of Comparative Law* (CUP 2024) 408–25, 408.

[28] Focusing on 'Orientalism' and 'Occidentalism' may give too much weight to geography as it leaves evolving global power dynamics in the dark. See Jedidiah Kroncke, 'Orientalism, Occidentalism and the Control of Law' (2021) *Ancilla Iuris* 172–88.

[29] See, eg, Tor Krever, 'The Rule of Law and the Rise of Capitalism' in Christopher May & Adam Winchester (eds), *Handbook on the Rule of Law* (Edward Elgar 2018) 184–200.

[30] For a concise analysis, see Jan-Erik Lane, 'What is the "West"?' (2023) 10 *Economic and Social Thought* 61–65.

[31] See Niall Ferguson, *Civilization* (Penguin 2010).

[32] Some negative attitudes can be traced back to drawing a line between the laws of the barbarians that were different from those of civilised Roman laws. See Carlos Lévy, 'Cicero, Law, and The Barbarians' in Katell Berthelot, *Legal Engagement* (Publications de l'École française de Rome 2021) doi.org/10.4000/books.efr.9388.

features of Western law.[33] For much later comparative law scholarship, this reveals the epistemic bottom line of separating 'us' and 'them', or the West and the Rest. The paradox of this kind of othering, as noted by Mauro Bussani, is that general features attached to the rule of law are not to be found in all Western systems.[34] We implicitly assume that this would be the case. However, some of those features are to be found in many non-Western societies, including in Islamic and autocratic ones, even though Westerners do not regard those societies as following the ideals of the rule of law.[35]

One area where the discussion on the rule of law reveals comparative law's othering situates in what can be labelled as Asian law. Of course, there is no Asian law in much the same way as there is no African or Nordic law: these macro-constructs are of course broad generalisations. For example, it would not make much sense to describe the legal systems of Egypt and South Africa simply as African. Consequently, I use the concept of Asian law here in a fashion that is familiar from macro-comparative law literature, fully aware of its problematic quality caused by its sweeping nature.

Asian law – or more broadly Asian legal systems and legal cultures – have always held a peculiar place in macro-comparative law. Commonly, comparative law scholarship typically starts out with two paradigmatic macro-constructs: common law and civil law. It is not argued that there would not be law outside these two legal families, but it is not difficult to see that everything beyond the spheres of common law and civil law seems residual, revealing its nature as 'the Rest'. In turn, the Rest does not belong to the cultural sphere of the West in living allegedly by government of laws. This can be seen, indirectly though, in classifications of legal families in which Asian law is discussed briefly or merely in passing. But there may of course be many reasons for this practice.

One of these reasons has very likely to do with the size of Asia, which in turn has produced paradoxical treatment. First, as an area of law Asia is too big to be ignored, despite language and cultural barriers. Second, comparatists have been compelled to say at least something about Asian law even though their knowledge about Asian law(s) has been less than satisfactory. A paradigmatic example is the grouping arranged by Zweigert and Kötz. Their classification of legal systems including (1998 edition) Romanistic, Germanic, Anglo-American, Nordic, Far Eastern, and religious law (Islamic, Hindu) became the macro-comparative mainstream during the last decades of the twentieth century.[36] Even though Zweigert and Kötz's private law-based grouping is more modern than earlier ones, it

[33] James Q Whitman, 'The World Historical Significance of European Legal History' in Heikki Pihlajamäki, Markus D Dubber & Mark Godfrey (eds), *The Oxford Handbook of European Legal History* (OUP 2018) 4–22.

[34] Even countries normally thought to adhere to the rule of law experience attacks against the rule of law. See, eg, Scott Cummings, 'Why Do Lawyers Attack the Rule of Law?' (2024) *International Journal of the Legal Profession* 19–44 (discusses 'Trump lawyers'). See also Hans Petter Graver & Petra Gyöngyi, 'Hidden Rule of Law Discontinuities' (2024) 20 *International Journal of Law in Context* 117–32.

[35] Mauro Bussani, 'Rule of Law and Globalization' in Smits et al (n 4) 353–60, 354.

[36] Zweigert & Kötz, (n 10) 67–73.

reserved a modest place for Asia.[37] Judged by the number of pages, it is evident that their opus is centred on civil law and common law as most of the ink is spilled on these two macro-constructs. However, this observation needs nuance in order to avoid being unfair. They were not blind to non-Western law; they just did not see it as being as important as Western law. Indeed, to exaggerate somewhat, why would a Western lawyer be interested in something that seemed to lack practical significance for their profession? This echoes the distinction between the lawyer and the scholar – discussed in the preceding chapter – but it also demonstrates how we construct the 'self' and the 'Other'.

The problem of size has another consequence as Asian legal systems are packed by comparatists into one large legal family lacking nuance and detail. Placing the whole of Asia into one or perhaps two compartments (typically, China and Japan) has been the bread and butter of macro-comparative law.[38] An important exception to this tendency is Werner Menski's thick comparative law volume that focuses on Asian and African systems but leaves Western law out, in true contrarian manner.[39] The problems of packing Asia into one legal family are not unknown and this mainstream practice has been rightly criticised.[40] Theoretical assumptions in comparative law scholarship are, nonetheless, changing even though the speed of these changes may seem a bit timid.[41] Scholarship on the rule of law in Asia appears to confirm the change but also its slow pace. Of course, discussing the rule of law against the backdrop of Asia as a whole makes very little sense as the scale renders any such approach impossible.[42] Nevertheless, modern China is an especially interesting illustration in this regard.

It seems evident that the contemporary Chinese understanding of the rule of law is not the same as it is within the Western sphere of law and legal thinking.[43] One of the key distinguishing factors is the role of the Chinese Communist Party, which uses law as a means to wield power, not so much to constrain the use of power. Importantly, it seems that the rule of law does not limit the Party's exercise of power. For comparative law, this creates something of a puzzle as the Chinese version of the rule of law does not replicate the qualities that are deemed important by Western legal scholars.[44] China has, more or less, created its own version

[37] For example Georges Sauser-Hall, *Fonction et méthode de droit comparé* (Kundig 1913) ('droits aryens et indo-européens, droits sémitiques, droits mongols, droits barbares') based grouping on race, thinking that that each race had its own legal evolution, ibid 63. He distinguished laws of the Aryan peoples (Indo-European peoples), Semitic peoples, Mongolian peoples (ie, Japan and China), and uncivilised (or barbarous) peoples that include, eg, the law of Negroes and the law of Melanesians.

[38] See Pargendler (n 7) 1056–60.

[39] Werner Menski, *Global Comparative Law*, 2nd edn (CUP 2006).

[40] See, eg, Andrew Harding, 'Comparative Public Law' in Andrew Harding and Esin Örücü (eds), *Comparative Law in the 21st Century* (Kluwer 2002) 249–66.

[41] See, eg, Luca Siliquini-Cinelli & Jaakko Husa, 'Introduction: The Philosophies of Comparative Law' (2021) 8 *Critical Analysis of Law* 1–8, cal.library.utoronto.ca/index.php/cal/article/view/37851.

[42] See, eg, Imelda Denla, *The Development of the Rule of Law in ASEAN* (CUP 2017).

[43] This is not to say that the rule of law would be identical in the West. See, eg, Martin Loughlin, *Foundations of Public Law* (OUP 2010) 312–41.

[44] See for more detailed discussion, Albert HY Chen, 'China's Long March towards Rule of Law or China's Turn against Law?' (2016) 4 *Chinese Journal of Comparative Law* 1–35.

of the rule of law, which is 'rule of law with Chinese characteristics'.[45] The Chinese adaptation places rule of law as a functional part of the 'socialist market economy'.[46] All this does not, however, mean that law would not be important in China. As Larry DiMatteo points out 'the Chinese government has an interest in the judiciary applying laws efficiently and properly'.[47] This does not, on the other hand, mean that growing judicial independence would change the Chinese conception of the rule of law and move closer to Western notions. In other words, it is quite unlikely that the Chinese rule of law would open the way for liberal democracy. For comparative law scholarship based on West-focused epistemology, this seems like an oxymoron that causes feelings of unease similar to those art circles in the early twentieth century who, when facing Cubism for the first time, experienced a sense of the familiar, yet strange.

Now, the key issue here is not Chinese law or the Chinese understanding of the rule of law but the setting that conceives Chinese as the Other, non-Western, as the opposite of the West. In the words of Teemu Ruskola, 'the West has constructed its cultural identity against China in terms of law'.[48] In essence, this othering is what the binary constellation between the West and the Rest is about. Binarity is not only a feature of comparative law theory but it extends to various sub-areas of comparative law, for example to constitutional law, where Anglo-Eurocentric ideas have shaped and 'despite critical voices, still shapes mainstream comparative constitutional studies' as Günter Frankenberg notes.[49] The same goes for administrative law as well: macro-comparative scholarship on classification of legal systems and administrative models typically omits non-Western law.[50] For my part, I draw attention to the epistemic dimensions of the binary constellation because I suspect it reveals something essential about the scholarly transformation in the comparative law of our ongoing century.

Despite critique and a growing understanding that a broader view is needed, it would be a mistake to argue that othering non-Western law would be a thing of the distant past in mainstream comparative law. An illustration of this kind of thinking can be found from the book by Peter de Cruz published in 2008 in which he starts the discussion on 'other types of law' by explaining that:

> There are, of course, other non-Western conceptions of 'law' such as the Muslim, Hindu, African, Chinese and Japanese conceptions of law. These are based on religious beliefs or

[45] This is not to say that the rule of law would be a simple thing in China as there are different camps and interpretations of what it means in the Chinese context. See Samuli Seppänen, *Ideological Conflict and the Rule of Law in Contemporary China* (CUP 2016).

[46] See, eg, Ignacio Castellucci, *Rule of Law and Legal Complexity in the Peoples Republic of China* (Università degli Studi di Trento 2012) 119–47.

[47] Larry A DiMatteo, "Rule of Law' in China' (2018) 51 *Cornell International Law Journal* 391–444, 444.

[48] Teemu Ruskola, 'Legal Orientalism' (2002) 101 *Michigan Law Review* 179–234, 184.

[49] Günter Frankenberg, 'Constitutions as Commodities' in Günter Frankenberg (ed), *Order from Transfer* (Edward Elgar 2013) 1–26, 2.

[50] Roberto Scarciglia, *Methods and Legal Comparison* (Edward Elgar 2023) 185. Scarciglia cites English, French, and Italian scholarship.

> customary law. It is not proposed to discuss these laws here, but salient points regarding Eastern laws, such as the Chinese and Japanese conceptions of law, will be highlighted.[51]

My point here is not to criticise de Cruz's modus operandi but, rather, to ponder what it reveals about mainstream comparative law more generally.[52] According to the analysis by William Twining, this approach to doing comparative law was particularly common in between 1945–1990. He argued, quite convincingly in my view, that comparative law was interested mostly in positive laws and 'official' legal systems. Importantly, the focus of scholarship was virtually exclusively on Western capitalist societies in Europe; there was no real interest in 'the East' consisting of former and surviving socialist countries, 'the South' - meaning poorer countries known today as the Global South - or even the wealthier countries of the Pacific Basin. Accordingly, comparative law concerned itself with the similarities and differences between the private laws of common law and civil law systems. In practice, this meant focusing routinely on France and Germany, England, and the United States. This was, in a way, understandable as comparatists were interested in describing similarities and differences in the area of doctrinal private law in order to learn how foreign systems had resolved essentially similar types of problems through law.[53] So, it was prudent or at least 'practical' to focus on the West and leave the Rest outside or to address it in passing. This conception worked well in tandem with the lawyerly way of grasping comparative study of law as a doctrinal and practical venture with little interest in epistemology or methodology.

One further point needs to be made on the West and the Rest. This binarity should not be understood as something that concerns merely geography. Crucially, it is about conceiving non-Western forms of law in a certain manner. A fitting illustration of this is the treatment of indigenous laws in macro-comparative law. Such legal traditions as Sámi, Māori, or Inuit are situated mostly within geographical regions governed by Western states. Yet these forms are indigenous and situated outside of the West in a legal-cultural sense. Only Patrick Glenn's macro-comparative scholarship on legal traditions of the world gives an equal place to this type of law.[54] For others, non-Western forms of law have been of lesser interest: a curiosity if you like. Nice to know and thus taking up only a limited number of pages in comparative law textbooks.

Against the above-discussed ways to deal with non-Western law are scholarly countermoves, ie contrarian reactions to the mainstream's way of depicting and relying on the binary epistemology of the West and the Rest. These are countermoves against epistemic Occidentalism.

[51] Peter de Cruz, *Comparative Law in a Changing World*, 3rd edn (Routledge 2008) 209.

[52] It has been pointed out that the Western vision of law has always been interested in other parts of the world and laws in other territories, Scarciglia (2023) 24–25.

[53] William Twining has discussed this in many of his publications as the idea of 'Country and Western' epistemology runs through much of his scholarly work in the twenty-first century. See, eg, Twining, 'Comparative Law and Legal Theory' in Ian Edge (ed), *Comparative Law in Global Perspective* (Brill/Nijhoff 2001) 21–76.

[54] H Patrick Glenn, *Legal Traditions of the World*, 5th edn (OUP 2014) ch 3 'a chthonic legal tradition'.

II. Countermoves

Finding contrarian views to 'West and the Rest' thinking is not particularly difficult. There are comparatists who have criticised the Western orientation by shifting the focus towards non-Western law. Their critique takes as its starting point an observation of how the West is automatically assumed as the centre.[55] Representing this kind of scholarship is an important book written by Menski.[56] His macro-comparative law draws from legal anthropology and socio-legal studies through which he reinterprets both Western legal theory and West-focused comparative law.[57] In essence, Menski illustrates and criticises the connection between the culture-specific nature of legal theory – where the implicit focus is on the West – and the Western concept of law.[58]

What is remarkable and original is that most of Menski's volume is dedicated to Other legal cultures: Hindu law gets some 80 pages, Islamic law gets 100 pages, African laws get over 100 pages, and Chinese law or legal culture gets some 60 pages. There are no chapters on European or North American systems at all. Crucially, Menski questions the legal-cultural supremacy of the West: 'The culture-specific nature of European natural law debates thus becomes deeply problematic when they claim universal validity'.[59] To that end, Menski is a contrarian in terms of how he treats Anglo-Eurocentrism in the field of comparative law. He turns the epistemic tables and demotes the West by promoting the Rest.

To be sure, Menski is not alone. There are whole areas in modern comparative law scholarship that present epistemic countermoves to the supremacy of Western law and legal thinking. This is indeed problematic if the comparatist aims for balanced comparisons. Both of these are relevant for discussion on the binarity of the West and the Rest. These are legal orientalism and decolonial comparative law. Both of them illustrate how comparative law as a field has changed in this century and how it has become growingly sensitive to detecting epistemic imbalances. These changes may not be mainstream quite yet, but they do exist and have at least some scholarly significance.

Legal orientalism concerns the epistemic attitude of comparatists that are based on an implicit colonial mindset. Legal orientalism has become a relevant issue in comparative law because the study of Chinese law and the significance of China as a world power have grown hand in hand. Consequently, much of comparative law

[55] 'The usual practice of comparative law takes the West as its centre', Tomasz Giaro, 'A Purely Western Tradition' in Luca Siliquini-Cinelli, Davide Gianti& Mauro Balestrieri (eds), *The Grand Strategy of Comparative Law* (Routledge 2024) 253–67, 253.

[56] Menski (n 39).

[57] The theoretical goal is to 'move the existing debates beyond false axioms and simplistic models to a deeper level of legal analysis and understanding', ibid 17.

[58] In the extensive theoretical part of the book Menski cites comparatists such as Annlise Riles, Esin Örücü, Roger Cotterrell, William Twining, ibid 25–190. The ambitious idea is to 'reassess the Eurocentric nature of mainstream legal theory', ibid 128.

[59] ibid 146.

work focuses on Chinese law.[60] The concept of orientalism and the postcolonial discussion are both connected to theoretical and methodological discussion in comparative law scholarship. Legal orientalism is not only a feature of comparative law as it can be seen as part of a larger scholarly movement that wants to dismantle normative universalism in international legal studies and reveal hidden biases of Western legal scholarship.[61] Even though the focus here is on comparative law it is useful to conceive comparative law's scholarly transformation as part of a broader movement in the study of law.

The key scholar in legal orientalism is Teemu Ruskola, who has criticised the notions of Western scholars about law and its role in China during different historical periods.[62] Ruskola, in short, argues that Western analyses have been characterised by the idea of Chinese stability, an idea that does not seem to hold water against the backdrop of the history of China. The problem is that the views of Western scholars on Chinese legal culture have not taken historical changes into account. These views – which could be described as negative stereotypes – have, according to Ruskola, fortified the idea of the superiority of European-American legal civilisation. The underlying theoretical idea has been that traditional Chinese legal culture has never been rational. This is seen quite differently from Western law. The contrarian claim is that 'Western representations of Chinese law…tell us far more about the Western idea, and ideology, of law than they do of any equivalent (or even nonequivalent) phenomenon in China.'[63] On closer inspection, this is about othering non-Western law on the basis of an implicitly assumed 'self'.

It is not clear how much othering is about real law and how much about our own images of law. Thomas Coendet summarises the view that legal orientalism shows how 'Eastern places are *imagined* from a *Western* perspective', meaning that Eastern law is observed through Western lenses.[64] The intellectual mode of imagining Eastern law is what the West and the Rest is about. One can, however, wonder: does this leave comparatists weaponless when it comes to applying a critical approach to Asian law? Does legal orientalism lead to comparative law having no ability in terms of critical study of non-Western law? Importantly – Coendet notes – critique of orientalism and Eurocentrism does not mean that one should defend non-Western legal traditions. It is more about dispelling imaginaries.[65] To put it otherwise, it is about recognising underlying epistemic contrarianism, not about blindly admiring what is different. In other words, it would not make sense simply to change from xenophobia to xenophilia.

[60] One example is the establishment of a flagship journal in 2013, the *Chinese Journal of Comparative Law* published by the Oxford University Press. Of the legal system of the People's Republic of China, see Albert HY Chen, *An Introduction to the Chinese Legal System* (LexisNexis 2019).

[61] This movement has been particularly vibrant in public international law. See, eg, Sundhya Pahuja, *Decolonising International Law* (CUP 2011).

[62] See Ruskola (n 48) and a more refined version Teemu Ruskola, *Legal Orientalism* (Harvard University Press 2013).

[63] Ruskola (n 48) 196.

[64] Thomas Coendet, 'Legal Orientalism' in Smits et al (n 4) Vol 2 (Edward Elgar 2023) 470–78, 470.

[65] ibid 476.

Decolonial comparative law is closely related to the issues which legal orientalism also discusses and – as one can see from the work of Ruskola – these forms of critical comparative law scholarship are overlapping. In a sense, they are both related to a post-colonial way of doing comparative law.[66] Their mindset is distinctly anti-mainstream. Nevertheless, decolonial comparative law covers a broader scope than legal orientalism as it is global and does not limit itself to Asia or what can be conceived as 'Eastern'. The novel field of decolonial comparative law can be seen as a further development of a broader 'colonialism and law' field of study. This form of scholarship was developed in the study of law in colonial contexts. The first steps having been taken by anthropologists, it grew into a form of scholarship that approaches the laws of colonised societies through their colonial history, showing how their laws were affected by – or even creations of – colonisation.[67] All this is, of course, relevant for modern self-aware comparative law.

The pivotal assumption on which decolonial comparative law is built is similar to that of scholarship on legal orientalism. Lena Salameh and Ralf Michaels put it like this: 'The discipline of comparative law, as it exists today, is structured and dominated by the Global North.'[68] This blunt statement nonetheless seems broadly an accurate one. Against this backdrop, it is no surprise, then, that – just like legal orientalism – decolonial comparative law is inspired by critical legal theory. One of the most important outcomes of decolonial thinking has taken place in the field of public international law under the banner of the Third World Approach to International Law (TWAIL).[69] However, the project of decolonial comparative law does not simply follow TWAIL scholarship because international law is a field of law whereas comparative law is not a field of law.[70] Moreover, even though colonisation and colonialism are relevant for decolonial comparative law, it goes beyond them. Instead of turning into a study in legal history, decolonial comparative law seeks to reveal the colonial elements in contemporary law and legal thinking.[71] It is about trying to detect comparative law's self.

In my reading, decolonial comparative law can highlight how colonial ideas may be inherently part of modern law and legal thinking. Shedding light on this is at least one of the objectives in decolonial thinking in comparative law scholarship. For the discussion on the West and the Rest, decolonial comparative law is important because it denounces the idea that any law – Western or otherwise – would

[66] About postcolonialism and comparative law, see Judith Schacherreiter, 'Postcolonial Theory and Comparative Law' (2016) 49 *Verfassung und Recht in Übersee* 291–312.

[67] Shane Chalmers, 'Colonialism and Law' in Smits et al (n 4), Vol 1 282–91.

[68] Lena Salameyh and Ralf Michaels, 'Decolonial Comparative Law' (2022) *Rabels Zeitschrift für ausländisches und internationales Privatrecht* 166–88, 167.

[69] See, eg, Antony Anghie, 'Rethinking International Law' (2023) 34 *European Journal of International Law* 7–112.

[70] Daniel Bonilla Maldonado puts the perspectives of TWAIL, postcolonial studies of law, and critical comparative law in the same basket as intellectual movements that challenge the mainstream. See Bonilla Maldonado, *Legal Barbarians: Identity, Modern Comparative Law and the Global South* (CUP 2021) ch 5.

[71] See also Upendra Baxi, 'The Colonialist Heritage' in Pierre Legrand and Roderick Munday (eds), *Comparative Legal Studies* (CUP 2003) 46–75.

be intrinsically superior to other forms of law.[72] In other words, the underlying idea – that the West (common law and civil law) can automatically claim superiority over other forms of law – is abandoned. In doing so, decolonial comparative law assumes a contrarian stance in its relation to mainstream comparative law. It launches a critique against the mainstream's inbred contrarian suspicion towards the Rest.

III. In Search of Balance?

Detecting the impact of Western law and legal thinking is not necessarily a walk in the park. As Mathias Siems and Po Jen Yap say, 'There can be a fine line in between identifying certain cultural differences and risking cultural stereotypes' such as 'East' and 'West'.[73] There have, notwithstanding, always been scholars who have sought to be balanced in their relationship to non-Western laws and legal systems. Their impact and relevance have grown in the current century. In fairness, we can also say that West-oriented epistemology has always had a stronger grip on scholarship published in English. For instance, the French tradition of 'grands systémes de droit contemporains' has aimed to be encyclopaedic as to its nature, which means that it has taken non-Western forms of law into account more broadly than English speaking scholarship. One of the reasons why British comparative law has not had an encyclopaedic character is because its origins stemmed from the practical need to assimilate laws of the dominions of the Empire.[74] Besides, encyclopaedism seems to be typically a French phenomenon quite different to what one could label as British pragmatism.

With the wisdom of hindsight, Ugo Mattei's seminal article published in the late 1990s paved the way to more balanced takes.[75] He created a classification consisting of professional law, political law, and traditional law.[76] Another, and most likely even more important, is Glenn's volume on legal traditions of the world – which placed comparative law in deeper interaction with legal history – that saw its first edition published in 2000.[77] Today, however, it would seem that even English-

[72] See Ralf Michaels, 'Decolonial Comparative Law: FAQ' in Jaakko Husa (ed), *A Research Agenda for Comparative Law* (Edward Elgar 2024) 61–86.

[73] Mathias Siems & Po Jen Yap, 'Introduction' in Mathias Siems & Po Jen Yap (n 27) 1–11, 2.

[74] See for more detailed discussion, John Cairns, 'Development of Comparative Law in Great Britain' in Reimann & Zimmermann (n 6) 111–47.

[75] Ugo Mattei, 'Three Patterns of Law' (1997) 45 *AJCL* 5–44. However, Mattei's classification is not free of problems when it comes to classifying Asian systems. For critique, see Harding (n 40) 253.

[76] Discussion of Mattei's classification, see Husa (n 7) 18–25 and Fekete (n 2) 115–16. For further elaboration see Ugo Mattei, 'The Legal Metaverse and Comparative Taxonomy' (2023) 71 *AJCL* 900–29 (revisits Three Patterns of Law).

[77] Glenn (n 5) describes and discusses on the basis of common law, civil law, Indigenous law (chthonic law), and religious law (Talmudic, Islamic, Hindu, Confucian). However, Glenn's influential volume also faced strong critique. See 'A Fresh Start for Comparative Legal Studies?' (2006) 1 *JCL*, the whole issue contains a collective review of the book's 2nd edition. For more positive views, see Jaakko Husa, 'Emancipation or Deprivation for the European Legal Mind?' (2006) 13 *Maastricht Journal of European and Comparative Law* 81–107 and Thomas Duve, 'Legal Traditions' (2018) 6 *Comparative Legal History* 15–33.

speaking comparative law scholarship is also more balanced in terms of what one may describe as the mainstream.

A massive volume by Uwe Kischel, though translated from German, illustrates this.[78] Kischel speaks of legal families and seeks to take their context into account. Part II, which is the largest portion of the book with more than 600 pages, contains the contexts of legal systems.[79] He discusses first common law and civil law, which takes up some 400 pages. After that, Kischel moves on to discuss African, Asian and religious law (mostly Islamic law) covering over 200 pages. The short last section of Part II deals with transnational law. This is clearly different from the approaches by Zweigert and Kötz or their predecessors Pierre Arminjon, Boris Nolde, and Martin Wolff.[80] Regardless, it is clear for the reader that Kischel's discussion on common law and civil law is more detailed than discussion on non-Western law. In any case, in comparison to the earlier mainstream it is evident that there has been a shift towards a more balanced approach. At the same time, it is another issue if the way to write about these macro-constructs is truly balanced or perhaps some kind of a subtle epistemic bias is included simply because Western law is more familiar to the author. The same risk no doubt concerns every comparatist who ventures outside the safety of their own law and legal culture because '[e]very comparatist is shaped by her background'.[81] Readers of this book have doubtless noticed that the author comes from the Global North, which in turn inevitably influences what is argued, regardless of any aspiration to remain neutral.

Another example of an approach that seeks to be balanced can be found in the *Cambridge Handbook of Comparative Law*, which seeks to apply what the editors describe as a cosmopolitan approach. This means rejecting not only the West and the Rest binarity but also abandoning the view that 'there is an irreconcilable gap between "us" and "them", which would make it impossible to understand foreign ideas and cultures.'[82] This kind of contemporary comparative law cosmopolitanism shows in the macro-comparative Part II of the handbook, in which the brief list of usual suspects - civil and common law - is supplemented by sections of similar size on former Soviet states, Latin America, the Middle East and North Africa, South Asia, and Sub Saharan Africa.[83] I read this as a an attempt to break free from the rudimentary distinction between the West and the Rest and to seek epistemic balance.

The Cambridge handbook is not alone in its search for a more global and balanced reach. A similar kind of scholarly spirit seems to have penetrated established comparative law more generally. The earlier published *Oxford Handbook of*

[78] Uwe Kischel, *Comparative Law* (OUP 2019).

[79] ibid 227 et seq.

[80] Zweigert & Kötz (1998) deal with 'Law in the Far East' and 'Religious Legal Systems' in some 40 pages (287–319). Arminjon, Nolde, Wolff discuss (*Traité de droit comparé*, Tome III, LGDJ 1951) Soviet law in the space of some 270 pages, Islamic law gets some 130 pages, and finally the law of India and Burma is discussed in the space of some 20 pages.

[81] Mathias Siems, *Comparative Law*, 3rd edn (CUP 2022) 13.

[82] Siems & Yap (n 27) 6.

[83] ibid 211 et seq.

Comparative Law has similar tendencies even though its list of contents is thematically more traditional in a kind of mainstream way as much of the volume is structured according to the orthodox fields of law.[84] Moreover, the third edition of the *Elgar Encyclopedia of Comparative Law* abandons mainstream divisions as it seeks to be genuinely global and to take non-Western laws into account.[85] The Elgar encyclopaedia has a traditional field of law-based entries but also entries on systems that reach beyond the West.[86] Comparing the three volumes, the Oxford handbook has a more mainstream list of authors than is the case with the Cambridge handbook and Elgar encyclopaedia, even though the differences are not drastic. One possible partial explanation may be that the editors of the Oxford handbook - Mathias Reimann and Reinhard Zimmermann - belong to a different comparatist generation than the editors of the other volumes. It is quite possible that age is a factor here as the younger generation seems more open to diversity, embracing more diverse ideas than the older generation of comparatists. Then again, as Twining and Frankenberg show, which generation one belongs to is not always decisive when it comes to scholarly preferences.

If the text above rings true, then it offers support to what I argue throughout this book: comparative law has changed in the course of the twentieth and into the twenty-first century and many central underlying ideas that were the bread and butter of twentieth century comparative law are moving away from the nexus of comparative law as a field of legal scholarship. Along similar lines, epistemic assumptions on which macro-comparative law have been based are slowly morphing and distancing from the West and the Rest dichotomy. Keeping a distance from this dichotomy is important because the language we use not only describes the law but also shapes the way we see the law.[87] The path to this has been pioneered by contrarian scholars who chose to oppose the unbalanced binary epistemology. The process of change is still on the move and, even though the direction of the transformation seems clear, it is perhaps too early to announce the results.

[84] Reimann & Zimmermann (n 6), 'Part III Subject Areas'. The second edition is remarkably similar to the first edition published in 2006.
[85] Smits et al (n 4) 3 vols.
[86] As to entries on legal systems, all the usual suspects are present but also entries on, eg, Chinese law, European small jurisdictions (Andorra, Liechtenstein, Monaco), Hong Kong, India, Islamic law, Israel, Japanese law, law in North African countries (Tunisia, Algeria, Morocco), Mauritius, Nigeria, Pakistan, Peru, Russian law, Singapore, South Korea, Taiwan etc.
[87] This is important especially when we speak of non-Western legal traditions. See for detailed discussion Lucille Jewel, 'Comparative Legal Rhetoric' (2021) 110 *Kentucky Law Journal* 107–72.

7

Area Experts and Generalists

Point of view is an important factor when we discuss comparative law as a branch of legal scholarship. As the previous chapters have shown, debates and critiques do not appear out of nowhere. Legal scholars with different pedigrees, areas of interest, and methodological toolboxes inevitably see and understand comparative law in varying ways. Legal scholars' theoretical and methodological assumptions influence the manner in which they grasp comparative law and how they define its purposes. If one observes comparative law scholars and their publications from the outside of their specialised sub-field, it may deceptively appear that all comparatists belong to the same academic tribe and dwell in the same scholarly territory. 'Tribe' in this case refers to a group of scholars who apparently work in the same discipline ('law'), share the same scholarly language ('legal scholarship') and research culture differently from other fields ('comparing'), and position in law schools and faculties ('non-doctrinalists'). This tends to be how the field of comparative law (broadly understood) is conceived, especially by other legal scholars. Of course – and this will be known by all readers, I believe – this is a simplification. The above chapters have shown, if nothing else, that comparative law is not a monolith. Modern comparative law is in many ways a pluralist venture forged in the fires of disagreement. As a result, today different schools and approaches exist side by side, reflecting the diverse state of the field.[1]

In other words, those who study and teach comparative law are clearly not a uniform disciplinary group in academia. One needs just to glance at the titles of volumes of the *American Journal of Comparative Law*, *Rabels Zeitschrift*, *Revue internationale de droit comparé*, *International and Comparative Law Quarterly*, and *Journal of Comparative Law* to see the wide scope of scholarly work in the area. Articles vary from doctrinal to decolonial, from socio-legal to historical, from feminist to economic, from private law to public law, and so on. Regardless, conceiving comparative law as a tribe-based law may catch something essential

[1] For a recent take on schools and methods, see Yenny Vega Cárdenas, *Methodology and Epistemology of Comparative Law* (LexisNexis 2024). See also Simone Glanert, Alexandra Mercescu & Geoffrey Samuel, *Rethinking Comparative Law* (Edward Elgar 2021) and Jaakko Husa (ed), *A Research Agenda for Comparative Law* (Edward Elgar 2024).

in its unashamed simplicity. Generally speaking, when we perceive fields of legal scholarship as tribe(s) we entertain a particular manner in which we conceive of fields that are close to our own but still not quite the same. In the sense of the late Wittgenstein, we may also speak of family resemblances between fields of legal scholarship.[2] This is something that is instinctively known among legal academics. That said, in our intrinsic tendency to generalise lies an unavoidable problem. Even though academic fields in general are distinguishable both from epistemological and sociological points of view – as fields of knowledge and scholarly territories – it seems too bold an exaggeration to present comparative law as a unified tribe occupying easily identifiable academic turf with visible borders.[3]

Making oneself familiar with the literature swiftly proves the simplified view to be misguided. A closer look, as we have already seen in the previous chapters, reveals subtleties and features that do not meet the eye if looked at from the outside. It is perhaps not too far-fetched to claim that scholarship on comparative law may give the impression of a rowdy bunch divided by apparently trivial schisms on issues such as functionalism and legal transplants (see chapters eight and nine).[4] This is, as one would expect, one of the reasons why comparatists may be characterised as contrarians. As scholars, comparatists appear to be haunted by a spirit of almost grumpy discontent. Discontent relates to theory and methodology but yet comparatists are able to exist amicably in conferences such as those organised by the International Academy of Comparative Law.[5] Then again, one could argue that big conferences are gatherings of mainstreamers, and the most ardent contrarians prefer to stay in their own smaller tribal circles. Indeed, it is easy to see that the most critical stay away from the huge conferences organised by the Academy.

The fact that a field of knowledge is not a monolith leads to various consequences. There are, no doubt, many sorts of divisions, meaning that as a tribe comparative law has subtribes. In a way, the whole idea behind this book is based on that aspect as the collisions I discuss are by and large internal clashes between – and sometimes within – comparatist subtribes. The subtribes this chapter will focus on are based on the division between different focuses. Even though these archetypes of the comparative law scholar do belong to the tribe of comparatists, they do not belong to the same subtribes because they have their own tribal styles and preferences even though some scholars may have a foot in several corners. To that end, some comparatists can change hats swimmingly despite their innate propensity to contrarianism. Then

[2] See for more detailed discussion, eg, Leon Pompa, 'Family Resemblance' (1967) 17 *Philosophical Quarterly* 63–69 and Hjalmar Wennerberg, 'The Concept of Family Resemblance in Wittgenstein's Later Philosophy' (1967) 33 *Theoria* 107–32.

[3] More about academic tribes and territories, see Tony Becher, *Academic Tribes and Territories* (Open University Press 1989). For further discussion, see Paul Trowler, 'Academic Tribes and Territories' (2014) 25 *Österreichische Zeitschrift für Geschichtswissenschaften* 17–26.

[4] See, eg, Robert Leckey, 'Review of Comparative Law' (2017) 26 *Social & Legal Studies* 3–24.

[5] The two first congresses of the International Academy of Comparative law were organised in 1932 and 1937. Since 1950 General Congresses have been held every four years. The Academy also organises thematic congresses.

again, one can be a contrarian in many ways. To be sure, comparatists have no difficulty in finding issues to oppose and challenge. The literature provides an abundance of matters to disagree with.

This chapter will address two kinds of comparative law sub-tribes, namely area expertise and generalist expertise. The suggestion implicit in this chapter is that the collision of these branches of expertise is real but also overstated.

I. Area Experts

When we speak of areas, we refer to particular places such as a piece of land or a country. In the field of law, an area expert may refer to many kinds of forms of expertise but here it means a set of skills and a high level of knowledge concerning a particular geographical area.[6] This is why Islamic law or Hindu law are not discussed as they are not limited by geography but, more importantly, by substance.[7] In practice, area expertise may refer to scholars who focus on a system of a country or a region that is not their own. Commonly, this means that they have received their legal education in a different place than the one they study. Typically, in this context the set of scholarly skills needed refers to language skills but also to deeper cross-cultural literacy that contains an understanding of foreign customs and traditions.[8] For example, German Max Planck institutes have traditionally represented this kind of specialised expertise that requires an area expert's skills in order to unearth the content of foreign legal systems.[9] The underlying justification comes close to that of anthropology and ethnography, where fieldwork is considered important because it enables the scholar to generate rich context-specific data which is difficult to acquire from the outside or without linguistic skills.[10]

For the discussion in this chapter, it is important to point out that specialist skills go beyond those of generalists but are, in turn, narrower.[11] Macro-comparatists, as

[6] Comparative law's relation to geography is a novel area of scholarship. This discussion leaves that dimension out. For more details, see Matteo Nicolini, *Legal Geography* (Springer 2022). Of course, religious and Indigenous laws also allow thematic area expertise.

[7] See generally, Stefan Hammer, 'Religion Impacting the Concept of Law' (2021) 7 *Interdisciplinary Journal for Religion* 3–12. From the point of view of comparative law, see Jaakko Husa, 'Comparative Law and Christianity' (2024) 44 *Oxford Journal of Legal Studies* 54–73.

[8] On cross-cultural literacy, see, eg, Steven F Arvizu and Marietta Sharavia-Shore, 'Cross-Cultural Literacy' (1990) 22 *Education and Urban Society* 364–76. In the context of study of law (eg, the rule of law), see Ivar Hannikainen et al, 'Are There Cross-Cultural Legal Principles?' (2021) 45 *Cognitive Science* DOI: 10.1111/cogs.13024

[9] One needs only to visit the websites of those Max Planck institutes where legal scholarship is practised. For instance, the institute in Frankfurt for Legal History and Legal Theory (www.lhlt.mpg.de/en) shows this if one looks at the academic staff in the various departments who largely consist of area or regional experts.

[10] See, eg, Conrad Watson, 'Introduction' in Conrad Watson (ed), *Being There: Fieldwork in Anthropology* (Pluto Press 1999) 1–24.

[11] Country experts may play a role in various legal processes, eg, when a country expert provides information to a deciding body. This can take place, eg, in the context of the asylum-seeking process. See, eg, Femke Vogelaar, 'A Legal Analysis of a Crucial Element in Country Guidance Determinations' (2019) 31 *International Journal of Refugee Law* 492–515.

archetypical generalists, commonly address legal families and entire legal systems, but they are not experts in all the areas they write about. Consequently, for example, a macro-comparatist who writes about Asian or African law is typically not an expert in any Asian or African language or a particular legal system situated in these regions.

In the literature we can see introductory books written about legal systems that present a legal system to outsiders.[12] Be that as it may, area expertise characteristically goes well beyond the introductory level. For example, a European scholar who focuses on Chinese law and can read Chinese language materials is an area expert. There are, in fact, many such scholars but an excellent illustration of such a scholar is Björn Ahl. He is a professor at a German university but his scholarly work focuses on the law – as broadly understood – of China. In a wide sense, his work falls under the heading of comparative law. Accordingly, it would appear that Ahl is apparently a member of the comparative law tribe. He has published on issues such as public international law, procedural law, human rights, and data protection in the Chinese context.[13] His publications have appeared on different academic forums and some of his work is published in comparative law journals. What is noteworthy is that theoretical issues which comparatists constantly address in their scholarly work are virtually absent even when Ahl publishes in journals dedicated to comparative study of law. He concentrates on a geographically restricted substantive area and has the necessary specialist skills to do so.

This, is of course, not a criticism of Ahl's work but an observation of a specialised scholar who exemplifies what an area expert in the field of comparative law means. In a sense, this also concerns the distinction between talkers and doers discussed above in chapter five. The scholarly outlook is different from that of generalists as the area expert's view is closer to an insider's view than that of the generalist. From there it follows that – instead of dwelling endlessly in epistemology and methodology or debating the identity, goals, or nature of comparative law or classification of legal families – the area expert focuses on Chinese law and Chinese legal culture. As a result, their scholarship on China is bound to delve deep and address subtle issues that do not find their place in the work of generalist comparatists who remain on the macro-level and speak to a potentially

[12] See, eg, Albert HY Chen, *An Introduction to the Legal System of the People's Republic of China* (LexisNexis 2018); Nigel Foster & Sula Satish, *German Legal System and Laws*, 4th edn (OUP 2010); John Bell, Sophie Boyron & Simon Whittaker, *Principles of French Law*, 2nd edn (OUP 2008); and Pia Letto-Vanamo, Ditlev Tamm & Bent Ole Gram Mortensen (eds), *Nordic Law in European Context* (Springer 2019).

[13] See, eg, 'International Law in Chinese Courts' in Ignacio De la Rasilla & Congyan Cai (eds), *The Cambridge Handbook of China and International Law* (CUP 2024) 113–30; 'Norm Taker oder Norm Maker?' (2023) 73 *Osteuropa* 209–26; 'The Development of the Due Process Principle in post-2013 China' (2022) 17 *JCL* 254–76; 'China's Evolving Data Protection Law and the Financial Credit Information System' (2021) 51 *Hong Kong Law Journal* 287–308; and 'Chinese Positions on Global Constitutionalism, Community of Common Destiny for Mankind, and the Future of International Law' (2021) 9 *Chinese Journal of Comparative Law* 304–27.

wider audience.[14] But because Ahl's epistemic home base is not China, his work is innately comparative as to its nature: that is, he is not ethnically or culturally a Chinese scholar. What the relationship of this sort of comparative law scholarship is to general comparative law is not crystal clear. There is overlap – but is that all there is to it?

There is no need to rely on hyperbole while discussing the issue. It seems evident that this sort of specialised scholarly work is not in visible conflict with general comparative law scholarship. We see few references to Zweigert and Kötz, Legrand, or to general textbooks – but that is where the overlap stops. Instead of opting for head-to-head confrontation or on-going discussion, the specialist may simply stay out of general tribal conflicts. The scholarly collision is an invisible one and can be sensed in wilful avoidance of general comparative law scholarship and its long-standing debates on issues such as legal transplants or functionalism. Whatever collision occurs is situated mostly under the surface and needs to be read between the lines as an act of avoidance. The work of an area specialist seems, in my reading, to belong to a different sub-tribe than that of a generalist. However, it is important to point out that being an area specialist does not necessarily mean focusing on one country or system as it may also mean focusing on a region while, at the same time, avoiding the generalist nature of scholarship. This type of area-specialist scholarly work is certainly not unheard of.

For instance, Andrew Harding epitomises the comparative law scholar who can be regarded as an area expert whose expertise is broader than a country expert's and who focuses on a certain geographical region, hence avoiding being a full-blooded generalist.[15] To simplify a great deal, his focus has been mostly on South-East Asian legal studies. Besides South-East Asian law in general, he has focused specifically on Malaysian law.[16] Moreover, beyond Malaysian law he has also published on Thai law and legal history.[17] However, unlike Ahl, Harding has been vocal in the area of generalist comparative law and has criticised the broad generalist assumptions of non-area specialist comparatists (or talkers, if you prefer). In part, his scholarly work has discussed the relationship between the global and the local against the backdrop of South-East Asia. Among other things,

[14] Typically, macro-comparatists confine Asian law discussion to China and Japan. See Gilles Cuniberti, *Grands systèmes de droit contemporains*, 4th edn (GLDJ 2019) ch 4 (*Droit chinois*) and ch 5 (*Droit japonais*) and Raymond Legeais, *Grands systèmes de droit contemporains*, 3rd edn (LexisNexis 2016) ch 5 §1 (*Le Japon et le droit*) and ch 5 §2 (*La Chine et le droit*).

[15] Regional comparative law may also mean focusing on regional collaboration through legal means. This dimension is not discussed here. See for more detailed analysis on this, Armin Cuyvers, 'Comparing Regional Law' in Mathias Siems & Po Jen Yap (eds), *Cambridge Handbook of Comparative Law* (CUP 2024) 649–73. Nordic legal cooperation is a good example of development of regional law. I discuss this in Jaakko Husa, 'History and Contextualisation of Nordic Cooperation and European Integration' in Graham Butler & Helle Krunke (eds), *Nordic Cooperation and the European Union* (Hart Publishing 2026) forthcoming.

[16] See, eg, Andrew Harding, *Law, Government and the Constitution in Malaysia* (Kluwer 1996); *Constitution of Malaysia* (Hart Publishing 2012); and Andrew Harding and Dian AH Shah (eds), *Law and Society in Malaysia* (Routledge 2019).

[17] Andrew Harding & Peter Leyland, *Constitution of Thailand* (Hart Publishing 2011); and Andrew Harding & Munin Pongsapan (eds), *Thai Legal History* (CUP 2021).

he has highlighted how local reality, or the facts of a society as it exists, ought to be meaningful when legal globalisation is discussed.[18] Even though he does not deny the possibility of convergence of legal systems, he also points out that there are many areas where legal pluralism is likely to remain.[19] More importantly, Harding has discussed the underground issue on the collision between the comparative law subtribes of area experts and generalists.[20]

Broadly speaking, Harding would seem like a classic comparatist, that is, a contrarian legal scholar on the basis of his critical take on macro-comparative law.[21] Significantly - adding more ambiguity - he criticises generalism in his capacity as an area expert but not as a generalist. This is yet another indication of how comparatists can don different hats while assuming the guise of a comparatist. Indeed, it is well-known that the comparatist can assume different identities.[22]

It is not a coincidence that Harding builds his critique on the basis of South-Asian law and legal culture. Dimensions I discuss in other chapters of this book concern the same underlying issues that are difficult to differentiate between. The same overall difficulty in terms of distinguishing between various dimensions is also faced here. Area expertise and generalist expertise can sometimes become entangled. Here, once again, comparative law stumbles upon the West and the Rest dichotomy discussed in the previous chapter, which overlaps with area expertise vs generalist expertise and deep-reaching issues such as the lasting impact of colonialism. Overlap makes it tricky to address the issue. According to one analysis, from the viewpoint of comparative constitutional law, the Western or Euro-American view unfairly holds an epistemic upper hand as the West manufactures the knowledge of the Rest, which acts as a kind of reservoir of raw data.[23] This view is critical of the heritage that resides in the elite Western institutions.[24] Without going into details of this critique, it seems safe to say that it appears by and large justified.[25] Although Harding's critique is not built directly on these kinds of assumptions, it well illustrates what the collision between area expertise and scholarly generalism is about and what it involves. His critique - directed towards generalism in comparative law - reveals how an area specialist conceives macro-comparative law's generalism as expressed in terms of legal families:

[18] Andrew Harding, 'Global Doctrine and Local Knowledge' (2002) 51 *ICLQ* 35–53.

[19] ibid 53.

[20] Andrew Harding, 'Comparative Public Law' in Andrew Harding & Esin Örücü (eds), *Comparative Law in the 21st Century* (Kluwer 2002) 249–66.

[21] Harding distinguishes between 'theoretical' and 'applied' forms of comparative law, ibid 262.

[22] According to a comparative law proverb, in one's home country one can bill as an expert in foreign law and in a foreign country one can bill as an expert in one's home law.

[23] Eugénie Mérieau, 'Area Studies and the Decolonisation of Comparative Law' (2020) 51 *International Quarterly for Asian Studies* 153–70.

[24] ibid 165.

[25] One way of doing this is to focus on the West and say briefly something about 'other types of law' and to briefly discuss Chinese and Japanese law as representing 'eastern legal conceptions', see Peter de Cruz, *Comparative Law in a Changing World*, 3rd edn (Routledge 2008) 209–17.

> Legal families tell us nothing about legal systems except as to their general style and method, and the idea makes no sense whatsoever amid the nomic din of South East Asia. To call the South East Asian legal systems any kind of a family or even members of a family is about as accurate and as interesting as calling *rojak* (a spicy, culturally mixed Malay salad) a kind of vegetable.[26]

In essence, Harding attacks macro-comparatists and comparative law generalism because he considers it unable to detect localities beyond general style and method. In short, there is not sufficient subtlety or nuance. As a result, generalist macro-comparative law produces trivial or downright banal results in the eyes of an area expert. This harsh take seems right but also then leads to suspecting the very existence of macro-comparative law and the spirit of generalism on which it is based. Importantly, much of comparative law literature is general as to its nature. Generalist comparative law will be discussed in the following section.

II. Generalists

To begin with, it is easy to understand that a generalist refers to a person who has varied or unspecialised scholarly interests in the area of comparative law.[27] In a comparative law tribal setting, these scholars feature as a kind of all-rounder. More specifically, these are the scholars – of which this author is an example – who write textbooks and edit handbooks and encyclopaedias.[28] Notwithstanding, generalists discuss and analyse laws of countries and also – especially in macro-comparative law – regions.[29] But what we mean by region is not always evident.[30] Or, as Armin Cuyvers asks, 'What, for example is Asia, Europe or Latin America, if these are regions at all?'[31]

It is not difficult to grasp that macro-comparatists are a case in point of comparative law generalists. In order to highlight the collision between area specialists and generalists I choose to focus on the scholarship of the late Patrick Glenn because his work combines several sorts of generalism: theory, methodology, and

[26] Harding (n 18) 49. Harding speaks of 'comparative lack of empirical socio-legal research', ibid 253.

[27] Besides regions this may, of course, also refer to sub-specialisations, eg in comparative law and society scholarship we can see different approaches based on non-legal disciplines: sociology, criminology, anthropology, economics, political economy, and psychology. See David Clark, *Comparative Law and Society* (Edward Elgar 2012).

[28] I am fully aware that it is possible to see these kinds of scholars as 'gatekeepers' even though this dimension is not discussed here. For a discussion on gatekeeping (from an American viewpoint), see Paul Campos, 'Legal Academia and the Blindness of Elites' (2014) 37 *Harvard Journal of Law and Public Policy* 179–86.

[29] For my part I can say that I have studied and published on Nordic law and legal culture. See, eg, Jaakko Husa, 'Nordic Law and Development' (2015) 60 *Scandinavian Studies in Law* (2015) 15–32; Jaakko Husa, 'Nordic Constitutionalism and European Human Rights' (2010) 55 *Scandinavian Studies in Law* 101–24; and Jaakko Husa, 'Constitutional Mentality' in Pia Letto-Vanamo et al (n 12), 41–60; and Husa (n 15).

[30] Here I have left out regionalism, which concerns decentralised territorial governance in multinational states. See Vito Breda, 'Regionalism' in Jan Smits, Jaakko Husa, Catherine Valcke & Madalena Narciso (eds), *Elgar Encyclopedia of Comparative Law* vol 3 (Edward Elgar 2023) 297–304.

[31] Cuyvers (n 15) 653.

macro-comparison. More than that, Glenn's work is intellectually stimulating and original despite the critical questions it also raises. As far as I can tell, it is a learned and modern version of macro-comparative law. Moreover, Glenn's *Legal Traditions of the World* has become an influential book in comparative law circles.[32] Without a doubt, it is an influential work in the field, regardless of what one thinks of it.

To begin with, Glenn's legal traditions approach is something of a paradox. This is because it is built on criticism of macro-comparativism but, in turn, is itself a form of macro-comparative law. Accordingly, Glenn pointed out that 'the number and diversity of our laws has led to an apparently irresistible process of aggregation and categorization'.[33] The beginning of aggregation and categorisation as an academic endeavour appears, I suspect, very strange in contemporary eyes. The pedigree of comparative law itself raises questions. At the beginning of the twentieth century, race, nationality, and alleged level of civilisation played a key role. For instance, Georges Sauser-Hall's macro-comparative law grouped the world's legal systems into the laws of the Aryan peoples (Indo-European peoples), Semitic peoples, Mongolian peoples (namely Japan and China), and uncivilised (or barbarous) peoples, which included, for example, the law of Negroes and the law of Melanesians.[34] This is - there is no way around it - a form of comparative law racism and has no place in modern comparative law.

The next step, taken by John Henry Wigmore, was less racist as his grouping was more historical and focused on legal cultures he regarded as important.[35] He distinguished 16 historic and later legal systems, namely Egyptian, Mesopotamian, Chinese, Hindu, Hebrew, Greek, maritime, Roman, Celtic, Germanic, canon, Japanese, Islamic, Slavic, civil, and English law.[36] The following steps were taken in the direction of private law's dominance as Pierre Arminjon, Boris Nolde, and Martin Wolff presented their classification in the 1950s.[37] Their macro-comparative law construction became influential through the famous volume by Kötz and Zweigert. There is something that deserves to be registered here. Doctrinally flavoured private law orientation left earlier historical and anthropological tendencies in the shadows of mainstream comparative law.[38] For the development of comparative law as a field, this change turned out to be essential. Much

[32] The manuscript of the book was awarded the inaugural *Canada Prize* of the International Academy of Comparative Law in 1998, two years before the first edition was published.

[33] H Patrick Glenn, 'Comparative Legal Families and Comparative Legal Traditions' in Mathias Reimann & Reinhard Zimmermann (eds), *The Oxford Handbook of Comparative Law* (OUP 2006) 421–40, 422.

[34] See Georges Sauser-Hall, *Fonction et méthode de droit comparé* (Kundig 1913) (*droits aryens et indo-européens, droits sémitiques, droits mongols, droits barbares*). According to him each race had its own internal legal development (*'qu'à l'intérieur de chaque race'*, ibid 63).

[35] For more details, see Annlise Riles, 'Wigmore's Treasure Box' (1999) 106 *Harvard Law Review* 723–40 (revisits Wigmore's scholarship).

[36] See John Henry Wigmore, *A Panorama of the World's Legal Systems* (West Publishing 1928) 1140–45.

[37] See Pierre Arminjon, Boris Nolde, and Martin Wolff, *Traité de droit comparé*, Vol I (LGDJ 1950). Their grouping consisted of seven legal families: French, German, Scandinavian, English, Russian, Islamic, and Hindu, ibid 49–53.

[38] Importantly, Glenn's work can be seen as a scholarly dialogue between comparative law and legal history even though this dimension is left out of the discussion here. See Thomas Duve, 'Legal Traditions' (2018) 6 *Comparative Legal History* 15–33.

of Glenn's endeavour was, as I see it, an attempt to step out of the shadows and to rebuild macro-comparative law on a less conflictual basis, abandon the intellectual heritage of private international law and move back towards historical and anthropological approaches.

Glenn sought to get rid of the epistemic and methodological problems of macro-comparative law by constructing a novel way of doing macro-comparative law.[39] His approach cleared some of the problems but was unable to shake off the epistemic shackles of generalism. A crucial conceptual tool for Glenn is the notion of legal tradition, which – he argues – is different from legal family or legal culture. In essence, 'tradition' in Glenn's reading is about transmitted information. Accordingly, legal tradition is culturally transmitted information concerning what law is, where we acquire knowledge of it, and the kind of techniques we use when seeking information about law. Importantly, Glenn's macro-construct is not like others, in the sense that it avoids placing legal traditions in pigeonholes (families, cultures) as he underlines the historical fact that legal traditions result from and are built on exchanges of information with other legal traditions. Legal tradition, however, has different dimensions of interchange of which the most important are internal and lateral. The underlying idea is to avoid compartmentalisation, unlike in the legal family approach.

The idea of internal traditions is built on the thought according to which there are no pure traditions. Consequently, all legal traditions contain other internal traditions as laws of different places have been in contact with each other throughout history. Lateral traditions, in turn, are not only part of any given tradition as they are traditions that exist within several broader traditions. Glenn mentions such lateral traditions as 'casuistry' (Roman, Talmudic, Islamic, and common law, even perhaps Hindu law). Moreover, Glenn discusses analogical reasoning (Islamic and common law), fundamentalism, and the tradition of the legal profession ('jurists' or legal scholars (academic as well as other legal experts and judges). The bottom line seems to be to offer a setting that places different legal traditions in peaceful interaction with each other rather than collisions.[40] In this sense, Glenn sought to break not only the shackles of compartmentalisation but also those of comparative law's contrarian intellectual spirit. On the other hand – bafflingly perhaps – his work is openly contrarian in its relationship to earlier macro-comparative law constructions.[41]

The theoretical part of Glenn's legal traditions approach is apparently different from typical macro-comparative law's theoretical – implicit or explicit – assumptions. However, when it comes to the legal traditions he actually addresses

[39] In this analysis of Glenn's legal traditions, I draw from my review essay of Glenn's *Legal Traditions of the World* (OUP 2004): Jaakko Husa, 'Emancipation or Deprivation for the European Legal Mind?' (2006) 13 *Maastricht Journal of European and Comparative Law* 81–107.

[40] He rejected the idea according to which legal traditions would be incommensurable. See, eg, H Patrick Glenn, 'Are Legal Traditions Incommensurable?' (2001) 49 *AJCL* 133–45.

[41] See, eg, how he attacked the notion of 'culture', in Glenn, 'Legal Cultures and Legal Traditions' in Mark Van Hoecke (ed), *Epistemology and Methodology of Comparative Law* (Hart Publishing 2004) 7–20.

in his book, the difference between other macro-constructions becomes uncertain and somewhat blurred. Glenn includes chthonic (Indigenous), Talmudic, civil law, Islamic, common law, Hindu, and Asian legal traditions.[42] Glenn manages to deal in a reasonably equal manner with distinctly different legal traditions and he does not seem to give epistemic preference to common law and/or civil law – the West, if you like. His modus operandi seems unprejudiced as each discussion starts from the general nature of the legal tradition addressed, then moves to justifications of it and continues to its view on change of the tradition and ends with its relationship to other legal traditions. Regardless, Glenn could not really escape the obvious methodological basic weakness of macro-comparativism: its innate generalism.[43] This is an inborn quality of generalist comparative law, as noted by Mark Van Hoecke when he says that '[c]onstructing legal families always is a reductionist operation'.[44] Generalist comparative law is doomed to present complicated legal systems in a simplified manner that is bound to look way too blunt for the area experts whose knowledge is more detailed and contextual. Or – as Ugo Mattei notes – generalising macro-constructs exists for 'merely proposing cardinal points'.[45] Cardinal points are, in short, what comparative law generalism is about. No wonder, then that this falls short of the ambit of area expertise.[46]

In a way – and certainly against Glenn's intentions – the legal traditions approach may be conceived as a continuation of the so-called 'grand tradition' type of approach. This is simply because the approach is so general and concerns general history and sweeping cultural abstractions. It may not be conflictual, but it certainly is encyclopaedic. This inborn weakness was, of course, noted by other comparatists soon after the book was published. To take an example, the *Journal of Comparative Law* dedicated an issue to a collective critical review of Glenn's book, but there is no need to rehash what was said.[47] For the sake of balance, it should also be noted that there are more positive views on Glenn's legacy in the field of comparative law.[48] Nevertheless, the focus here is on the generalist nature of Glenn's contribution because the scope is so wide, making it impossible to really take into account the rich empirical context-specific reality and subtleties of different legal traditions. And because of this, Glenn's approach ended up using old, slightly altered nametags which tell us little about the reality filled with details which are, instead, squeezed within the frames of mainstream's 'grand tradition'

[42] H Patrick Glenn, *Legal Traditions of the World*, 4th edn (OUP 2014) chs 3–9.

[43] I posed this question to Glenn on several occasions: In the end, how different is this from legal families? I was left with the impression that despite his good-humoured and witty replies he never really liked this comparison.

[44] Mark Van Hoecke, 'Macro Comparative Law' in Smits et al (n 30), Vol 2 3–9, 4.

[45] Ugo Mattei, 'Three Patterns of Law' (1997) 45 *AJCL* 5-44, 17.

[46] Duve (n 38), 33 notes that Glenn's approach 'tends to be essentialist, it underrates the need of translation into different contexts, it is not sensitive for the significance of institutions, and it does not provide clear criteria for the distinction of what is and what is not part of a legal tradition'.

[47] William Twining et al, 'A Fresh Start for Comparative Legal Studies? A Collective Review of Patrick Glenn's Legal Traditions of the World, 2nd edition' (2006) 1 *JCL* 100–99.

[48] See Helge Dedek (ed), *A Cosmopolitan Jurisprudence: Essays in Memory of H. Patrick Glenn* (CUP 2022).

approach.[49] Cardinal points are, after all, meant to be cardinal and leave out the details even if a non-conflictual framework would be theoretically subtle.

In fairness, as already pointed out above, Glenn's basic tenor differs from earlier macro-constructions since he specifically takes into account ideas of pluralism and interaction between cultures.[50] In that sense, the legal traditions approach evades at least some of the critique by Harding, as Glenn avoided compartments in the sense that he paid attention to the relations and interactions between legal traditions.[51] Where all this leaves us with the discussion on specialist vs generalist confrontation is unclear. In any case, one thing seems possible to say. In macro-comparative law it is impossible to reach the level of detail that is possible in micro-comparison even though – as John Bell points out – these two have a meaningful relationship between them.[52] Indeed, despite collisions there is also overlap and interaction that seems to weaken the significance of scholarly collisions. Perhaps it is possible to find a middle way and to look beyond apparent disagreements.

III. Defusing the Collision?

The above discussion reflects the present state of generalist comparative law, which is not easy to pinpoint because the literature is so vast. Of course, abandoning the nationalist view on law has always been part of the challenge of comparativism – micro and macro alike – that much is clear.[53] Where are we now as comparatists? On the whole it seems justified to assume that the comparative law of this century has 'arrived at a much richer, especially more nuanced and dynamic, view of the world map of law than we had in 1950.'[54] Today's key macro-constructs are legal family, legal culture, and legal tradition. These macro-constructs overlap even though the methodologies or theoretical commitments on which they are based may differ.[55] As pointed out above, there seems to be interaction, with generalists and area experts making the distinction

[49] cf Harding (n 18) 48–50.

[50] Other legal-culturally sensitive approaches also give the interaction between legal cultures much less attention. See Sören Koch and Jørn Øyrehagen Sunde (eds), *Comparing Legal Culture*, 2nd edn (Fagbokforlaget 2020). This book provides theoretical and methodological grounds and then moves on to provide pictures of chosen legal cultures: Norwegian, Finnish, Estonian, German, Polish, English/Welsh, Scottish, Belgian, French, Austrian, Italian, Romanian, Australian, and Chinese.

[51] 'Comparative law does not need compartments; it needs profound understanding of local knowledge and global doctrine', ibid 49.

[52] John Bell, 'The Value of Micro-Comparison' (n 48) 64–82 points to how Glenn's macro-comparison illustrated the way different legal traditions are able to operate in combination and across borders between legal systems, thus challenging the compartmentalised view of legal traditions.

[53] cf Kjell-Åke Modéer, 'Abandoning the Nationalist Framework' in Heikki Pihlajamäki, Markus D Dubber & Mark Godfrey (eds), *The Oxford Handbook of European Legal History* (OUP 2018) 100–14.

[54] Mathias Reimann, 'The Progress and Failure of Comparative Law in the Second Half of the Twentieth Century' (2002) 50 *AJCL* 671–700, 679.

[55] See for more detailed discussion, Jaakko Husa, 'Macro-Comparative Law – Reloaded' (2018) 131 *Tidsskrift for rettsvitenskap* 410–47.

between generalists and area experts quite hazy. The question is, nevertheless, how this interaction takes place and is it sufficient to alleviate collision?

First, it makes sense to register the present situation in mainstream comparative law. To take an example, Uwe Kischel starts the chapter on Asian law in his thick volume by saying that 'Asia is a geographic category, not a legal one' and a bit later he continues by stating that Asia's 'cultural, religious, historical, and political systems are too diverse, as are the foreign and domestic influences on legal systems in the region'.[56] His chapter on Asia covers China, Taiwan, South Korea, India, and Indonesia.[57] Despite generality, Kischel's extensive book is filled with more detailed discussions and analyses, which in turn means that it would not be fair to argue that the volume is merely about generalising. There are subtleties, too. General and specific interact as the details influence how generalisations are made, and vice versa. As a result, specialism and generalism are difficult to tell apart.

Second, we need to accept that generalising comparative law cannot escape the quality of being open to critique. As generalisations, macro-constructs are, in all honesty, helplessly vulnerable to the detailed criticism of area experts. In this sense, for an area expert, criticising macro-constructs is like shooting fish in a barrel. Collision with area expertise or micro-comparative expertise reveals unsparingly the vulnerability of generalising comparativism. This raises a question on the usefulness of general comparative law expertise. Of course, one possible way to avoid the problem is to say that notions like legal families are not really about research as their main purpose is to serve teaching of law.[58] This is, in my view, one possible way to make the issue disappear, although it seems a bit too evasive. Macro-constructs are not, perhaps, without research-related purpose as they seek to describe global legal diversity and indirectly influence our understanding of global legal diversity. If this holds, then, generalising comparative law may still have a place in the field of comparative law studies.[59]

Consequently, if one studies common law or civil law, one is equipped with notions about what they are because there is already an epistemic structure, as well as theoretical language that guides the comparatist. Therefore, while it is true that legal families as generalising macro-constructs are best suited for describing and generalising civil law, common law, and (Western or Western-influenced) mixed legal families, they may be of use if renewed from time to time. This explains why we also need other kinds of conceptualisations of which Glenn's legal traditions are one example. Abandoning legal families underlining the parentage and frameworks based on Western private law speaks for other kinds of conceptualisations

[56] Uwe Kischel, *Comparative Law* (OUP 2019) 675.

[57] ibid ch 9.

[58] According to Bogdan, a macro-construct such as a legal family is a 'very basic pedagogical instrument', Michael Bogdan, *Comparative Law* (Norstedt 1994) 86. cf Cuniberti (n 14) 27–28.

[59] Again it is crucial to keep in mind that comparative law has many purposes. For example, we can separate three kinds of core areas: (1) description of foreign law, ie, giving information about foreign legal systems, (2) mapping law into different models of families, cultures or traditions, and (3) comparing law, ie, using, creating, and criticising different types of methods and approaches in comparative law. See Reimann (n 54).

and epistemic packaging.[60] With the change of conceptual framework, some collisions are defused, others not. This is unavoidable because macro-concepts are crafted for the purpose of simplification.[61] To that end, macro-concepts are not even meant to provide detailed empirical descriptions but to make a group of legal systems less complicated and therefore easier for an outsider to understand.

Nevertheless, as the very purpose of generalisations is to generalise, macro-comparative law will never be able to successfully respond to the detail-based critique of area experts and micro-comparatists. The collision runs deep as it rests upon a juxtaposition of underlying methodological assumptions: area expertise – and micro-comparativism in general – rely on individualism whereas generalist comparativism rests on holism. This collision seems to be elementary as to its nature but is not necessarily an insurmountable obstacle.[62] In my view, the collision exists in the literature and in research practice(s), but it may be somewhat overstated. There are also approaches that seek to combine elements of micro and macro. The legal formants approach, invented by Rodolfo Sacco, is an example of legal comparativism that is difficult to place in the discussion on area expertise vs generalist expertise.[63] The idea with legal formants is not to focus on norms but to see them as components of law that are connected by the agency of different actors. Legal formants highlight the actions of legislators, civil servants, legal scholars, and others who connect various components and elements of law.[64] Legal formants are, however, difficult to place in the confrontational situation between area expertise and generalist expertise. Nevertheless, legal formants scholarship is contrarian in its relation to rule-focused forms of comparative law as Sacco's idea was to abandon legal formalism in the comparative study of law.[65] At the same time, the legal formants approach does seem more original than contrarian as it combines rather than collides micro- and macro-levels.

It is important to keep in mind that the collision is about different levels of comparative law and there is, indeed, nothing that would require any comparatist to limit their study to a single level only.[66] Reading comparative law literature, however, may give the impression that these two are like East and West in Rudyard Kipling's famous poem and never the twain shall meet.[67] This verdict appears to be

[60] See for more detailed discussion on this, Jaakko Husa, 'Legal Families' in Smits et al, (n 30), Vol 2, 443–52.

[61] cf Esin Örücü, 'Mixed and Mixing Systems' in Esin Örücü & Elspeth Attwooll (eds), *Studies in Legal Systems* (Kluwer 1996) 335–52, 335.

[62] cf Van Hoecke (n 44) 7.

[63] See, eg, Rodolfo Sacco, 'Legal Formants' (1991) 39 *AJCL* 1–34. See also Michele Graziadei, 'Rodolfo Sacco's Theoretical Contribution to Comparative Law' (2024) 37 *International Journal for the Semiotics of Law* 1471–84.

[64] For a concise discussion on legal formants, see Antonio Gambaro and Michele Graziadei, 'Legal Formants' in Smits et al (n 30) Vol 2 452–58.

[65] Gambaro and Graziadei describe Sacco's approach as being 'as distant from legal positivism as cubism is from figurative art', ibid 453.

[66] cf Cárdenas (n 1) 27.

[67] Rudyard Kipling, 'The Ballad of East and West' (1889) in *Rudyard Kipling's Verse: Definitive Edition* (Garden City 1940) 234–38. The verse starts like this: 'Oh, East is East, and West is West, and never the twain shall meet; Till Earth and Sky stand presently at God's great Judgment Seat'.

an exaggeration. Despite collisions, area expertise and macro-comparative generalism are in interaction as in a hermeneutic circle. In short, our understanding of a single legal system as a whole is based on our understanding of its individual parts.[68] My claim is that even though a great deal of comparative law contrarianism is involved, our understanding of foreign law and legal systems (broadly understood) is built upon a hermeneutical process of understanding. That said, this does not mean that the comparatist would ever gain a full understanding as there will be continuous movement back and forth between the details and the overall view.

Comparative law's hermeneutic circle is always on the move, as indeed are legal families, cultures, and traditions. Collisions, however, prevent us from creating a suitable and sophisticated comparative law language following universal grammar.[69] Besides, universal grammar seems like too ambitious a goal. If we are to truly embrace global legal pluralism, then it may be prudent to reject overly ambitious ideas about universal comparative law grammar.[70] This is simply because, as Paul Schiff Berman puts it, '[t]he world is simply messier than many hope it will be'.[71] Messiness in this context means simply that the global world of law is characterised by disorder which, in turn, makes lawyers almost instinctively shrink back from universal grammar. On the bright side, comparative study of law has countless matters to investigate, and comparatists have a lot to learn. In the best case scenario, comparative law is a continuous process between area and generalist expertise, leading to new insights and perspectives. In the end, it all boils down to being curious about foreign law. Curiosity may have killed the cat, but it is still the driving force that keeps comparative study of law alive and kicking.

[68] For this argument in full, see Jaakko Husa, 'Legal Families in Comparative Law' (2001) 24 *Retfærd* 15–24.

[69] As to the idea of this kind of language, see Harding (n 20) 252. The idea of common legal language is, indeed, a tall order. See, eg, Simone Glanert, 'Europe, Aporetically' (2012) 5 *Erasmus Law Review* 135–50.

[70] See Paul Schiff Berman, *Global Legal Pluralism* (CUP 2012). Berman's book is based on an idea according to which there are 'complexities of law in a world where a single act or actor is potentially regulated by multiple legal or quasi-legal regimes', ibid 4.

[71] ibid 323.

8

Functionalism – Proponents and Opponents

Functional comparative law, with its multiple meanings, has occupied a central role in modern comparative law scholarship. Virtually everyone involved with comparative law has, in one way or another, an opinion about it. Sometimes it has played the role of villain and sometimes the role of hero on the stage of legal comparativism. Much has been written on what functional comparative law is, or what it should be, what are its pros and cons, and what is its role in modern comparative law. I speak of 'modern' for lack of a better word, referring to this century because functionalism used to be a kind of paradigm in the latter decades of the twentieth century.[1] The story of comparative law's functionalism is an intriguing one for many reasons. First, it is a tale of the rise and fall of an archetypical mainstream dogma. Second, it reveals plainly the contrarian nature of comparative law scholarship and how it builds on and draws from colliding theoretical ambitions.[2] Third, despite its being declared dead it continues to play a part in comparative law scholarship as it still stirs sufficient discord for scholars to debate over it. These three reasons alone explain the need to discuss functionalism and its antagonists in a book that tells the story of modern comparative law through the collisions that have shaped it. Without a shadow of doubt, functionalism has played a pivotal role – as an ally or an enemy – in modern comparative law's formation.

Importantly, comparative law functionalism differs from many other collisions I discuss in this book as it has created openly colliding views that seem to create an oddly passionate and staunch scholarship. Unmasked discord has consequences for outlining the lines of battle.[3] In comparison to some other collisions, functionalism is

[1] Functionalism is 'seen as one of the most important features of traditional comparative law', Mathias Siems, *Comparative Law*, 3rd edn (CUP 2022) 17.

[2] According to one description, comparative law functionalism is 'historically one of the most influential approaches to the study of comparative law, and perhaps the most controversial', Christopher Whytock, 'Legal Origins, Functionalism, and the Future of Comparative Law' (2009) *Brigham Young University Law Review* 1879–1905.

[3] For a useful (critical) overview, see Michele Graziadei, 'The Functionalist Heritage' in Pierre Legrand & Roderick Munday (eds), *Comparative Legal Studies* (CUP 2003) 100–26.

easier to analyse because of its rich literature; moreover, scholars have not pulled their punches even though much of the debate has perhaps been shadow boxing against self-constructed straw men. Then again – this is my intuition – building straw men may be an innate quality of the contrarian mentality. In some ways, debating over functionalism in comparative law brings to mind a phrase known in politics: 'you are either with us, or you are against us.' In this kind of setting, images tend to play an important role.

Before I can delve deeper into comparative law functionalism, I need to define what it is that functionalism in comparative law means.[4] This is, unfortunately, not a walk in the park as there are many ideas about functionalism. Any commentator hoping to get a comprehensive grip may find themselves in the role of Procrustes, stretching functionalisms or cutting them so as to force them to fit into their scholarly framework. When addressing functionalism in comparative law it is necessary to bear in mind its conceptual diversity.[5] Functionalism has many meanings. Despite the difficulties, it is possible to pinpoint roughly what functionalism means against the backdrop of comparative law scholarship. First, it seems clear that functionalism in comparative law does not mean the same as it does in other fields of knowledge.[6] Second, there are generally speaking – here I follow Esin Örücü's take – two main streams of functionalism in comparative law.[7] These two are certainly not the only ones but they cover a great deal of the relevant scholarly terrain.[8]

The functional-institutional approach seeks to find out which institution in a system performs an equivalent function to the one under survey in another system. Essentially, the comparatist attempts to identify institutions that fulfil a similar role in that they seek to address the same socio-legal issue. The problem-solving approach asks, instead, how a socio-legal problem is resolved in the systems being compared. This approach shares the same belief as with the functional-institutional approach because it also assumes that similar problems have similar solutions across legal systems even though solutions are reached by different routes. The justification for comparison is that the problem in the system compared is believed to be more or less the same. Accordingly, the first approach looks for the purpose of an institution whereas the latter focuses on solutions ('functional equivalents')

[4] See, eg, Roberto Scarciglia, *Methods and Legal Comparison* (Edward Elgar 2023) 99–102.

[5] See, eg, Yenny Vega Cárdenas, *Methodology and Epistemology of Comparative Law* (LexisNexis 2024) 41–47.

[6] There is no need to discuss this further in this chapter as the focus lies elsewhere. But I have discussed this elsewhere, see Jaakko Husa, 'Functionalism' in MT Gibbons (ed), *The Encyclopedia of Political Thought* (Wiley 2014) doi.org/10.1002/9781118474396.wbept0398 and Jaakko Husa, 'Functional Method in Comparative Law' (2013) 2 *European Property Law Journal* 4–21.

[7] Esin Örücü, 'Methodologies for Comparative Law' in Jan Smits, Jaakko Husa, Catherine Valcke & Madalena Narciso (eds), *Elgar Encyclopedia of Comparative Law*, Vol 3 (Edward Elgar 2023) 42–50.

[8] Another, more refined, way to distinguish notions of functionalism is to discuss no less than nine versions: finalism, adaptionism, constructivist version, classical version, instrumentalism, refined version, epistemological version, equivalence version, and finally comparative law's functionalism as synthesis or eclecticism. See Ralf Michaels, 'The Functional Method of Comparative Law' in Mathias Reimann & Reinhard Zimmermann (eds), *The Oxford Handbook of Comparative Law*, 2nd edn (OUP 2019) 345–89, 348–67. See also Siems (n 1) 31–35.

in resolving the same issue.[9] Of course, in practice, telling these two apart may be difficult as these approaches are based on broadly similar thinking about law and society.[10] They may not be identical, but they are intimately related and entangled with each other.[11]

There are certain underlying ideas about law. In essence, comparative law functionalism conceives law as a kind of *system* whose components are held together by functions. Even though functionalism in comparative law is not as strictly systemic as functionalism in sociology, it nevertheless shares at least some general ideas of sociological functionalism.[12] Regardless, comparative law functionalism does look like a homespun methodology in comparison to more refined functionalisms in other fields.[13] What is more, my inkling is that functionalism has been mostly a stimulus for comparatists who have sharpened their scholarly nails while seeking to look like serious comparative law scholars. To that end, in order to give an impression of a modern comparative law scholar, one may have assumed that attacking functionalism was, more or less, the expectation. Functionalism has been a good enemy, so to speak. In that sense, functionalism shares similarities with the law in books and law in action distinction discussed in chapter two; beyond methodology, it has to do with the self-image of the comparatist.[14] The following sections will examine functionalism's defence, discuss critiques of functionalism, and finally investigate whether the collision has lost its potential significance for contemporary scholarship, which has embraced pluralist ideas about itself and law in general.

I. The Basic Principle and its Defence

Unlike some other collisions discussed in this book, no need arises here to unearth a deeper hidden meaning in scholarly texts. Elucidating beyond what is explicitly stated appears virtually unnecessary; no complicated exegesis is required. We need only, once again, to turn to Zweigert and Kötz's influential volume and its

[9] These dimensions are difficult to tell apart; eg, Richard Hyland manages to identify only one dimension in his otherwise excellent discussion on functionalism. He sees functionalism as what one might call purposivism that focuses on law's articulated purposes. See Richard Hyland, *Gifts* (OUP 2009) 96. See also Maurice Adams & John Griffiths, 'Against 'Comparative Method' in Maurice Adams & Jacco Bomhoff (eds), *Practice and Theory in Comparative Law* (CUP 2012) 279–301, 284 'broad use of the idea of "function" confuses what a rule does as a matter of fact ("solves those problems") with (legislative) purpose ("attempt to satisfy a particular legal need")'.

[10] Hyland (n 9) 43–44.

[11] The functional approach is very close to structural comparison, which is left out of discussion here. See, eg, Birke Häcker, *Consequences of Impaired Consent Transfers* (Hart Publishing 2013).

[12] Sociological functionalism in general, see Alan Barnard, *History and Theory in Anthropology* (CUP 2021) 62–80.

[13] See Husa (n 6).

[14] About the link between functionalism and American legal realism, see Samuel Mermin, 'Legal Functionalism' (1973) 17 *Annuario de Filosofía del Derecho* 81–92.

outspoken theoretical part.[15] They make their point very clearly. The core passage becomes some kind of a credo, or a mantra as Ralf Michaels calls it,[16] for the comparative law mainstream:

> The basic methodological principle of all comparative law is that of functionality. From this basic principle stem all the other rules which determine the choice of laws to compare, the scope of the undertaking, the creation of a system of comparative law, and so on.[17]

In particular, the first sentence of the quote has been cited countless times. Some may cite it approvingly, so that it also expresses how they conceive the methodological foundation of comparative law. Others, as we shall see in the following section, have cited it – or the message it conveys – in order to attack it. Importantly, as Michaels notes, for the supporters of functionalism it 'is the most, perhaps the only, fruitful method'.[18] Functionalism is so important for comparative study of law because it takes a firm stance on the key issue regarding studying law comparatively; indeed, as Zweigert and Kötz argue, 'the only things which are comparable are those which fulfil the same function'.[19] The worrying issue concerns first and foremost *comparability*. Concentration on comparability took root in comparative law from the 1970s. In 1999 Kötz argued that '[i]t is recognized generally today that the basic methodological principle of all comparative law is that of functionality'.[20] Along similar lines, a group of comparatists declared that functionalism in comparative law is 'comparative law's principal gift to twentieth century legal science'.[21]

As is typical of comparative law scholarship, ideas tend to be brewed in contrarian fashion. Indeed, functionalism itself was originally crafted as a contrarian move against earlier scholarship on comparative law methodology.[22] It emerged from scholarly dissatisfaction. With the wisdom of hindsight, we may claim that functionalism was constructed as a step forward, not a step backward. As it sought to step forward, it aspired to renew the discipline in the spirit of scientific endeavour accompanied by its own narrative about law and its nature. Its basic principle grew out of this kind of 'scientific' mentality, not as an attempt to conserve previous ideas about methodology.

As a basic principle, functionalism is a kind of a postulate from which all methodological ideas should ideally be derived as it defines the fundamental requirements for allegedly meaningful comparison. As Balázs Fekete also notes,

[15] However, functionalism was outlined much earlier by Zweigert on the basis of Ernst Rabel & Rudolf von Jhering's work. See Balázs Fekete, *Paradigms in Modern European Comparative Law* (Hart Publishing 2021) 123–24.

[16] Michaels (n 8) 345–89, 346 (he also calls it '*bête noire*').

[17] Konrad Zweigert and Hein Kötz, *An Introduction to Comparative Law*, 2nd edn (OUP 1998) 34.

[18] Michaels (n 8) 346.

[19] Zweigert & Kötz (n 17) 34.

[20] Hein Kötz, 'Comparative Law in Germany' (1999) 51 *Revue internationale de droit comparé* 753–58, 755.

[21] Mary Ann Glendon, Michael Gordon & Paolo Carozza, *Comparative Legal Traditions in a Nutshell* (West Group 1999) 9.

[22] Zweigert & Kötz (n 17) 33.

the basic principle was an attempt to build comparative law on a novel basis that would be free from the problems of earlier methodologies.[23] In a way, it was an attempt to create some distance from the doctrinal approach. In essence, functionalism contains an epistemic and methodological assumption about comparative law. In practice, functionalism is about an approach which builds on deceptively simple ideas about what and how to compare.[24] Today it can be considered as a traditional method of comparative law that still exists but has a number of rivals and variations.[25] 'Traditional' refers here to a number of qualities, such as a tendency to focus on Western private law from a more or less doctrinal framework.

In the late 1990s it was claimed that Zweigert and Kötz offered a balanced synthesis of comparative law literature while providing the most advanced approach to comparative law.[26] This claim made sense as it stemmed, among other things, from the fact that functionalist ideas were endorsed by numerous comparative law scholars who were engaged in methodological debate.[27] So, what does comparative law functionalism mean in actual research? According to the functional understanding of comparative law, the key aspect is, as noted by Geoffrey Samuel, to look at a specific problem – for example in case law or litigation – in one legal system and then inquire how that problem is resolved in another legal system.[28] The underlying methodological idea was to reach comparability of rules and institutions by studying them as part of a larger socio-legal context and placing them in an external comparative framework (pompously titled *tertium comparationis*) constructed by the comparatist.[29] The driving force behind functionalism was and is the fear of incomparability.[30] Functional comparatists believe strongly in the idiom claiming that one cannot compare apples and oranges.[31] By extension, this dread stems from the urge of twentieth century comparatists' desire to be truly 'scientific' as discussed above in chapter three. Accordingly, if one is to believe in functionalism's

[23] Fekete (n 15) 124.

[24] The following part of this section builds on Jaakko Husa, 'Traditional Methods' in Mathias Siems & Po Yen Jap (eds), *The Cambridge Handbook of Comparative Law* (CUP 2024) 15–31. I also draw from Jaakko Husa, 'Farewell to Functionalism of Methodological Tolerance?' (2003) 67 *Rabels Zeitschrift für ausländisches und internationales Privatrecht* 419–47.

[25] See Siems (n 1) 15–49.

[26] Mark Van Hoecke & Mark Warrington, 'Legal Cultures, Legal Paradigms and Legal Doctrine' (1998) 47 *ICLQ* 495–536, 495.

[27] Fekete (n 15) 121.

[28] Geoffrey Samuel, *An Introduction to Comparative Law Theory and Method* (Hart Publishing 2014) 67.

[29] There has been much discussion on *tertium comparationis*, which refers to the third part of comparison, ie the common yardstick used in comparison. On the term, see Lei Zhu, 'On the Origin of the Term Tertium Comparationis' (2017) 60 *Language & History* 35–52. In comparative law discussion, see eg Michael Bogdan, 'Some Reflections on the Comparability of Laws Based on Different Socio-economic Systems' (2015) 61 *Scandinavian Studies in Law* 105–12.

[30] The concept is also known outside legal academia where it also refers to shared commonality between things compared, see Ulla Connor & Ana Moreno, 'Tertium Comparationis' in Paul Bruthiaux et al (eds), *Directions in Applied Linguistics* (Clevedon 2005) 153–64.

[31] This is clearly a wrong assumption. From certain points of view apples and oranges are equivalent: they grow from seeds, they are juicy and sweet, and have a seed-bearing core. They make great low-calorie snacks that are high in antioxidants and contain other beneficial compounds. Moreover, they are typically eaten raw and can be peeled.

underlying idea, the comparatist cannot compare what is incomparable and, moreover, 'in law the only things which are comparable are those which fulfil the same function'.[32] Functionalism, in this sense, is a kind of solution to comparative law's bad conscience about not being 'scientific' enough. Importantly, and to avoid anachronism, comparative law functionalism is beneficial to conceive as a contrarian move towards the allegedly unscientific nature of earlier comparativism.[33]

The core idea was that the comparatist should become epistemically detached from their innate preconceptions and to come up with more neutral concepts allowing them to study legal problems comparatively.[34] The supposed focus ought to be on social problems that are resolved by means of law. Zweigert and Kötz, nevertheless, did not stop there but went further and argued that 'different countries meet the same need in different ways, we must ask why'.[35] Without going into details and repeating what is argued in the large amount of literature, we can say that functionalism's key assumption is that *if* the comparatist follows a functional scheme, *then* they need to construct an external framework so that they are able to compare different answers or ways to answer the same problem. All this is supposed to ensure comparability, hence the quality of being a 'scientific' study of law.[36]

Many comparative law scholars have followed the functionalist methodology or at least its key ideas. For example, Peter de Cruz constructed his methodological framework on functional building blocks.[37] De Cruz's blueprint by and large coincides with Zweigert and Kötz's view – although it has more details as it is more refined – in that they both take a similar basic view. Of course, de Cruz has not been the only one. Many comparative law scholars have outlined the research process in the same functionalist manner. For example, echoing Zweigert and Kötz, WJ Kamba distinguished the main phases in the comparative study of law in the mid-1970s in a way that comes close to functionalism.[38] Later, Michael Bogdan's view of a comparative method built on functionalism because rules – to be meaningfully compared – 'must be comparable to each other functionally'.[39] Another similar type of methodology is that of John Reitz, who provided methodological principles outlining the research process in comparative law in a more or less functionalist manner.[40] I have characterised these loose methodologies as 'traditional' because they are apparently West-centred and stem mostly from doctrinally flavoured private law despite their socio-legally flavoured vocabulary.[41]

[32] Zweigert & Kötz (n 17) 34.

[33] We can speak of the shortcomings of the normative-dogmatic approach which prompted comparative legal scholars to develop functional comparative law, George Mousorakis, *Comparative Law and Legal Traditions* (Springer 2019) 115.

[34] See Hyland (n 9) 64–68.

[35] Zweigert & Kötz (n 17) 44.

[36] This seems to be meant to work especially in the fields of property law, contract law, and tort law. This point is made by Fekete (n 15) 126.

[37] Peter de Cruz, *Comparative Law in a Changing World*, 3rd edn (Routledge 2008) 242–46.

[38] WJ Kamba, 'Comparative Law: A Theoretical Framework' (1974) 23 *ICLQ* 485.

[39] Michael Bogdan, *Comparative Law* (Kluwer 1994) 60.

[40] John C Reitz, 'How to do Comparative Law?' (1998) 46 *AJCL* 617, 618.

[41] See Husa, 'Traditional Methods' (n 24).

One further point needs to be made before moving on to the rejection of functionalism as a basic principle of comparative law. Now, functionalism in comparative law has always been intimately connected to Europe and in particular European private law scholarship. In this sense, comparative law's functionalism is related to the distinction between the West and the Rest, discussed in chapter six, and the division between private law and public law, addressed in chapter four. After World War II, earlier anthropologically and historically flavoured approaches were more or less sidelined as the needs of European economic integration took over and harmoniser comparatists stepped forth.[42] This development – which later reached its peak in the 1980s and 1990s – was one of the reasons why functionalism rose to such a focal role. Europe's 'common core' projects relied on functionalism's basic ideas as it was an effective method in terms of enhancing integration through law.[43] The general aim was to find commonalities. The common core approach, first developed by Rudolf Schlesinger in the 1960s, shares a basic understanding of law with comparative law functionalism(s) as it assumes that legal systems share a common – that is, similar – *core* despite the fact of technical variations in terms of how similar problems are resolved through law.[44] In Schlesinger's words:

> when confronted with the same problem, decision-makers A and B, though independent of each other and widely separated by time and space, more often than not will respond in similar way.[45]

These ideas later became part and parcel of mainstream comparative law. For example, when the former (2014-2022) President of the International Academy of Comparative Law Katharina Boele-Woelki, explained the method in the creation of Principles of the European Family, one of the research steps was explained in the following manner: 'questions are posed in purely functional terms without any reference to the concepts of a specific legal system, thus asking what is the underlying problem that a certain legal provision aims to redress'.[46] This is not to criticise Boele-Wolki but to underline how comparative law's ideas about the functional approach have been an innate part of common core projects.[47] To that end, Kötz – in the preface to his volume on European contract law – noted that 'If Europe is to be economically unified as a Single Market, there is no doubt that its private law will also have to be unified, at least to

[42] cf Martti Koskenniemi & Ville Kari, 'A More Elevated Patriotism' in Heikki Pihlajamäki, Markus D Dubber & Mark Godfrey (eds), *The Oxford Handbook of European Legal History* (OUP 2018) 974–99, 997.

[43] cf Esin Örücü, 'Developing Comparative Law' in Esin Örücü & David Nelken (eds), *Comparative Law: A Handbook* (Hart Publishing 2007) 43–65, 51.

[44] See, eg, Matthias E Storme, 'Common Core Projects' in Smits et al (n 7) Vol 1 306–17. Storme shows how functionalism or different versions of functional comparative law have been an important part of common core project-related methodologies. See also Fekete (n 15) 134–36; Siems (n 1) 38.

[45] Rudolf Schlesinger, 'The Common Core of Legal Systems' in Kurt Nadelmann, Arthur von Mehren & John Hazard (eds), *XXth Century Comparative and Conflicts Law* (AW Sythoff 1961) 65–79, 66.

[46] Katharina Boele-Woelki, 'The Principles of European family Law' (2005) 1 *Utrecht Law Review* 160–168, 165.

[47] On another occasion, she urges comparatists to be realistic about interdisciplinary requirements as '[m]uch is possible, but not everything', Katharina Boele-Woelki, 'Rechtsvergelijking en multidisciplinariteit' in Constantin Kelk, Frans Koenraadt, Dina Siegel & Chrisje Brants (eds), *Veelzijdige gedachten* (Boom 2013) 375–86, 386.

some extent.'[48] Functionalism offered a kind of a common method to a pan-European methodology for creating more unification.[49] The justification for this is understandable because systems are different; hence it makes sense to focus on what can be seen as the common functions of law. Notwithstanding, functionalist analysis alone is arguably inadequate even for the purposes of harmonisation.[50] Noteworthily, as we will see in the following section, functionalism's ideas about comparative law and cherished commonalities have certainly not been taken lying down.

II. Rejecting the Basic Principle

The first major and in many ways ground-breaking contrarian criticism of functional comparative law saw daylight in the mid-1980s when Günter Frankenberg published his seminal article that called for a rethink of comparative law.[51] It later became probably the most cited critical article in the debates over comparative law functionalism. There is neither need nor space here to address the rich literature and debate that this article prompted. It is, nevertheless, important to register that Frankenberg's article can be considered truly one of the most eminent expressions of what one might call the crisis of mainstream comparative law of the late twentieth century.[52]

Frankenberg's critique was based on a simple but somewhat accurate observation according to which functionalism's practice differs greatly from its theoretical presumptions. Crucially, he argued, functionalism is actually a methodological principle that guides comparison but it camouflages the true aim of functionalism, which is to uphold the political status quo.[53] Frankenberg expanded discussion from method and methodology and investigated the very motives behind comparative study of law and posed the question 'Why should anyone undertake the difficult and complex task of studying the law comparatively?'[54] Clearly this was an ambitious attempt to look below the methodological surface of functionalism and to grasp what its ideological assumptions and aims were truly about (see chapter eleven, s II). Of course, even though Frankenberg's critique was seminal, he has not been alone in an ideology-focused critique, as especially David Kennedy's views show, even though Frankenberg's thoughts have been more influential in

[48] Hein Kötz, *European Contract Law I* (Clarendon Press 1997) iv.

[49] See, eg, Stefan Vogenauer, 'Eine gemeineuropäische Methodenlehre des Rechts' (2005) 13 *Zeitschrift für Europäisches Privatrecht* 234–63.

[50] Roger Cotterrell, 'too many unanalysed assumptions stand behind', 'Is It So Bad to be Different?' in Örücü & Nelken (n 43) 133–54, 142.

[51] Günter Frankenberg, 'Critical Comparisons' (1985) 26 *Harvard International Law Journal* 411–56.

[52] See, eg, Peer Zumbansen, 'Comparative Law's Coming of Age?' (2005) 6 *German Law Journal* 1073–84 ('shattering critique of the wide-ranging absence of theory in comparative law and…the ultimate lack of critical self-examination', ibid 1074).

[53] Frankenberg (n 51) 439–40.

[54] ibid 416.

comparative law circles.[55] This may be because Frankenberg has been conceived as a comparatist whereas Kennedy has been conceived more as a critical international law scholar with an interest in comparative law as well.

What is clear is that comparative law functionalism was in Frankenberg's eyes a dominant paradigm, a worthy opponent for a contrarian to oppose. On theoretical grounds, he noted that functional comparative law was 'a vulgar version of sociological functionalism' which claimed to analyse law in two basic elements: law in books and law in action. In his analysis, the idea that legal texts and institutions are solutions for problems of life in organised societies is problematic because legal systems should be seen more holistically.[56] In particular, what stirred his disapproval was Zweigert and Kötz's presumption of similarity. Frankenberg argued that '[g]rand similarities and not differences in detail are what the functionalist is out for.'[57] Such synthetic vision is enhanced, he argued, by the presumption that all practical results are similar. There is no denying that much of this critique was, more or less, spot on.

Functional comparative law was deemed to be too formal, thus giving too much weight to law as a formal technique of conflict resolution, a tendency that strips law of its innate political and moral elements. The gist of this criticism was aimed at the narrow way of understanding law, limiting it to formal law and its institutions. In a genuine contrarian spirit, Frankenberg asserted that functionalism has no eye for informal law. Importantly, it would seem, Frankenberg was aware that this kind of research-practice stood against what the theory of functional comparative law was about. Overall, and in no uncertain terms, the main target of critique was the practice of comparative law under self-professed functionalism.[58] It is not a surprise, then, that Frankenberg speaks of 'the functionalist fallacy' which (falsely) aids the comparatist in moving from system to system on the basis of imagined similarities.[59]

Another central contrarian critic of functionalism has been Pierre Legrand. His critique is built on a general philosophically-animated distrust of method and methodology. From the early stages of his comparative law scholarship he held that comparative law as a discipline was too focused on method, which in turn exerted 'a negative and potentially stultifying impact on comparative law as an intellectual discipline'.[60] The contrarian idea – going against mainstream's alleged method-fixation – was based on a view according to which comparative study of law would have more to offer than 'some relatively sterile methodological endeavours may have led us to believe'.[61] From this point of view, functionalism as a fundamentally methodological and somewhat technical approach was bound to

[55] See, eg, David Kennedy, 'The Methods and Politics of Comparative Law' in Pierre Legrand & Roderick Munday (eds), *Comparative Legal Studies* (CUP 2003) 345–433.

[56] Frankenberg (n 51) 426–28; 434–35.

[57] ibid 436.

[58] ibid 437–38.

[59] Günter Frankenberg, 'Comparing Constitutions' (2006) 4 *International Journal of Constitutional Law* 439–59, 445.

[60] Pierre Legrand, 'Beyond Method: Comparative Law as Perspective' (book review) (1988) 36 *AJCL* 788–98, 789.

[61] ibid 791.

look suspicious and insufficient.[62] In this view, seeking similarities is an epistemic cardinal sin. Later, Legrand continued along these lines and refined his critique of functionalism, pointing out functionalism's positivistic way of conceiving law comparatively. Positivism is something that Legrand regards as a fundamentally insufficient intellectual foundation for comparative study of law. In his own words:

> As regards foreign law, then, positivism, even on a most charitable reading of what it is able to achieve, can only ever allow one to identify the law in force. It cannot do more, and it cannot reasonably be expected to do more. When it comes to foreign law, positivism is thus seen to behave in stationary intellectual fashion.[63]

Instead of attacking functionalism on a more technical methodological basis, Legrand seeks to look beyond the surface and tackle fundamental issues and intellectual challenges. Underneath the mainstream, he finds, in essence, positivistic attitudes about the endeavour of studying law comparatively. Accordingly, he sees positivism's attitude regarding culture as 'autistic', which in turn stems from its inborn epistemic limitations that do not allow the comparatist to create the required sensitivity to foreign law. In short, '[p]ositivism simply lacks this kind of epistemic momentum'.[64] In this view, functionalism is seen as coupled with legal positivism. This, no doubt, seems like a well-grounded view even if one would not agree on its philosophical basis.

In practice, Legrand's one target of contrarian critique is James Gordley and the methodological ideas that – so Legrand argues – Gordley represents.[65] Gordley, in turn, conceives that Legrand's attack is actually against functionalism.[66] Indeed, this seems to be the case.[67] Unsurprisingly, Legrand has constantly proposed an assumption of *dissimilarity* instead of an assumption of functionalism's similarity.[68] Now, even though Gordley does recognise the contradictions between cultural and functional approaches, he does not accept Legrand's critique fully and defends the key ideas of functionalism, arguing that functional comparative law is not blind to

[62] For a more detailed critical discussion on method/methodology in comparative law, see Simone Glanert, 'Method?' in Pier Giuseppe Monateri (ed), *Methods of Comparative Law* (Edward Elgar 2012) 61–81 ('I have wanted to challenge the ideology of method prevailing in the field of comparative law', ibid 81).

[63] Pierre Legrand, 'Jameses at Play: A Tractation on the Comparison of Laws' (2017) 65 *AJCL* 1–132, 90.

[64] ibid 91.

[65] Gordley's view on functionalism seems generally speaking a positive one. See, eg, James Gordley, 'The Functional Method' in Monateri (n 62) 107–19.

[66] 'According to Pierre Legrand, there is an orthodox method in comparative legal studies that he calls "positivism," although it is properly called functionalism', see James Gordley, 'Comparison, Law, and Culture' (2017) 65 *AJCL* 133–80, 133.

[67] Michaels (n 8) 347 makes a good point as he says that the functional method 'merely serves as shorthand for traditional comparative law'.

[68] One example out of many, 'Only if it [comparative law] is prepared to move beyond the juxtaposition of substantive and adjectival posited law and if it is willing to overcome its seemingly obsessional drive to suppress difference across laws can comparative research about law meaningfully influence the ongoing conversation concerning legal uniformity', Pierre Legrand, 'The Return of the Repressed' (2001) 75 *Tulane Law Review* 1033–51, 1037 (against the backdrop of legal integration in Europe). Legrand also speaks about the contrarian position in comparative law scholarship: 'Contrarianism questions certain overly choreographed or patterned practices and enables a clearer, if disconcerting, awareness of the restricted reach of these practices', ibid 1034.

differences: 'anyone using the functionalist approach should be aware that sometimes purposes may be different'. In the end, in Gordley's view, '[t]he object of the functionalist approach is to clarify the purposes the law serves. In doing so, it enables a better understanding of how the law should be applied.'[69] This does not fall far short of what I have argued elsewhere.[70] Notwithstanding, it would seem that no version of functionalism is safe from relentless critique. Against the backdrop of contrarian critique it makes sense, nonetheless, to ask if the collision still exists or whether something has changed in more recent comparative law scholarship.

III. Storm in a Teacup?

The difficulty of addressing functionalism in comparative law is that one cannot ascertain the extent to which scholarly takes have been able to contribute to the actual practice of all that is done under the broad umbrella of comparative law. Discussion has been like trench warfare in which scholars have dug elaborate networks of trenches. How much or many of the combative views and debate has found its way into research practices of comparative lawyers is all but clear, just as it is with the attempt to study law in action (see chapter two). Michaels observes – speaking generally about functionalism in comparative law – that functional comparative law studies are actually rare.[71] With this caveat it is nevertheless possible to discuss the nature of the collisions in terms of – what I have labelled above in a generalising fashion as – functional comparative law. Discussion here concerns talking about comparative law rather than actually doing it (see chapter five above).

Debate on functionalism, whatever conclusion one draws from it, aptly demonstrates the scholarly nature of comparatists as contrarians. First, functionalism was crafted by Zweigert, following in the footsteps of Rabel, who sought to rebuild the methodological basis and to abandon earlier methodological poverty.

Second, functionalism became the target of contrarian critique that painted it as a dreadful failure and a monstrously misguided way to think about comparative law. In my reading, however, much of the later contrarian critique seems like a storm in a teacup; a relatively small group of scholars fighting among the tribe of comparatists. To put it otherwise, there has been a lot of unnecessary and exaggerated indignation over something that has been wilfully misunderstood or, at any rate, is less important than contrarian critics persuaded themselves to believe. For the sake of analysis here, it is possible to abridge the discussion on functionalism to two major modifications. The first is about redefining functionalism so that it would be freed from Zweigert and Kötz's view and further developed. The second concerns the pluralistic turn in comparative law and its way of conceiving functionalism merely as one tool in the comparatist's methodological toolbox. Needless

[69] ibid 179.
[70] See Husa (n 24).
[71] Michaels (n 8) 347.

to say, both of them look suspicious if seen from the viewpoint of functionalism's impenitent antagonists. I find myself unable to deflect these suspicions within the scope of the present discussion, which is based on acceptance of methodological pluralism in the form of an idea of a toolbox of methods. In other words, perhaps we have produced a lot of hot air about functionalism in comparative law. As Örücü notes, the simple fact that all things can be compared has not prevented broad and meandering discussion on comparability initiated and upheld by supporters and opponents of comparative law functionalism.[72]

A key observation is that modern functional comparative law scholarship does not blindly follow the old mainstream. For instance, Maurice Adams and John Griffiths developed an approach they call 'casting the net wide'.[73] This approach is built on functionalistic foundations, but is more refined, and they note that Zweigert and Kötz's use of the term is 'simplistic and unfortunate'.[74] What Adams and Griffiths study is euthanasia and law for which they reformulate ideas of functional comparative law. It follows, then, that 'the idea of "function" was just an analytic tool that makes it possible to achieve some kind of comparability in the rules, the institution and the behavior with which we were concerned'.[75] Instead of 'scientific research' they speak modestly about 'some kind of comparability'. This is no more than toning down the debate over functionalism.

Along similar lines, Gordley – labelled by Legrand as a defender of functionalism – seems to take a rather realistic view of functionalism in comparative law. Depicting Gordley as a one-eyed champion of blunt functionalism seems like a contrarian exaggeration. Gordley discusses the popularity and impact of functionalism in comparative law and asserts that:

> The reason is not that its theoretical foundations are clear and compelling. The reason is that they find it helps them to make sense of some of the similarities and differences among different legal systems.[76]

Conceived like this, functionalism is a heuristic tool, a kind of rule of thumb rather than a refined methodology or hermeneutical legal theory.[77] Perhaps more interesting and potentially fruitful is to consider how functionalism's role in comparative law has been diminished generally. Today it is seen as one possible way out of many through which to study law comparatively. For example, in his thick comparative law textbook Yves-Marie Laithier presents, side-by-side, a functional approach and a contextual approach as the two principal methods of

[72] Esin Örücü, *The Enigma of Comparative Law* (Martinus Nijhoff 2004) 20.

[73] See Adams & Griffiths (n 9).

[74] ibid 283.

[75] ibid 284–85. This is simply because '[i]t is necessary for comparative research to simplify reality in order to be able to explain it', Olive Sabiiti, 'New Institutional Economics' in Siems & Jen Yap (n 24) 133–56, 144.

[76] Gordley (n 65) 107.

[77] I discuss this point more thoroughly in Husa (n 6 above) and Husa, 'Research-Designs of Comparative Law' in Maurice Adams & Dirk Heirbaut (eds), *The Method and Culture of Comparative Law* (Hart Publishing 2014) 53–68.

comparative law.[78] Another illustration is Samuel's balanced view in which he identifies possible approaches to comparative law. The functional method forms part of a collection of alternatives.[79] Samuel does not seek to eradicate functionalism in a contrarian manner but, rather, recognises its role as one possible way to study law comparatively.[80] Mark Van Hoecke's take is similar in the sense that he recognises the innate pluralism of modern comparative law scholarship.[81] We can also count Mathias Siems's modern comparative law scholarship in this group because his conception of comparative study of law allows many approaches as it builds on the idea of flexibility.[82] Besides, there have always been competing approaches that are not functional even if they come close to it. For instance, Rodolfo Sacco's 'legal formants' seems to share certain features with functionalism but it 'intends to go beyond the mere description of functional solutions.'[83]

So, where are we with our discussion on functionalism in comparative law scholarship? There are still comparatists who see – if sufficiently refined – a bright future for functionalism in comparative law. One may, for example, hold that comparative law should continue to build on the legacy of functionalism because it holds virtues and valuable applications.[84] In short, one can hold that functionality as a methodological principle can still be useful if developed further.[85] Jan Smits duly clarifies this attitude:

> there is nothing wrong with functionalism as long as it is taken seriously. It is fine to develop rules of thumb and abstain from a robust methodology if one compares jurisdictions with a view to drawing inspiration for one's own jurisdiction. However, if one's aim is to identify similarities and differences, the functional method still has a future. How bright this future will be is dependent on the extent to which comparatists are able to reshape the functionalist method.[86]

Smits's point is simply that there is nothing wrong with the functional approach if done correctly.[87] This does not mean uncritical wholesale acceptance of what has

[78] Yves-Marie Laithier, *Droit comparé* (LGDJ 2024) 425 ff.

[79] Discussion on functional method, see Samuel (n 28 above) 65–78. In certain respects, Samuel comes close to Michaels (n 8 above, 388) who notes that the 'functional method remains of crucial importance to comparative law'.

[80] Samuel explicitly says that the functional method is 'a hugely influential method' (n 28 above) 78.

[81] Mark Van Hoecke, 'Is There Now a Comparative Legal Scholarship?' (2017) 12 *JCL* 271–80.

[82] '[T]here is a high degree of flexibility in the method and scope of comparative law', Siems (n 1) 445.

[83] Elena Ioriatti, 'Comparative Law Method and Legal Formants' in Luca Siliquini-Cinelli, Davide Gianti & Mauro Balestrieri (eds), *The Grand Strategy of Comparative Law* (Routledge 2024) 39–54, 40. Sacco's approach is more structuralist but functionalism in other fields and structuralism are close to each other, see Husa (n 6).

[84] Oliver Brand, 'Conceptual Comparisons' (2007) 32 *Brooklyn Journal of International Law* 405–66, 411.

[85] Catherine Valcke & Matthew Grellette, 'Three Functions of Function in Comparative Legal Studies' in Adams Heirbaut (n 67) 99–111, 111.

[86] Jan Smits, 'Taking Functionalism Seriously' (2011) 18 *Maastricht Journal of European and Comparative Law* 554–58. Smits's paper is a reply to Jaakko Husa, 'Metamorphosis of Functionalism' (2011) *18 Maastricht Journal of European and Comparative Law* 548–53.

[87] See Jan Smits, 'De toekomst van de functionele methode van rechtsvergelijking' (2024) 61 *Tijdschrift voor Privaatrecht* 709–17 ('There is nothing wrong with correctly applied functional method of (legal) comparison', ibid 716).

been done or argued under the banner of functional comparative law. Along similar lines, Michaels claims that if functional comparative law is properly understood it also – like the contextual or cultural approach – assumes that 'legal rules are culturally embedded'.[88] In this sense, one may be able to combine functionalism and culturalism.[89] This would also mean mitigating the collision between the defenders and critics of functionalism by admitting the existing overlap.

In my earlier work I defended functionalism but with certain reservations, especially concerning the presumed similarity and the alleged scientific nature of comparative law scholarship.[90] In the field of contrarians, however, taking a kind of middle position leads to a no man's land where some view 'the centrist' critically as a functionalist whereas others may say that one has yielded too much to critique.[91] In fact, it is impossible to know how one's scholarship is seen in a field divided as to proponents and antagonists.[92] And as we saw above, Gordley was painted – unfairly in my view – as some kind of a die-hard functionalist lacking subtlety. Apparently, arguing that functionalism is a heuristic tool is also too much or too little, depending on who speaks.[93] The 'if you are not with us, then you are against us' type of logic has been applied to scholars who have taken part in the discussion on functionalism in comparative law.

This brings me back to the question of contrarianism and to comparatists as contrarian legal scholars as broadly defined in chapter one. The contrarian nature of the debate seems to create dead ends. One is either an insensitive functionalist or a sensitive culturalist/contextualist; one either supports or opposes traditional comparative law. In this sense, developing a notion like 'interpretative functionalism' cannot be forward leading as in the eyes of a critic it will remain too mainstream.[94] Then again, what else can one expect if the field is divided and there is no middle ground: one is either a proponent or an antagonist. In the end, functionalism – if nothing else – displays in no uncertain terms the contrarian quality of comparatists. Regardless, despite its duration and tenacity much of the debate still seems like a storm in a teacup. If one embraces methodological diversity, then it seems that there has been a lot of fuss over a matter that seems increasingly trivial today. Then again, much depends on how one sees the nature of law and legal systems, as we will see in the next chapter.

[88] Michaels (n 8) 369.

[89] See also Qian Xiangyang, 'Culture and Comparative Law' in Siems & Jen Yap (n 24) 72–90.

[90] See Husa (n 24) and Husa (n 6). See also Alessandro Somma, *Introduzione al diritto comparato*, 3rd edn (Giappichelli 2025) 316–22.

[91] See Julie de Coninck, 'The Functional Method of Comparative Law' (2010) 74 *Rabels Zeitschrift für ausländisches un internationales Privatrecht* 318–59, 337 (Husa and Michaels painted as defenders of functionalism) and Michaels (n 8) 375. See also Michaels's response to de Coninck, 'Explanation and Interpretation in Functionalistic Comparative Law' (2010) 74 *Rabels Zeitschrift für ausländisches und internationales Privatrecht* 351–59.

[92] For Fekete (n 15) 131 this author is a 'skeptical voice' when it comes to functionalism. Maurice & Griffiths (n 9) 283, fn 11 say in turn that my 2003 article makes 'important qualifications' concerning functionalism in comparative law.

[93] See de Coninck (n 91) 339. See also Xiangyang (n 89) 90.

[94] About interpretative functionalism, see Michaels (n 8) 386–88.

9

Legal System – Closed or Open?

As we have seen in the previous chapters, comparative study of law is certainly not a monolith. To describe it as a field of legal scholarship using a metaphor, I would say it was a jungle rather than a neatly organised academic garden.[1] This is not to argue that comparative law cannot be civilised, but to recognise the situation where the comparatist faces an almost impenetrably tangled mass of scholarly literature. Of course, some might argue that comparative law should be a unified scholarly field. However, that is a normative argument and does not reflect today's reality as discussed in previous chapters. On many points, comparatists disagree openly or more discreetly. Some even doubt comparative law as a field altogether or want to end its alleged or pursued autonomy.[2] For an observer the situation is twofold. Some collisions are easy to detect – for example functionalism, discussed in the previous chapter – whereas others are more subtle and require reading between the lines. In any case, I hope by now to have established that there are many debates and contrarian dissent.[3]

In some cases, debate circles around questions that arise from deeper issues of a fundamental nature. Furthermore, disagreements often overlap with each other, making it difficult to deduce which disagreement is about a fundamental issue and which is more technical as to its nature. In that sense, comparative law scholarship is like an iceberg, meaning that only a portion of the issues are above the surface. Some debates may be of a technical or conceptual nature but those are not the issues investigated here. It is safe to say that one of the most elemental disputes concerns law – what it is or what it is not.[4] Consequently, whether law even exists is an issue

[1] See Jaakko Husa, 'Introduction' in Jaakko Husa (ed), *A Research Agenda for Comparative Law* (Edward Elgar 2024) 1–14.

[2] See, eg, David Kennedy, 'The Method and the Politics of Comparative Law' in Pierre Legrand & Roderick Munday (eds), *Comparative Legal Studies* (CUP 2003) 345–433; and Mathias Reimann, 'The End of Comparative Law as an Autonomous Subject' (1996) 11 *Tulane European & Civil Law Forum* 49–72.

[3] For an overall view of the debates, see Robert Leckey, 'Review of Comparative Law' (2017) 26 *Social & Legal Studies* 3–24 (identifies 13 areas of comparative law scholarship, ibid 4–6).

[4] See also Geoffrey Samuel, *An Introduction to Comparative Law Theory and Method* (Hart Publishing 2014) ('Comparative law is about comparing laws, but what is meant, in this context, by the term "law"? Such a question takes one, of course, into the field of jurisprudence (legal theory and legal philosophy), since this is an area of legal studies that is devoted to the very question about the nature of law. Yet the concerns of the comparatist are different', ibid 121).

of interest to the comparatist.[5] This is, of course, also a question of legal philosophy. However, comparatists are not legal philosophers, at least not in any conventional sense.[6] Regardless, all comparatists have a view on this issue, even though many do not explicitly define what it is exactly that they understand the concept of law to consist of.[7] Many comparatists seem to leave the issue to legal philosophers more or less willingly as they rely on a tacit doctrinal understanding of law. They seem to prefer to compare hands-on without further ado. But if one compares laws, then one *must have* an idea about what law is and what it is not in order to know what kinds of materials to include and what to leave out. Even though this seems like a deeply theoretical question, it is also a practical one: do legislation, precedents, and doctrinal writing suffice or is it also necessary to take the context(s) of law into account and venture into the realm of non-legal disciplines? Should one read, for example, general history or political science studies too? More importantly, what do choices over these matters tell us about the nature of law and legal systems from a comparative point of view?[8]

I. The Mirror Thesis

As we saw in the preceding chapters, placing the focus of comparative research is an issue that can be answered in different ways. Some focus on positive law, others on how law works empirically, but there also many who think that both of these dimensions are of importance and that the comparatist should be a methodological pluralist rather than leaning on any fixed framework to understand law.[9] However, the question is not only about what comparatists understand by law itself but also how law is conceived in relation to its surroundings. Is law perhaps a special social category that is, more or less, autonomous in relation to its surrounding society?

[5] See Geoffrey Samuel, 'The Epistemological Challenge' in Simone Glanert, Alexandra Mercescu & Geoffrey Samuel, *Rethinking Comparative Law* (Edward Elgar 2021) ch 1.

[6] This is not about creating a comparative law-based definition of law, which is a different issue altogether. See, eg, Ronald L Akers, 'Toward a Comparative Definition of Law' (1965) 56 *Journal of Criminal Law and Criminology* 301–06. One can even hold that comparative law 'is essential for an accurate definition of law as a social phenomenon and for the understanding of the nature of law and its function in society generally', WJ Kamba, 'Comparative Law: A Theoretical Framework' (1974) 23 *ICLQ* 485–519, 494. See even Mark Van Hoecke, 'Do "Legal Systems" Exist?' in Seán Patrick Donlan & Lukas Heckendorn Urscheler (eds), *Concepts of Law* (Routledge 2014) 4–57.

[7] Here the legal philosophical discussion on the so-called separation thesis that concerns the relationship between law and morality is not touched upon. However, see Andrei Marmor, 'What Is Law and What Counts as Law?' in Torben Spaak & Patricia Mindus (eds), *The Cambridge Companion to Legal Positivism* (CUP 2021) 465–86.

[8] How to define a legal system theoretically see, eg, Joseph Raz, *The Concept of Legal System*, 2nd edn (OUP 1980). See also Sean Coyle, 'Hart, Raz and the Concept of a Legal System' (2002) 21 *Law and Philosophy* 275–304.

[9] 'The general view among comparative law nowadays is simply that a "variety of methods" can be chosen from', Marieke Oderkerk, 'The Need for a Methodological Framework for Comparative Legal Research' (2015) 79 *Rabels Zeitschrift für ausländisches und internationales Privatrecht* 589–623, 590. For a more detailed analysis, see Yenny Vega Cárdenas, *Methodology and Epistemology of Comparative Law* (LexisNexis 2024); Roberto Scarciglia, *Legal Methods and Comparison* (Edward Elgar 2023); Jaakko Husa, *Interdisciplinary Comparative Law* (Edward Elgar 2022).

Or is law perhaps something that needs to be perceived as a part of the social fabric? This is no simple quiz and, as we have seen in the above chapters, answers vary. In essence, colliding views are in effect specific views of law and its nature. A particularly fruitful debate to analyse in this regard is the juxtaposition between law – or more broadly a legal system – as a *closed entity* or as an *open entity* in the shape of the disagreement on legal transplants. Despite the fact that debate on legal transplants has been ongoing for decades, it still is part of today's comparative law scholarship.[10] A legal transplant is a comparative law evergreen as its popularity in terms of something to disagree about does not wane, no matter how many years or even decades pass. A legal transplant, no matter what one thinks about it, hits a nerve for many comparatists. This is no surprise, as legal transplants tell us a great deal about the nature of law.[11] Along these lines, I agree with Mindy Chen-Wishart's view, according to which 'at the heart of comparative law is the study of relationships – between law and society, between the social discourse in the originating and receiving cultures, and between the evolution of the law in the originating and receiving systems.'[12] This is why discussion on transplants remains relevant for comparatists.

Colliding views on legal transplants are seemingly of a conceptual nature but, on closer inspection, the collision concerns law's relationship to its environment.[13] To be sure, disagreement is not only about which concept to use because use of a certain concept is also a choice in terms of highlighting a certain aspect of legal transfers.[14] In part, a collision is a kind of proxy war where the major powers do not themselves become directly involved. The backdrop is, I will insist, the so-called mirror thesis or theory that assumes an inescapable reflexive link between a society and its law. This view sees law and its related legal system responding to and being developed by forces that are external to law. For comparative law scholarship, this assumption is of utmost relevance as it contains an answer to the question what is the law that one compares and what kind of sources to use.

This is a complicated issue that also concerns sociology of law and legal philosophy. However, here my focus is on the ramifications of the mirror thesis in the field of comparative law. To simplify a great deal, the mirror thesis argues that law does not possess an autonomous existence.[15] The skeletal sociological idea is

[10] For example, *The Cambridge Handbook of Comparative Law* (CUP 2024) has two chapters (21 and 22) dedicated to legal transplants placed under the heading of 'Central Themes in Comparative Law.' Besides, legal transplants are discussed in several other chapters.

[11] cf Alan Watson, *Society and Legal Change* (Scottish Academic Press 1977) 98.

[12] Mindy Chen-Wishart, 'Legal Transplant and Undue Influence' (2013) 62 *ICLQ* 1–30, 30.

[13] There are competing concepts. See, eg, Esin Örücü, 'Law as Transposition' (2002) 51 *ICLQ* 205–3 and Máximo Langer, 'From Legal Transplants to Legal Translations' (2004) 45 *Harvard International Law Journal* 1–64.

[14] cf Langer (n 13) 63.

[15] There is no need here to discuss the deeper roots of this thinking and to address Charles-Louis de Secondat Montesquieu or Emile Durkheim. See for discussion, Donald L Levine, 'Montesquieu and Durkheim' in Howard G Schneiderman (ed), *Dialogical Social Theory* (Routledge 2018) ch 11.

that law is a mirror of society.[16] As William Ewald summarises the idea, 'law is the mirror of some set of forces (social, political, economic, whatever) external to law'.[17] In short, the argument is that law or a legal system reflects society's customs and morality even though it is also recognised that some gaps exist between law and society.[18] For the purposes of this chapter, I chose to investigate the mirror thesis through the legal transplant as a kind of a litmus test for comparative law.

In my estimation, legal transplant debates are exceptionally fruitful for three reasons. First, a legal transplant is an evergreen in comparative law scholarship: it has generated and still generates opinions pro and contra, even beyond comparative law circles. Its ability to generate colliding views is virtually unparalleled. Second, debates on legal transplants touch upon one of the most crucial questions in comparative study of law; what is law's relation to its environment? One dimension of this is the separation, already discussed, between law in books and law in action. Third, debates on legal transplant reflect the scholarly nature of comparative law in general as a field of contrarians. The basic situation is not too difficult to grasp. Brian Tamanaha explains the underlying collision between the mirror thesis and legal transplants: '[l]egal transplantation, whether by voluntary borrowing or by imposition, poses an obvious problem for the mirror thesis: how can positive law reflect society if it is derived from elsewhere?'[19] For some, failed transplants are evidence of the mirror thesis, whereas others may draw opposite conclusions. In order to analyse the debate as a collision that has shaped comparative law, it is useful to start from the pivotal opening gambit.

II. Watson's Gambit – Insulation Thesis

When it comes to the mirror theory, its most ardent and influential opponent was Alan Watson. Of course, he is not alone but his work stirred most reactions in the field of comparative law.[20] We return to his ideas just as we return to Zweigert and Kötz in terms of functionalism. Watson was an extremely productive legal scholar who published mostly about the legal history of civil law systems from the point of view of Roman law.[21] However, his work has been described as controversial.[22] As

[16] Kermit L Hall, 'Mirror Theory' in David S Clark (ed), *Encyclopedia of Law and Society* (Sage 2007) 1025–26.

[17] William Ewald, 'Comparative Jurisprudence (II)' (1995) 43 *AJCL* 489–510, 491.

[18] See for more detailed discussion, eg, Mark A Edwards, 'The Alignment of Law and Norms' (2014) 10 *Florida International University Law Review* 19–51.

[19] Brian Z Tamanaha, *A General Jurisprudence of Law and Society* (OUP 2001) 107.

[20] See, eg, Margit Cohn, 'Legal Transplants' in Mathias Siems & Po Jen Yap (eds), *The Cambridge Handbook of Comparative Law* CUP 2024) 426–52, 427–30.

[21] Ewald (n 17) fn 1 offers a good overview of Watson's works to the mid-1990s. See also Mathias Siems, *Comparative Law*, 3rd edn (CUP 2022) ('Watson's view was shaped by having been a legal historian and Roman lawyer, in particular his insight that the private law of many countries is significantly based on the reception of Roman law', ibid 295).

[22] Gary Francione, 'Alan Watson's Controversial Contribution to Legal Scholarship' (2002) 31 *Georgia Journal of International and Comparative Law* 59– 63 ('he remains a controversial figure in academia', ibid 62).

a comparative law scholar, he has not been a mainstream character even though his focus was on doctrinally-flavoured Western private law.[23] As a member of the comparative law tribe, Watson exemplifies what a contrarian legal scholar means. As Gary Francione puts it, rejection by mainstream scholars became 'something of a point of pride' for Watson.[24] This may sound strange but it is something one understands intuitively when reading Watson's scholarship as he was not one to pull his punches.[25] In this sense, he was a Contrarian with a big C: a towering but disputed figure.

As to Watson's ideas opposing the mirror theory, he occupies a unique position in many senses. One of those is his almost jubilant contrarianism, or – as Ewald says – his 'theory flies in the face of some of the most treasured preconceptions of modern legal thought'.[26] Watson's scholarship on legal transplants is the tip of the iceberg of his legal thinking and holds great value for comparative law scholarship regardless of what one thinks about it.[27] It also crucial to keep in mind that decades of discussion means that comparative law debates have developed far beyond the initial discussion that started in 1974 when the first edition of *Legal Transplants* was published. This also means that discussion has gone in various and unexpected directions that Watson could never have been able to foresee in the 1970s.[28] In many ways, the 1974 book was like a stone dropped in the relatively tranquil pond of comparative law and the ripples it created are still moving. This discussion is one of the many ripples that Watson's stone created but instead of throwing a new stone I seek to register some of the biggest waves.

As a scholar, Watson is easy – and often annoying – to read. There is very little one needs to read between the lines as he argues in a straight line without muddying the waters with complicated theoretical language. Watson's view of law and society has radical implications because it makes a strong claim that is intuitively felt to be misguided by comparatists – this author included – as it argues that 'legal rules can be easily transported from society to society'.[29] It is worth pausing over what he assumes about the nonchalance of transplanting law. For many, I assume, the word 'easily' is particularly vexing. Importantly, Watson's view on the (absence of a) relationship between law and society is part of a broader idea about comparative law as a field. For him, fuelled by insights on Roman law, '[c]omparative Law

[23] Scholarship on legal transplants has long since expanded from narrow Western private law to other thematic and geographic regions. See, eg, Vito Breda (ed), *Legal Transplants in East Asia and Oceania* (CUP 2019).

[24] Francione (n 22) 62.

[25] '[A]ttacking Watson is like shooting fish in a barrel', Lawrence Friedmann, 'Some Comments on Cotterrell and Legal Transplants' in David Nelken & Jonathan Feest (eds), *Adapting Legal Cultures* (Hart Publishing 2001) 93–99, 93.

[26] Ewald (n 17) 490.

[27] He was also an important figure in Roman law (and legal history) but here the focus is on the comparative law side.

[28] cf John W Cairns, 'Watson, Walton, and the History of Legal Transplants' (2013) 41 *Georgia Journal of International and Comparative Law* 637–96, 639.

[29] Ewald (n 17) 490.

is Legal History concerned with the relationship between legal systems.'[30] I leave out of the discussion the obvious weakness, namely that this view leaves out study of systems that have no such relationship. Accepting this view thoroughly would mean an impoverished comparative study of law or setting the bar for 'relationship' very low in order to make up ground for comparative law. That does not seem like the right way to proceed.

What is important is that Watson's anti-mirror thesis is, perhaps surprisingly, subtle in the sense that it assigns a special role for lawyers and lawmakers as the legal elite. It is this very elite that holds the key role in terms of law, hence the rest of society plays only a minor role: '[t]he input of the society often bears little relation to the output of the legal elite' says Watson.[31] The implied idea is to elevate the legal profession, as the legal elite, to an unusually high position in terms of development of law. This view is no coincidence, as he explicitly rejects the mirror thesis despite the fact that one could choose to support either a strong thesis (no relation) or a weaker version (some relation).[32] In focus is the legal transfer labelled as a legal transplant which means – according to Watson's seminal definition – simply 'the moving of a rule or a system of law from one country to another, or from one people to another'.[33] Along these lines, Watson conceives law as a special kind of social category which is 'largely autonomous and not shaped by societal needs'.[34] This goes against the idea of mirroring, that is, a relationship in which formal law and legal practices match, more or less, morals and customs practiced by the people of a particular society.[35] And, needless to say, this view seems strangely to exclude the idea of law as a form of tailored social engineering.[36] If one denies the connection between legal change and society, then the attempt to govern social change by regulating the future development and behaviour of a society appears, more or less, unviable. Watson's view also says very little about how legal transplants are actually used when drafting legislation or deciding a case.[37] Moreover, this kind of view excludes public law even though one can possibly argue that *ius publicum* influenced the development of constitutional law.[38]

On the other hand, there is one simple but strong argument that speaks for Watson's view, which Jan Smits puts like this: '[i]f a legal solution for a specific problem has already been devised in another country, then it would, after all,

[30] Alan Watson, *Legal Transplants*, 2nd edn (University of Georgia Press 1993) 6.

[31] Alan Watson, *The Evolution of Law* (Johns Hopkins University Press 1985) 17. This view does not concern only law and modern society because of the thought that even in primitive societies law did not fit society particularly well, ibid 116.

[32] Tamanaha (n 19) 109 notes that 'Watson rejects not just the mirror thesis, but also to a significant extent the selective mirror thesis as well'.

[33] Watson (n 30) 21.

[34] Watson (n 31) 119.

[35] This kind of an idea of mirroring is what Tamanaha (n 19) 131 calls the 'fullest sense of mirroring'.

[36] See Roscoe Pound, 'The Lawyer as a Social Engineer' (1954) 3 *Journal of Public Law* 292–303; and Adam Podgorecki, 'Law and Social Engineering' (1962) 21 *Human Organisation* 177–81.

[37] See, eg, Helen Xanthaki, 'Legal Transplants in Legislation' (2008) 57 *ICLQ* 659–73.

[38] See, eg, Erida Pejo & Esmeralda Kolaneci, 'The Role of Roman Law in the Formation of the State and Modern Law' (2024) 45 *Statute Law Review*, doi.org/10.1093/slr/hmae027.

be inefficient not to benefit from it in one's own country'.[39] Without addressing the pragmatic point further it is, regardless, easy to see that Smits' point is valid as such. Stated shortly, reinventing the wheel makes very little sense even in the world of law. Then again, this would also mean assuming a relationship between law and society because why import law if it if would not be considered suitable?

Watson's scholarship dealt with broad areas and issues. However, as a comparatist Watson considers law, by and large, as an autonomous entity that develops by transplantation. This view strips the agency of society as it holds that legal rules are not created because of societal needs but because the legal elite is aware of a non-national legal rule and recognises the benefits that adopting it may bring about. In short, Watson's picture of the relationship between society and legal rules is such that one cannot really argue that legal rules (especially in the field of private law) would reflect a society's desires, needs, or aspirations.[40] But this does not exclude the idea that elements in a society may determine the options known and hence, available, but he says these do not predetermine the outcome.[41] It is hardly a surprise that these views have been criticised by socio-legally oriented legal scholars. More than that, Watson's thinking defies both legal pluralist ideas and interdisciplinarity if interdisciplinarity ventures beyond legal history, which is Watson's own field. In many ways - and despite some softening elaborations - his idea of a legal transplant is not far from insularity in terms of the relationship between society and law.

III. Waves of Opposition

The discussion on criticism of legal transplants needs to be approached with some caution, especially because the criticisms addressed are by no means exhaustive as the literature is nothing but voluminous. Then again, some scholars possess a central role in the debate, which makes it easier to identify the key criticisms. The most influential and, in my view, also most interesting critic of Watson's views was Otto Kahn-Freund, who reacted early to Watson's views.[42] Additionally, the distinctively contrarian critique by Pierre Legrand holds a relevant opposing view that goes directly against the very idea of transplantation.[43] One can argue that, in a sense, Kahn-Freund paved the way to Legrand's stark contrarian view.[44] Then again, Legrand defines law in a way that is very different from Kahn-Freund's more practical take. Another important critique was made by Günther Teubner.[45] What

[39] Jan Smits, *The Making of European Private Law* (Intersentia 2002) 60.

[40] See Alan Watson, 'Comparative Law and Legal Change' (1978) 37 *Cambridge Law Journal* 313–36.

[41] ibid 334–35.

[42] Otto Kahn-Freund, 'On Use and Misuse of Comparative Law' (1974) 37 *MLR* 1–27. Of this critique see discussion by Cairns (n 28) 642–8.

[43] Pierre Legrand, 'The Impossibility of Legal Transplants' (1997) 4 *Maastricht Journal of European and Comparative Law* 111–24 and Pierre Legrand, 'What "Legal Transplants"?' in Nelken & Feest (n 25) 55–70.

[44] cf Cohn (n 20) 428.

[45] Gunther Teubner, 'Legal Irritants' (1998) 61 *MLR* 11–32.

is relevant for the discussion here is that these critiques are based, more or less, on the mirror theory and much or many of the contra-arguments are drawn from an assumption of the existing relationship between law or a legal system and society. Moreover, they are related to critical voices presented especially by socio-legal scholars or comparatists who are somewhat socio-legally inclined.[46]

For Kahn-Freund, Watson's biggest mistake was to disregard the significance of the social context of law. To put the point in basic terms: the concept of transplant failed simply because one 'cannot take for granted that rules or institutions are transplantable'.[47] This is the fertile foundation upon which most of the later critique is based. In my reading, debates look on the surface like disagreement about whether legal transplants are possible or not but what is really at stake is the deeper issue about the *relationship* between law and its socio-political environment or, if you prefer, context. In other words, are legal rules just rules in the lawyerly sense of the word or should the comparatist regard them as something more than just rules narrowly understood? Two intrinsic questions are entangled here. First, what is law or a legal system? Second, based on the view of law or legal system, what is it that the comparatist should study? Scholarly collisions on legal transplants are about these cardinal questions and different reactions to them.

To Legrand, Watson's view is fundamentally flawed as – so he maintains – it refuses to take the cultural context of law into account. This is not to accept the mirror thesis as such but simply to underline the importance of law's cultural context. This critique is based on a legal-philosophical idea about the law: a legal rule is not a string of words but something much more. In essence, Legrand underlines the connection between the existence of a rule or legal system and its meaning, which only truly exists in the context of a given rule or legal system. The meaning of a rule is possible only in a certain context.[48] Accordingly, legal transplants do not happen because '[n]o rule in the borrowing jurisdiction can have any significance as regards the rule in the jurisdiction from which it is borrowed'.[49] I find this view extreme but also a theoretically interesting and intellectually intriguing form of legal philosophy.

In the foregoing, I have noted that Watson and Legrand conceive 'legal rule' differently as they hold contrarian views in relation to each other. Legrand does not shy away from stating the opposition in plain terms as '[r]ules are just not what they are represented as being by Watson…because of what they effectively are, rules cannot travel. Accordingly, legal transplants are impossible'.[50] Michele

[46] See, eg, Jen Hendry, '"By Your Powers Combined"' in Jaakko Husa (n 1) 109–27 ('I take the view that comparative approaches…are generally and positively enhanced by socio-legal practices and reflections', 127).

[47] Kahn-Freund (n 42) 9.

[48] There is no need here to investigate further but this idea is not that far from the arch-functionalist Ernst Rabel's ideas about the relationship between law and legal rules. See Jaakko Husa, 'Comparative Law, Legal Linguistics, and Methodology of Legal Doctrine' in Mark Van Hoecke (ed), *Methodologies of Legal Research* (Hart Publishing 2011) 209–28.

[49] Legrand (n 43) 120.

[50] ibid 122.

Graziadei aptly summarises Legrand's take as he says that in Legrand's view 'law does not have a determinate content apart from a given culture'.[51] This is a highly demanding and specific way to understand what law – and thus legal rule – means. Then again, it is this very idea that forms the basis of Legrand's legal philosophy, which in essence is about the 'priority of difference'.[52] This line of thinking is difficult if not impossible to reconcile with Watson's more technical view of law.

In my reading, Watson and Legrand are the extreme contrarian ends of the debate.[53] Other forms of critique situate themselves somewhere in between the extreme ends even though they also circle around the underlying question on the relationship between law and society. Some critiques propose abandoning the concept of legal transplant altogether and adopting a new one. Again, we see that contrarian legal scholars have no difficulty when it comes to suggesting new conceptualisations.

Teubner's worry, in turn, is not so much about whether a legal transfer is possible or not, but what actually happens when transfers are attempted. This means broadening the scope of analysis beyond the transfer and highlighting what happens after the transfer has taken place. He rejects the concept of transplant and claims that the concept of irritant better captures the transfer of legal rules. In this way, Teubner connects what Watson kept separate, namely law and society. His concrete illustration concerns the central principle of civil law 'good faith' (*Treu und Glauben*) in English law which he sees as a failed legal transfer. Transferring private law rules from one economic culture to another is not without problems, as the essential features of Anglo-American economic culture are different from those of the civil law world. Teubner's key point is that it is not possible to domesticate legal transfers because:

> they are not transformed from something alien into something familiar, not adapted to a new cultural context, rather they will unleash an evolutionary dynamic in which the external rule's meaning will be reconstructed and the internal context will undergo fundamental change.[54]

In short, Teubner underlines the risks involved in legal transplantation. Accordingly, when risks enter into the equation one should speak of irritant, not transplant. No wonder, then, that the legal transfer is a dear child of comparative law that has many names. Máximo Langer, in genuine contrarian style, abandons both concepts and claims that translation would be 'a superior heuristic device to analyze the circulation of legal ideas, rules, and institutions'.[55]

A further general point that needs to be made concerns the sociological dimension of the issue. Above, I have touched upon the comparative law critique of the

[51] Michele Graziadei, 'Comparative Law, Transplants, and Receptions' in Mathias Reimann & Reinhard Zimmermann (eds), *The Oxford Handbook of Comparative Law*, 2nd edn (OUP 2019) 442–73.

[52] Pierre Legrand, 'The Same and the Different' in Legrand & Munday (n 2), 240–311, 286.

[53] Seeing their relation as 'binary' is, indeed, very much justified. See Andrew Harding, 'The Legal Transplant Debate' in Vito Breda (ed), *Legal Transplants in East Asia and Oceania* (CUP 2019) 13–33.

[54] Teubner (n 45) 12.

[55] Langer (n 13) 32.

idea of law's autonomy; but there are also critiques that come from the socio-legal corner of the tribe of comparatists. These are linked by defence of the idea about the rudimentary relationship between law and its societal environment. Now, these critiques do not necessarily accept any crude form of the mirror thesis, but they are nonetheless highly suspicious of the autonomy thesis. For instance, Roger Cotterrell thinks that Watson (and Ewald) oversimplify sociological scholarship about law and make it a kind of straw man simply holding that law mirrors society. Importantly, Cotterrell presumes that one cannot hold a view according to which development of law is not connected to society. Making this kind of argument believably would, in any case, require the comparatist to do actual socio-legal research.[56] Indeed, if we are to speak of legal transplants with more subtlety, there clearly is a need to undertake empirical research in order to find out how transplanted rules and institutions really work.[57]

Along similar lines, Lawrence Friedman sees that legal history does not offer enough support to discuss the link between law and society. Commenting on Cotterrell, Friedman also sees that one should study actual contemporary legal systems in order to be able to make far-reaching claims about the relationship between law and society. More concretely, Friedman is critical about the concept of the legal transplant and suggests that we should use different conceptualisations and start speaking about more socio-legally sensible things such as diffusion, borrowing, and imposition.[58] Andrew Harding, in turn, points out that Watson is a legal historian and Legrand a legal philosopher and for that very reason they do not rely on actual comparative research: 'Reference to research of this kind is missing in their work'.[59] This observation is, of course, closely related to the collision between generalists and area experts addressed in chapter seven above. Perhaps it is simply too tall an order, though, to ask contrarians to move towards the middle ground. Then again, it may be the case that contrarians are not interested in changing their scholarly allegiances when it comes to the mirror theory. It is difficult to fully avoid the impression that some aspects of the transplant debate embody a kind of 'high horse' attitude.

IV. Finding a Balance?

The above discussed binary contrarianism does not, however, agree with the present – seemingly pluralist – spirit of comparative law. We can see that scholarship has transformed and become more diversity-embracing. For instance, Tamanaha, who is a socio-legally oriented legal scholar, is critical of the mirror thesis. Yet his criticism does not come from an extremist binary position. He does not support the idea of autonomous legal systems in terms of the relationship between law and

[56] Roger Cotterrell, 'Is There a Logic of Legal Transplants?' in Nelken & Feest (n 25) 70–92.
[57] cf Michael Palmer, 'For Comparative Legal Studies' in Jaakko Husa (n 1) 129–55, 51–52.
[58] Friedman (n 25).
[59] Harding (n 53) 14.

society. He takes into account factors that problematise the mirror thesis, giving space to legal pluralism and globalisation. Both of these factors bring subtlety and complications to the discussion on the idea of law mirroring society. This view does not emanate from Roman private law (Watson) or legal philosophy (Legrand). In Tamanaha's view, the mirror thesis is an idealised theoretical description between law and society.[60] This view benefits from its realistic take, making it more plausible and suitable for modern comparative law.

George Mousorakis, in turn, concludes discussion on legal transplants by saying that 'the view that legal transplants are impossible, as some scholars have asserted, is too extreme and betrays an exaggeration of cultural diversity'.[61] Moreover, if one accepts an extreme position, there is always the risk that one's stance contains inconsistencies.[62] If one cannot transplant law, then how can transplants have an impact in the receiving legal system? This seems like circular reasoning with no way out.

Mention must of course be made of some of the other voices that abandon the contrarian extremes.[63] Margit Cohn discusses legal transplant scholarship and notes, correctly in my view, that both extreme views 'have long collapsed' into a middle ground that rejects both Watson's optimism and Legrand's pessimism as too absolutist.[64] This public law-fuelled view fits well in contemporary comparative law scholarship that has become increasingly allergic to rigid extreme views. Along similar lines, Harding also rejects the extremes and makes a point through the prism of socio-empirical reality, saying that extreme views do not concern 'the development of law as project but rather with legal theory'.[65] This view suggests that comparative law would be wise not to transform into abstract legal theory. Or, as Chen-Wishart puts it, '[t]here is no alternative to careful case studies to identify the factors at work in particular areas of the law.'[66] To put it otherwise, it needs to be recognised that generalism has its inborn limitations.

Both Cohn and Harding seem to speak from the middle ground and against strict contrarian views. Cohn draws from a case study of a single public law doctrine (margin of appreciation) whereas Harding draws from South East Asian experience. Cohn and Harding base their views, like Teubner, on actual cases (doing it) whereas Legrand's views are of a theoretical nature (talking about it). Watson, in turn, developed the legal transplant on the basis of legal history but limiting his

[60] Tamanaha (n 19) 132.

[61] George Mousorakis, 'Legal Transplants and Legal Development' (2013) 54 *Acta Juridica Hungarica* 219–36, 236.

[62] One may suspect, eg, that Legrand's cultural critique is inconsistent in the sense that if legal cultures are robust and legal transplants are impossible, then how can transplants change legal cultures if they are supposed to be impossible? See Ralf Michaels, '"One Size Can Fit All"', in Günter Frankenberg (ed), *Order From Transfer* (Edward Elgar 2013) 56–78, 65.

[63] In fact, as Siems (n 21) 296 notes correctly, '[u]nlike both Watson and Legrand, most scholars take an intermediate position'.

[64] Cohn (n 20) 428.

[65] Harding (n 53).

[66] Chen-Wishart (n 12) 27.

scope to private law flowing from the tradition of Roman law. For instance, the spread of constitutional adjudication demonstrates how legal transplants can also take place in the field of public law.[67]

No surprise, then, that Watson's approach, as Uwe Kischel points out, 'has very little to do with the reality of what comparative lawyers ordinarily do' as it seems that his approach has been 'to a certain extent tailored to Watson himself'.[68] This is a relevant point as it shows how assuming a fixed view is bound to be limited in more than one way. Consequently, fixed views seem incompatible with contemporary methodological and theoretical pluralism.

Notwithstanding, it is possible to read Watson in a different light and stress the way he sees rules. Geoffrey Samuel, who is no stranger to Roman law, highlights that Watson's way of understanding rules is not as atomistic as one might think as rules 'exist in systematised blocks often independently of any social context'.[69] Along similar lines, Mathias Siems's benevolent reading tones down contrarian views and says that 'Watson claims that transplants are often "simply" about copying. By contrast, Legrand puts more emphasis on the complexities of this process.'[70] I would add that it is important to see that there are different situations in terms of legal transfer. Accordingly, some rules may indeed have a complex relationship to culture, as Legrand insists, whereas other rules may be more technical and potentially less bound by culture.[71] This would simply mean accepting that there are differences between legal rules and their embeddedness in certain cultures. Besides, Watson himself also admitted that 'law exists and flourishes at the level of idea, and is part of culture'.[72] This seems to suggest that holding coherently contrarian views is not that easy. Against this backdrop it is not unexpected that, in his reply to Legrand, Watson claims that 'from early days I have argued that a rule once transplanted is different in its new home'.[73] This is what Chen-Wishart seems to mean when she discusses the undue influence doctrine and does not describe transplantation as a success or a failure but notes that the contents of the doctrine are culturally adjusted: 'Singaporeanised.'[74] It would appear that the process of adjusting always forms part of legal transfer as a process regardless of what one thinks it is that is being transplanted: rules as solutions to particular legal issues or merely strings of words.

Have we reached an impasse in the discussion on legal transplants and the mirror theory? How is it possible to find a balance in the face of so many views and

[67] See, eg, Leonard Besselink, 'The Proliferation of Constitutional Law and Constitutional Adjudication' (2013) 9 *Utrecht Law Review* 19–35; and Doreen Lustig & JHH Weiler, 'Judicial Review in the Contemporary World' (2018) 16 *International Journal of Constitutional Law* 315–72.

[68] Uwe Kischel, *Comparative Law* (OUP 2019) 30.

[69] Samuel (n 4) 123–24. Samuel's reading underlines structural elements of Watson's view.

[70] Siems (n 21) 296.

[71] cf Harding (n 53) 22.

[72] Alan Watson, 'Legal Change' (1982–1983) 131 *University of Pennsylvania Law Review* 1121–58, 1152.

[73] Alan Watson, 'Legal Transplants and European Private Law', published originally in *Electronic Journal of Comparative Law* 2000 issue 4.

[74] Chen-Wishart (n 12) 28.

when some of the most vocal views are in direct opposition to each other? I would like to think that one can find some kind of middle ground that may be acceptable for many, if not for all. But what does it mean to accept a middle ground? Harding puts it well as he notes that legal transplants are possible 'although the process is not easy'.[75] This is an important notion as it combines two things. First, it admits that legal transfers take place, and it is against our practical experience to argue that it would be completely impossible.[76] Second, it does not follow the extreme view stemming from Roman law-based private law that legal transfer would take place 'easily' as Teubner also points out.[77] Moreover, accepting the middle ground would seem to be able to accommodate Teubner's idea that the economic regime is an important factor to be taken into account when attempting to transplant central private law principles from civil law to common law. Indeed, transplantation may lead to a situation where the intended transplant ends up being an irritant. Where does this leave us with the underlying issue on law's relationship to society?

V. Resolution?

An essential part of accepting the middle ground is to admit that Watson's theory, despite its obvious shortcomings, possesses remarkable strength and even though it is expressed uncompromisingly it has been and continues to be of value to comparatists and, I suspect, to legal historians as well. This may be difficult to admit if one supports the mirror thesis. Or, as Michele Graziadei aptly describes the situation from the point of view of mirror thesis scholars: '[f]or adherents of that tradition, it can be unsettling to recognize that much of the law in one society is imported from another'.[78] Regardless, while trying to find the middle ground, I would not go as far as John Cairns, who says that the 'ultimate success of legal transplants as an approach to comparative law is clear'.[79] Instead, I find Graziadei's conclusion to be what I regard as a pluralist non-contrarian middle ground: '[c]omparative law shows that legal orders owe their existence to both original innovation and borrowing'.[80] Indeed, as Siems rightly states in a Watsonian tone, '[d]iffusion of law has been a core element of legal evolution'.[81] This may be against a deep philosophical take; but, regardless, it reflects real legal history and human experience as I among many others understand it. Perhaps, indeed, what is transplanted is merely strings of words – but why would this mean that those words would be meaningless in their new environment?

[75] Harding (n 53) 31.

[76] In his vexed reply to Legrand, Watson offers a string of examples against the idea of impossibility of legal transplants. See Watson (n 73).

[77] Of course, one may note that Teubner's counter point is based on one example which concerns a specific European private law doctrine.

[78] Graziadei (n 51) 465.

[79] Cairns (n 28) 686.

[80] Graziadei (n 51) 472.

[81] Siems (n 21) 111.

It may be the case that Ralf Michaels has a point when he discusses legal transplants and concludes that if comparatists 'insist on the cultural specificity and locality of legal rules' they 'may be both romantic and elitist'.[82] Holding, like Legrand, that legal transplants are logically impossible may be true but only if one accepts the underlying legal philosophy. What we have seen over centuries tells us a different story as all sorts of transplants have occurred without connections to any socio-political or economic context.[83] Legal ideas do travel over borders of many kinds; countries, languages, cultures, and so on. It is a different issue to debate whether these transplantations have been successes or failures, or what it is that is actually transferred.[84] Having said that, I need to add that none of this is to deny that foreign law will always remain 'other' for the comparatist, as indeed Legrand holds while stressing the importance of alterity.[85] However, in discussing reception of Roman law, declaring firmly that what has been transplanted is 'a meaningless form of words' looks wilfully contrarian and dubious.[86] An army of Roman law scholars would argue against such a statement, and for good reason. [87] For instance, in the civil law legal family it is easy to see that Roman law has indeed moved across borders of many kinds over the centuries.[88] To be sure, the reason why modern civil law systems have so much commonality is because they are derived from Roman law and that is the reason why they are so different from common law.[89]

Indeed, comparatists do not need to assume an extreme view that is inherently contrarian to other views. Our logic need not be a binary one. This is a bit like what Patrick Glenn spoke of when he discussed multivalent logic that is capable of including apparently conflicting views.[90] I would tend to agree, insofar as contrarianism appears to lead to odd extremities and rigidity. Accordingly, in terms of legal transplants there is no compelling black-or-white logic implying that there are only two options when discussing legal transfer. If one accepts multivalent logic, then everything is a matter of degree.[91] But, if I am right, the innate scholarly nature of comparatists is a factor that will quite likely animate contrarian views in the future despite diversity and pluralism.

[82] Michaels (n 62) 78.

[83] Typology of legal transplants, see Jonathan Miller, 'A Typology of Legal Transplants' (2003) 51 *AJCL* 839–85.

[84] Further discussion on this, see eg, Randall Peerenboom, 'Toward Methodology for Successful Legal Transplants' (2013) 1 *Chinese Journal of Comparative Law* 4–20.

[85] See, eg, Pierre Legrand, *Fragments on Law-as-Culture* (Tjeenk Willink 1999) ch 1.

[86] Legrand (n 43) 64.

[87] Here it suffices to refer to the scholarly work of Reinhard Zimmermann and what he said about the civil law tradition. See, eg, Reinhard Zimmermann, *Roman Law, Contemporary Law, European Law* (OUP 2001).

[88] See, eg, Helmut Coing, 'The Roman Law as Ius Commune on the Continent' (1973) 89 *Law Quarterly Review* 505–17.

[89] See Peter Stein, 'Roman Law, Common Law, and Civil Law' (1991–92) 66 *Tulane Law Review* 1591–1604.

[90] See H Patrick Glenn, *Legal Traditions of the World*, 5th edn (OUP 2014) ch 10. For more detailed discussion, see H Patrick Glenn, 'Choice of Logic and Choice of Law' in H Patrick Glenn & Lionel D Smith (eds), *Law and the New Logics* (CUP 2017) 162–67.

[91] Glenn (n 90) 315.

In my view, Watson's idea according to which it is possible to discuss law detached from its original context is clearly possible. However, this does not mean that there would not be some kind of relationship between law and society beyond the small legal elite. If we abandon contrarian extremes, it may be possible to have one's cake and eat it if we just eat half of it.[92] To put it otherwise, it is possible to regard a legal system as open or closed in its relation to its society depending on which area of law or which particular legal issue one focuses on. Why would it not be less difficult to transplant technical rules of company law than to transplant culturally conditioned rules of inheritance law? But accepting this would require comparatists to rely increasingly on interdisciplinary views without locking themselves into extremities and insisting on eating the whole cake as the contrarians maintain.[93]

Finally, as much as the comparatist can learn from Roman private law-based logic or anti-positivist legal philosophy, it is the real life of law and professional practices of lawyers that we must give the final word to. In this way, then, the comparatist cannot avoid looking at the actual life of law in different legal systems. As Justice Oliver Wendell Holmes famously said, 'the life of the law has not been logic: it has been experience'.[94] Without going deeper into Holmes's legal philosophy, we can at least admit that his words act as a reminder not to lose touch with what actually happens in the legal systems that we seek to study comparatively. Lawyers, judges, and legislators borrow ideas over borders no matter what legal scholars think or how they choose to conceptualise what they think takes place. To put it otherwise, legal transplants are like bees in the sense that they should perhaps not be able to fly according to normal laws of aviation. In practice, bees do fly as the aerodynamics involved are more complex than meets the eye. Perhaps this is the case with legal transfers too?

[92] Watson himself has given reason to believe that his stance on the mirror thesis is not as rigid as may seem at first glance. So, he has noted that 'social, economic, and political conditions that affect other groups within society are important, of course, but their impact on the legal rules must not be exaggerated', Watson (n 72) 1154.

[93] cf Siems (n 21) 32.

[94] Oliver Wendell Holmes, *The Common Law*, 1st edn (Little Brown & Company 1963, originally published 1881) 5.

10

Individualisers and Generalisers – *Methodenstreit* of Our Time?

The previous chapters reveal time and again that comparative law scholars have contrasting ideas about the proper methodology and object of research – among other major issues they disagree about. This is not necessarily a problem. On the contrary, the broad church of legal comparativism is to be expected against the backdrop of various fields of law, diversity of compared systems, research skills, as well as scholarly preferences and interests. In the earlier chapters, it has been maintained that diversity and plurality is not to be considered problematic in today's world. We have mostly abandoned – or are about to do so – past dreams of a unified discipline having a place of honour in legal academia. Contemporary comparative law scholars tend to have less ambitious views of the field when it comes to the academic status of legal comparativism. This is not a defeat as it is evident that legal scholarship is done increasingly in comparative fashion even though those who do it do not necessarily identify as comparatists. On another occasion, I have characterised this situation as a kind of a pyrrhic victory for comparative law.[1] Pyrrhic, that is, against the backdrop of past academic aspirations; more comparisons but fewer scholars who identify primarily as comparatists.

What is left of past ambitions is not insignificant, though. Instead of a unified autonomous discipline it is more down to earth to wish that those who study law comparatively commit to using methods of investigation and analysis that meet their intellectual border-crossing curiosity. The unavoidable plurality is – even though it may appear odd at first sight in tradition-bound legal academia – a fruitful manner to adapt to today's global pluralism, where we deal with many kinds of normativities (see chapter twelve). One important qualification needs to be made concerning the way that pluralism is understood here. Pluralism stands for diversity – not for chaos or radical relativism. Tribalisation of comparative law, despite its problematic nature, is one indication of implicit vitality growing from down below.

[1] Jaakko Husa, 'Comparative Law's Pyrrhic Victory?' (2023) 30 *Maastricht Journal of European and Comparative Law* 680–88.

So, things have changed in comparative law. But – as the saying goes – the more things change the more they stay the same.[2] Despite pluralism, we still discuss and debate over methods in comparative study of law, at least that much is clear from the literature. Debating endlessly over fundamental issues seems to be an innate feature of comparative law scholarship. Perhaps comparatists have invented a perpetual motion machine that needs no more energy than what scholarly comparative law collisions generate all by themselves? There is more to it, though, as collisions about methods in comparative law may be a sign of *methodolatry* which means a tendency to privilege methodological concerns over other concerns.[3] I freely admit that this observation is not wildly off the mark. Much of theoretically oriented comparative law scholarship really does focus on methods and methodology. This has to do, of course, with the collision between doing it and talking about it, addressed in chapter five above. In a way, collisions on what to compare, what area of law to focus on, stressing practical or scholarly dimensions, expanding beyond the West, choosing between micro and macro, focusing on functions or culture, all concern methodology, directly or indirectly. It may be methodololatry, but even so it is hard to avoid when the legal scholar crosses borders of legal systems and the (doctrinal) basic method learned in one's own country cannot be trusted any more.

Beyond commonplace collisions, one distinguishable encounter concerns a fundamental methodological issue as it is about the very nature of comparative law as a field of study. In other words, to which tribe does a comparatist really belong? Is it the empirical field or more akin to classic humanities perhaps? This issue has crept slowly into comparative law scholarship in the present century although it is familiar from neighbouring fields, as the old juxtaposition between the qualitative and quantitative approach showcases.[4] The same collision is reflected in comparative law in a number of ways. Some comparatists wish to expand the scope of methods towards (other) social sciences, wanting to bring in quantification. Others oppose this as a wrong kind of expansion even if they themselves would be critical of the overly doctrinal legacy of legal scholarship. Contrarianism seems to be a layered factor as we choose to oppose or to support in ways that are not necessarily coherent.

[2] A saying that can be traced back to Alphonse Karr is '*plus ça change, plus c'est la même chose*', and his article published in 1849 in *Les Guêpes*. In essence, its message is that despite apparent changes or even advancements in society, fundamental features or patterns remain unchanged.

[3] See, eg, Valerie Janesick, 'The Dance of Qualitative Research Design' in Norman Denzin & Yvonna Lincoln (eds), *Handbook of Qualitative Research* (Sage 1994) 209–19 ('combination of method and idolatry, to describe a preoccupation with selecting and defending methods to the exclusion of the actual substance of the story being told. Methodolatry is the slavish attachment and devotion to method that so often overtakes the discourse', ibid 215).

[4] See, eg, Barry Glassner & Jonathan Moreno (eds), *The Qualitative-Quantitative Distinction in the Social Sciences* (Springer 1989). In comparative law, see Mathias Siems, 'Numerical Comparative Law' (2005) 13 *Cardozo Journal of International and Comparative Law* 521–40 (discussion against the backdrop of comparative company/corporate law).

I. What *Methodenstreit?*

Conceiving quality as the opposite of quantity seems like a cardinal methodological confrontation concerning the way research should be conducted. Accordingly, qualitative and quantitative approaches look quite different. Both of these approaches have a similar general aim of course, namely knowledge acquisition, they just choose different paths to pursue what seems like the same goal. Law as a discipline has traditionally been qualitative as to its nature because it has focused on phenomena that are not numerically measured.[5] For instance, how a court should interpret a statutory rule in the case at hand or how one identifies which judgments are to be given weight as precedents and which are of lesser guiding value are not numerical questions.[6] To be sure, determining what is the *ratio decidendi* of a case in common law is not based on numerical data.[7] Legal scholars do not tend to collect or conceive this kind of data in the form of numbers. The quantitative approach, in turn, is numeric as to its nature and seeks to rely on statistical analyses based on data transformed into numerical form.[8]

In short, and speaking generally, qualitative research focuses on words and meanings instead of numbers and statistics. The qualitative approach seeks to understand in a way that individualises the study object, whereas the quantitative approach seeks to generalise and unearth causalities. This is no simple contradiction as it is not only about the size of the data analysed, however. The same collision is increasingly part of the modern discussion on comparative law methods, but its intellectual roots go much deeper than the relatively recent social science contradiction between qualitative and quantitative.

In part, the collision I am referring to brings to mind the Latin phrase *nihil sub sole novum* which claims that there is nothing new under the sun. The phrase concerns actions and social inventions of humankind as every seemingly pathbreaking idea tends to have some kind of precedent or an echo of reminiscence from the past. In law, what the phrase argues seems to hold water. It is certainly not impossible – if there is no language barrier – for legal scholars of today to grasp what legal scholars wrote 200 years ago and vice versa, whereas in medicine or

[5] Then again, one also can separate doctrinal legal research and qualitative legal research, see P Ishwara Bhat, *Idea and Methods of Legal Research* (OUP 2020) chs 5 and 12.

[6] More generally, qualitative methods may be described as methods applied in the social sciences 'used to explore, describe, or explain social phenomenon; unpack the meanings people ascribe to activities, situations, events, or artefacts; build a depth of understanding about some aspect of social life; build 'thick descriptions'…of people in naturalistic settings; explore new or underresearched areas; or make micro–macro links (illuminate connections between individuals–groups and institutional and/or cultural contexts)', Patricia Leavy, 'Introduction' in Patricia Leavy (ed), *The Oxford Handbook of Qualitative Research* (OUP 2014) 1–14, 2 (cites Clifford Geertz).

[7] See, eg, AL Goodhart, 'The Ratio Decidendi of a Case' (1959) 22 *MLR* 117–24.

[8] For an overview of quantitative methodology see, eg, David Kaplan (ed), *The SAGE Handbook of Quantitative Methodology for the Social Sciences* (Sage 2004). The handbook discusses scaling, testing and measurement, models for categorical data, models for multilevel data, models for latent variables of qualitative experience and applying among types of statistical methods, and theoretical issues related to the quantitative approach.

natural sciences it would be a different story.[9] Legal scholars have been discussing topics such as property and contract for hundreds of years, whereas scientists started to talk about DNA and antibiotics only in the past century. In the case of numerical comparative law, the methodological echo comes not from a hugely distant past, but goes back to German academia of the late nineteenth and early twentieth century. The echo in question is the famous *Methodenstreit* concerning a dispute over methods. I believe that the dispute over methods offers a fruitful way to frame the discussion in this chapter. The underlying philosophical assumptions of today's discussion and those of *Methodenstreit* may not be identical, but they overlap to a significant degree.

Put in a nutshell, *Methodenstreit* was a longstanding debate among German scholars concerning the methodological contradictions between the natural sciences (*Naturwissenschaften*) and the social and historical sciences (*Geisteswissenschaften*).[10] Whereas *Naturwissenschaften* translates swiftly as natural sciences, *Geisteswissenschaften* translates more ambiguously as 'human sciences'.[11] The nexus of the debate was on the difference between separate ways of grasping research, namely interpretative understanding (*verstehen*) and the nomothetic law-seeking explanatory approach (*erklären*). The gist of the debate was the idea according to which social sciences (broadly understood) are different from natural sciences because they seek to reach a comprehensive understanding of social phenomena that go beyond mere causal explanations. Those who defended the autonomy of interpretative understanding of social and historical sciences were interested in social and cultural manifestations that are conceived as both purposive and interconnected. In relation to each other, *verstehen* and *erklären* are contrarian as the German words themselves seem to suggest opposition and controversy.[12] Importantly, they are not methods as such but more like rudimentary epistemological and methodological assumptions about how to conduct research and what results to seek. In the wider tribe of social sciences, they dwell in different corners of the tribal lands, glancing at each other furtively at a scholarly distance. In the world of comparative law, they generate a different distinction from the distinctions between doctrinal and contextual or science and practice, discussed above.

Traditionally, law as a field of study occupies a peculiar place in the contradiction between *verstehen* and *erklären*.[13] Seeing law as a social science requires

[9] However, one needs to keep in mind that past and present are not the same even if we might understand past law. See Derek Roebuck, 'The Past is Another Country' (1994) 3 *Asia Pacific Law Review* 9–23 (argues that legal history is a form of comparative law).

[10] 'Methodenstreit' in Craig Calhoun (ed), *Dictionary of the Social Sciences* (OUP 2002) www.oxfordreference.com/display/10.1093/acref/9780195123715.001.0001/acref-9780195123715-e-1070?rskey=JYc9p7&result=1071

[11] This is the translation used in Hans-Georg Gadamer's *Truth and Method*, 2nd revised edn (Continuum 1994) [First edition *Wahrheit und Methode* 1960]. See also Guy Oakes's translator's introduction to Heinrich Rickert, *The Limits of Concept Formation in Natural Science* (CUP 1986) vii–xxxii.

[12] Jan Bransen, 'Verstehen and erklären; the philosophy of' in Neil Smelser & Paul Baltes (eds), *International Encyclopedia of Social & Behavioral Sciences* (Elsevier 2001) 16165–70.

[13] In the eyes of philosophical hermeneutics, legal hermeneutics seems like a bit of an exceptional case. See Gadamer (n 11) 517–18.

a bit of a stretch. Law as a field has grown on the basis of legal doctrine and it belongs clearly to the general tradition of *Geisteswissenschaften*.[14] Accordingly, the knowledge that law as a discipline produces is, as to its nature, interpretative understanding, not causal explanation. The general underlying idea is that social and cultural matters are different from research objects in the natural world as human actors and products of their cultures are not merely results of causal forces.[15] Those who see law as an interpretative discipline tend to describe it as hermeneutics or some kind of exegesis.[16] This is, however, not to say that law as a discipline would be like the Exegetical School in the nineteenth century that reduced legal scholarship to an exact and literal explanation of codified law.[17] In law it is about 'understanding' in a broader way. This is easy to grasp and makes sense as the key question of hermeneutics is how to understand a text.[18]

For a legal scholar, hermeneutics means first and foremost how to understand a legal text as a source of normative information. Normativity means simply that law prescribes how things should be instead of how they are; law embodies the feature of 'ought'. In the case of comparatists, it is predominantly about how to understand legal texts that belong to a foreign legal system.[19] Described like this, comparative law belongs to the *verstehen* type of scholarship. Consequently, its instinctive place is among *Geisteswissenschaften* even though legal doctrine is a rather unique form of research which shares similarities with certain strands of theology.[20] This is simply because, as disciplines, law and theology are founded on the authority of given texts.[21]

Noteworthy comparative law scholars have described comparative study of law as a form of study that is, as to its nature, hermeneutical. When it comes to the method of law more generally, it has been conceived as legal hermeneutics focusing on the interpretation and normative meaning of law in written form.[22] However, in recent decades voices that seek to expand comparative law towards a more scientific or numerical direction, in the spirit of *erklären*, have increasingly gained ground. Moreover, a pluralistic understanding of comparative law seems

[14] See, eg, Klaus Obermeyer, 'Rechtswissenschaft als Geisteswissenschaft' (1987) 42 *JuristenZeitung* 691–96; and Dieter Simon, 'Die Rechtswissenschaft als Geisteswissenschaft' (1992) *Rechtshistorisches Journal* 351–66.

[15] See, eg, Larry Ray, 'Verstehen' in George Ritzer (ed), *The Blackwell Encyclopedia of Sociology* (Blackwell 2007) 5195–96.

[16] For a more detailed discussion on this, see Peter Goodrich, 'Historical Aspects of Legal Interpretation' (1986) *Indiana Law Journal* 331–54.

[17] Raoul Van Caenegem, *Judges, Legislators, and Professors* (CUP 1987) 89–90.

[18] See Paul Ricoeur, *Hermeneutics and the Human Sciences*, tr John B Thompson (CUP 1981) 43–62.

[19] This also concerns understanding foreign languages as translating forms an important part of comparative law. I discuss this issue in Jaakko Husa, 'Translating Legal Language and Comparative Law' (2017) 30 *International Journal for the Semiotics of Law* 261–72.

[20] See, eg, Werner Jeanrond, *Theological Hermeneutics* (MacMillan 1991) ch 1.

[21] This is connected to 'the authority paradigm'. See Geoffrey Samuel, 'Interdisciplinarity and the Authority Paradigm' (2009) 36 *Journal of Law and Society* 431–59 ('For both law and theology are founded, as disciplines, on the authority of given texts', ibid 441).

[22] See, eg, Gerald Bruns, 'Law and Language' in George Leyh (ed), *Legal Hermeneutics* (University of California Press 1992) 23–40; Peter Goodrich, 'Legal Hermeneutics' in *Routledge Encyclopedia of Philosophy* (Taylor and Francis 1998) doi:10.4324/9780415249126-T016-1

also to include the *erklären* type of approach. Nevertheless, *erklären*'s path to comparative law scholarship has not been without difficulty as it has met critique from those factions of the comparative law tribe who prefer to define comparative law primarily as a hermeneutic scholarly practice and text-oriented way to study law. Without saying it out loud, most comparatists seem to tacitly assume that law as a field belongs to *Geisteswissenschaften* even though it may be a special kind of hermeneutics.[23]

What is the modern collision between *verstehen* and *erklären* about? If I am not mistaken, *verstehen*-type arguments can be conceived as an individualising form of scholarship, whereas *erklären*-type arguments can be conceived as seeking to generalise and find causalities. Even though it would be intriguing to ponder why *Methodenstreit* arrived so late to the comparative law methodology debate, I leave this issue out because it would need considerable further investigation going beyond the theme of this volume, which focuses on scholarly collisions in comparative law itself.

II. Comparative Law as an Individualising Form of Legal Scholarship

Individualising a thing means making it different from other things and giving it a recognisable identity. In many ways, the hermeneutic approach seeks to do that as it avoids generalising and quantification. It seems to abhor numbers. Sometimes, nevertheless, it is difficult to keep these two separate, as legal families illustrate. Legal families are based on generalisations of several legal systems but the knowledge they convey individualises groups of legal systems from other groups of legal systems.[24] In this section, the focus is on individualising comparative law scholarship that can – rightly in my view – be characterised broadly as hermeneutics. Without seeking to offer an exhaustive definition or venturing deep into philosophy, hermeneutics can be understood as the theory of interpretation that concerns achieving an understanding of text.[25] This general definition works sufficiently well for the purposes of this chapter and in the context of legal scholarship in general, in particular comparative law. By and large, comparatists deal with legal texts of foreign origin: legislation, judgments, preparatory works, and legal literature.

[23] An important discussion about legal hermeneutics as a form of hermeneutics is by Hans-Georg Gadamer in *Truth and Method* (n 11). For further discussion, see Jean Grondin, 'Gadamer's Interest for Legal Hermeneutics' in Simone Glanert & Fabien Girard (eds), *Law's Hermeneutics* (Routledge 2017) 48–62.

[24] I have argued elsewhere that legal families are, as to their nature, like Max Weber's so-called Ideal Types that combine qualitative and quantitative elements. See Jaakko Husa, 'Legal families in Comparative Law' (2001) 24 *Retfærd* 15–24.

[25] See, eg, Michael Forster, 'Hermeneutic' in Michael Rosen & Brian Leiter (eds), *The Oxford Handbook of Continental Philosophy* (OUP 2007) 30–74 ('the theory of interpretation, ie the theory of achieving an understanding of texts, utterances, and so on' ibid 30).

As noted above, hermeneutics is one way to characterise comparative law as a field of legal study. Geoffrey Samuel speaks – drawing from sociological epistemology – of schemes of intelligibility. These schemes refer to the way the comparatist sees phenomena.[26] When Samuel discusses the hermeneutical approach, he focuses on Pierre Legrand's ideas, describing them generally as a 'deep hermeneutical approach to comparative law and legal culture'.[27] However, as Samuel observes, Legrand's hermeneutical take is more a philosophy than a method.[28] In this sense, Legrand's view fits in the tradition of philosophical hermeneutics rather than in the methodology of *Geisteswissenschaften*.[29] For this reason, I focus on another important comparatist who conceives comparative law as hermeneutics more clearly as a certain way to do comparative research and as a way to describe what comparative law is about as a field of study. The scholar in question is John Bell, whose scholarship has not been discussed in the above chapters partly because his work is difficult to characterise through the framework of collisions or contrarianism.[30] Regardless, his view of comparative law as a hermeneutic field fits well in the underlying juxtaposition between *verstehen* and *erklären*.

To begin with, Bell argues that comparative law is not significantly different from other fields of legal scholarship.[31] This is a central assumption with far-reaching consequences. He is not, of course, alone in this idea even though comparatists normally seek almost obsessively to underline the special character of their field.[32] One of the key features Bell regards as distinctive of comparative law is its *interpretative character*, which makes it hermeneutical as to its basic nature.[33] This characterisation is more profound than mere textual exegesis as legal texts on their own cannot be relied on: texts are parts of legal systems. In turn, this means that the comparatist needs to construct meaning in their research by going beyond the text itself.[34] For instance, how a lawyer reads precedents requires them to go beyond the mere textual surface.[35] This, in turn, requires thinking like a lawyer.[36] A similar type of issue was also highlighted through the law in books and law in action dichotomy, addressed in chapter two above. Moreover, going beyond the surface of the text is entangled with many comparative law collisions as it concerns

[26] Geoffrey Samuel, *An Introduction to Comparative Law Theory and Method* (Hart Publishing 2014) 81–92.

[27] ibid 108.

[28] ibid 115.

[29] Gadamer (n 11) xxi says that 'The hermeneutic phenomenon is basically not a problem of method at all'.

[30] For a comprehensive view of Bell's scholarship, see Sophie Turenne, 'John Bell's Principal Publications' in Sophie Turenne (ed), *Reasons and Context in Comparative Law* (CUP 2023) 275–81.

[31] John Bell, 'Legal Research and Distinctiveness of Comparative Law' in Mark Van Hoecke (ed), *Methodologies of Legal Research* (Hart Publishing 2011) 155–76, 155.

[32] cf Stephen A Smith, 'Comparative Legal Scholarship as Ordinary Legal Scholarship' (2013) 1 *European Journal of Comparative Law and Governance* DOI 10.1163/22134514-00101007

[33] Bell (n 31) 158.

[34] ibid 165.

[35] See, eg, Neil MacCormick & Robert Summers (eds), *Interpreting Precedents* (Dartmouth 1997).

[36] See, eg, Frederick Schauer, *Thinking Like a Lawyer* (Harvard University Press 2009). In essence, Schauer underlines the importance of legal reasoning as a distinct mode of thought.

the way the comparatist understands 'the law'. In essence, comparative law is about reading and interpreting texts that are sources of legal rules.[37]

According to Bell's view, comparative law is hermeneutic because it takes – or at least seeks to take – an insider's view of the legal systems studied, despite the fact that the comparatist perceives foreign law from the viewpoint of an outsider. However, it should be clear that comparatists do not miraculously transform into lawyers of the foreign systems they study; hence, they remain epistemic outsiders even if perhaps well-informed outsiders.[38]

Externality is next to impossible to avoid, as being a comparatist means being an outsider; yet, looking from the outside may come with the benefit that insiders may remain blind to things that well-informed outsiders may detect from the outside. As a result, the comparatist's view 'may not directly reflect what the national lawyer would say about his or her own system'.[39] It should go without saying, though, that the comparatist's take and that of the national lawyer's cannot be drastically different, as a considerable overlap is needed. Nevertheless, it is of importance to grasp that that these two takes are not identical, even if the comparatist were to do their very best. The outsider's view is never authentic, despite what the comparatist may claim, but that does not mean that this view would be worthless or uninteresting. Besides, being authentic is a complicated issue as one can argue that a constitutional lawyer is not truly able to grasp intricate private law issues authentically even though they might belong to the same legal culture and work in the same legal system.

Moreover, Bell rejects Legrand's view about the fundamental problem of otherness, which Bell recognises but refuses to give it such a decisive weight as Legrand.[40] For me, this is a pivotal common-sense modification. Overall, Bell's conclusion seems balanced and well thought through: 'Identifying difference is valuable and important, but enabling the reader to bridge the distance so as to gain a point of access into the other system is an essential task'.[41] Accepting this kind of a common-sense hermeneutical view of comparative law also means taking on the unavoidable imperfection of comparative study. Regardless, what the comparatist should be able to do is to reconstruct a description of the foreign law that someone who does not know the system can understand even though the description is not identical to those that internal lawyers would provide.[42] I have argued elsewhere that the comparatist simulates the internal point of view of a lawyer who operates within the system.[43] This means that, in one way or

[37] John Bell, 'Comparative Law and Legal Theory' in Werner Krawietz & Neil MacCormick (eds), *Prescriptive Formality and Normative Rationality in Modern Legal Systems* (Duncker & Humblot 1994) 23–31, 26.

[38] Günter Frankenberg has spoken critically of an imagined 'magic carpet' in this context, 'Comparing Constitutions' (2006) 4 *International Journal of Constitutional Law* 439–59, 445.

[39] Bell (n 31) 167.

[40] ibid 168–69.

[41] ibid 175.

[42] ibid 176.

[43] Jaakko Husa, *Introduction to Comparative Law*, 2nd edn (Hart Publishing 2023) 38.

another, the comparatist is both an epistemic outsider and an insider at the same time.[44] All this fits with the view according to which doing comparative legal research is essentially some form of hermeneutics, belonging to the *verstehen* type of scholarship.

There is one special feature in the idea of method in traditional comparative law that needs to be mentioned before moving on to the *erklären* type of comparative law. Traditional here does not mean age-old but a habitual kind of way to deal with textual materials being studied, without further thought. Philosophers speak of tacit knowledge, which exists but is difficult to articulate.[45] Something similar concerns much of legal comparativism. The blueprints or collections of research steps suggested by the comparatists all seem to make one key assumption according to which the comparatist studies legal *texts*. These may vary from a narrowly understood black-letter-law view to taking into account preparatory materials or political contexts of law (eg debates in the legislature or dissenting court opinions).[46] Other kinds of materials (or data if you like) may support the tacit basic approach – but they come after or on top of the silently assumed basic approach. In the end, it is my belief that in comparative law scholarship the *verstehen* type of way to deal with texts is *implicitly assumed* without further ado. This, like all inarticulate assumptions, has certain consequences that we as legal scholars tend to accept as normality.

In practice, hermeneutic study of legal texts is silently suggested, though not directly expressed. This is the reason why there are so few scholars, like Bell or Samuel, who explicitly define comparative law as a form of hermeneutic research in methodological terms.[47] There simply is no reason to state it because it is tacitly assumed that lawyers master the basic approach of analysing legal texts. Why this is hermeneutics instead of mere exegesis is because the modern comparatist seeks to interpret the legal meaning of a given text within its socio-historical context. No matter which comparative law faction one belongs to, it is difficult not to register the significant shift from a black-letter-law focus towards more contextual and less doctrinal approaches. Nevertheless, from the point of view of the nomothetic type of scholarship, this implicit way to grasp method is problematic. It is problematic because it fails to recognise the need for plural methodology and the concomitant idea of a toolbox. This problem is identified by Esin Örücü:

> The classical technique of legal methodology of reading texts of all kinds and hoping for insight has serious limitations for collecting data to serve comparative inquiry adequately. Unless there is collaboration between legal and social science researchers,

[44] Annlise Riles, 'Comparative Law and Socio-Legal Studies' in Mathias Reimann & Reinhard Zimmermann (eds), *The Oxford Handbook of Comparative Law*, 2nd edn (OUP 2019) 773–804, 795.

[45] See, eg, Abida Malik, 'Tacit Knowing' (2023) 20 *Episteme* 349–66.

[46] For more detailed discussion on traditional approach and understanding of comparative law, see Jaakko Husa, 'Traditional Methods' in Mathias Siems & Po Jen Yap (eds) *The Cambridge Handbook of Comparative Law* (CUP 2024) 15–31.

[47] This is not to imply that Bell and Samuel would agree on everything. They are, nevertheless, examples of comparatists who discuss comparative law and hermeneutics from the viewpoint of methods and methodology.

> comparative law falls short of its function, not only as a way of enhancing understanding and knowledge of law in context, but also as a source of models and of empirical information and knowledge.[48]

If the idea of pluralistic methodology of comparative law is taken seriously, as Örücü urges us to do, then non-idiographic approaches should also be considered by comparatists. It is about having a range of approaches instead of just one method. An increasing amount of scholarship is making the argument for moving closer to social science methods in one way or another. Numbers, as arithmetic values representing quantity, play a significant role in this. An important trend among these arguments focuses on what one might label as empirical or quantitative comparative law. In essence, these voices tend to argue that comparative law needs also to include the *erklären* type of scholarship and to step beyond hermeneutics based on the doctrinal way of grasping law.

III. Comparative Law as a Generalising Form of Legal Scholarship

Generalising forms of legal scholarship are still very much minority forms of research because law as a discipline has grown on the foundation of doctrinal study that, as to its nature, belongs to *verstehen* camp. One way to describe generalising research is that it is based on searching for general laws and the study of large numerical data.[49] In essence, it differs from the lawyer's tacit basic method as it relies on experiments, surveys, statistical analysis, and quantifiable information. In essence, quantitative comparative law means research that 'entails the collection and analysis of quantitative data with the aim of comparing legal systems or jurisdictions.'[50] Interestingly, this idea is not a recent one even though it has gained a proper foothold only in this century.[51] John Henry Merryman was – surprisingly perhaps – an early proponent of *erklären*-type research projects. For early Merryman, the most important goal of comparative study was 'explanation'. This idea was based on the alleged need for the comparatist to test general hypotheses by empirical data leading to explanations.[52] This is clearly an *erklären*-type vision

[48] Esin Örücü, 'Developing Comparative Law' in Esin Örücü & David Nelken (eds), *Comparative Law* (Hart Publishing 2007) 43–65, 49.

[49] For a concise description of the idiographic and nomothetic approach, see 'idiographic/nomothetic methods' in Simon Blackburn (ed), *A Dictionary of Philosophy* (OUP 2005) 178. See also James Lamiell, 'Nomothetic and Idiographic Approaches' in Thomas Teo (ed), *Encyclopedia of Critical Psychology* (Springer 2014) 1248–53.

[50] Ryan Whalen, 'Quantitative Methods in Comparative Law' in Jan Smits, Jaakko Husa, Catherine Valcke & Madalena Narciso (eds), *Elgar Encyclopedia of Comparative Law*, vol 3 (Edward Elgar 2023) 277–83, 277.

[51] See, eg, Chang, Yun-chien, *Property Law: Comparative, Empirical, and Economic Analyses* (CUP 2023) ch 1 (comparative empirical overview of property law).

[52] John Henry Merryman, 'Comparative Law and Scientific Explanation', in John Hazard & Wenceslas Wagner (eds), *Law in the United States of America in Social and Technological Revolution* (Bruylant 1974) 81–104.

of comparative law. In honesty, Merryman's idea never really got off the ground. There have been some attempts to do comparative law numerically, but that form of scholarship has never been mainstream.[53]

As is typical for comparative law, the call for empirical research can also be made in a more or less contrarian fashion. Han-wei Ho, Patrick Chung-Chia Huang, and Yun-chien Chang put it like this: 'Comparative law should go empirical. The traditional method is not wrong, but limited, with marginal returns accruing to empirical methods likely increasing'.[54] This is essentially a normative statement but nonetheless it avoids sharp contrarianism even when the message is clearly normative ('should go').

These scholars speak about the study of legal families but the arguments they present apply more broadly as points speaking for a nomothetic approach against the backdrop of alleged idiographic deficiencies. According to them, the coding process of data constrains the subjectivity of researchers. In their view, quantification is crucial as coding requires back-and-forth revisions to capture nuances, thus making claims possible based on objective data not on subjective judgements. Yet – as Ho, Huang, and Chang admit – subjective elements cannot be entirely weeded out, although the scope of subjectivity can be constrained. They continue, arguing that 'a transparent coding process facilitates scholarly discussions by breaking down high-level debate into manageable and verifiable issues'.[55] In many ways, what they say rehearses the core of *erklären* arguments presented in the *Methodenstreit*. Now, their call for quantitative approach(es) is certainly not the only one. The call has been presented in varying forms and against different backdrops.

For instance, Ralf Michaels makes the argument against the backdrop of legal origins scholarship as he is worried that comparative lawyers have largely ignored developments in economic research even though comparative law knowledge is incorporated by economists in their research on economic efficiency.[56] Michaels points out that the legal origins thesis, according to which common law is better for economic growth than civil law, 'has created hundreds of papers and citation numbers unheard of among comparative lawyers'.[57] He urges comparatists to engage with economic research because the political success of the legal origins thesis and the *Doing Business* reports shows how comparative law's political importance has declined in terms of issues situated beyond European private law harmonisation.[58] This is an issue, Michaels claims, because comparatists should actually be happy

[53] See also, Yenny Vega Cárdenas, *Methodology and Epistemology of Comparative Law* (LexisNexis 2024) 119–20.

[54] Han-wei Ho, Patrick Chung-Chia Huang & Yun-chien Chang' Machine-Learning Methods' in Siems & Yap (n 46) 177–208, 178.

[55] ibid 178.

[56] Ralf Michaels, 'Comparative Law by Numbers?' (2009) 57 *AJCL* 765–95. See also Siems (n 4).

[57] ibid 766.

[58] This view seems to echo the role of Max Planck Institute's traditional role of providing information of foreign law to German actors. See the Hamburg Guidelines (*Hamburger Leitlinien*) about providing information of foreign law: www.mpipriv.de/hamburger-leitlinien.

about the newly re-emerged interest of economists in law.[59] Importantly, he speaks for interdisciplinary approaches that would result in scholars having a better understanding and wielding an influence on economic research when economics deals with legal issues and questions that have been the bread-and-butter of comparative law scholarship for a long time. In short, Michaels does not advocate comparatists becoming like economists but instead he speaks for broadening the methodological constitution of comparative law so that it would retain its relevance as a border-crossing form of legal knowledge. When it comes to empirical data and measurements, '[t]raditional comparative lawyers have a lot to learn here' he argues.[60]

A less ambiguous call for empirical comparative law is made by Holger Spamann, who sees the *erklären* type of scholarship in a more positive light than Michaels, whose view is a bit more reserved.[61] In essence, Spamann argues that quantitative research designs look promising as they can provide interesting insights for comparative study of law. He does not argue that quantitative research designs should or could replace comparative law. Instead, what he argues is that comparatists should seek to deploy quantitative research designs for the benefit of comparative study of law. This would also mean that comparatists could then be able to contribute their expertise to other fields so that those other fields could do better quantitative comparative legal studies. In the end, Spamann concludes that:

> What matters is whether such studies can help answer relevant questions, and whether they benefit from the input of researchers with knowledge of the law of different countries and with an appreciation for the difficulties of comparison. I think the answer is yes on both counts.[62]

What exactly is it that those who speak for quantification and the *erklären* type of comparative law research think could be achieved? In short, why quantification and numbers? The impression one gets from the literature is that calls for quantification assume that it is capable of producing more comparative knowledge about law. Speaking for the use of numerical approaches, Pier Giuseppe Monateri and Mauro Balestrieri claim that:

> Quantitative methods such as statistical analysis, econometrics, and machine learning have been used to analyze large amounts of data and identify patterns and trends in legal systems. Of course, this can be useful in comparative law as it can help to identify in various ways the similarities and differences between legal systems and to test hypotheses about the impact of legal rules and institutions on economic growth, development, and other outcomes.[63]

[59] Michaels (n 56) 791–92.

[60] ibid 786.

[61] Holger Spamann, 'Large-Sample, Quantitative Research Designs for Comparative Law?' (2009) 57 *AJCL* 797–810. See also Spamann, 'Empirical Comparative Law' (2015) 11 *Annual Review of Law and Social Science* 131–53 (stresses the importance of establishing comparative findings through high-quality data collection).

[62] ibid 810.

[63] Pier Giuseppe Monateri & Marco Balestrieri, *Quantitative Methods in Comparative Law* (Edward Elgar 2023) xi. See also Monika Leszczyńska, 'Empirical Methods in Contract Law' in Yuliya Chernykh & Joshua Karton (eds), *Research Methods for Contract Law and Scholarship* (Edward Elgar 2025) 136–57.

Monateri and Balestrieri are not alone with this view as, for example, Mathias Siems's take comes close to this basic idea.[64] He discusses various areas that would work for numerical comparative law and mentions aspects such as measuring the impact of foreign legal ideas, measuring similarities and differences, and measuring the quality of legal rules and institutions. Siems concludes his discussion on quantitative comparative law by saying that it can contribute to the study of such core topics as legal transplants, legal families, and using comparisons for making policy recommendations.[65] Along similar lines, Ryan Whalen says that quantitative methods provide the potential to empirically test the hypotheses that comparative legal theory makes.[66] This is, no doubt, an *erklären* type of argument as empirical testing of hypotheses has certainly not been a part of legal hermeneutics no matter how it has been practised and understood.

Comparative constitutional law, besides legal origins scholarship, is an example of a specialised field of comparative law where the call for numerical approaches has been more successful than in other areas of comparative law.[67] Against this backdrop, Uwe Kischel's contrarian depiction seems overly belittling as he argues that statistical comparative law 'has attracted in some narrow areas of business law, but which has remained largely unknown in the broader field of comparative law'.[68] Constitutional law is a counter example unless, of course, one does think that comparative study is not for public law. Regardless, it would seem, attitudes towards quantification in general seem to be softening. However, finding a balance is not an easy task in the field of contrarians.[69] Fitting hermeneutics and statistics into the same comparative framework remains a tough assignment.

IV. Finding a Balance?

It seems that quantification and numerical approaches have gained some ground in comparative law scholarship. That said, however, it would be an exaggeration to claim that the *erklären* type of approaches would have been welcomed with open arms.[70] Indeed, there is also a principled *verstehen* type of culturalist critique on the very possibility of quantifying law. Comparative lawyers still

[64] See Mathias Siems, *Comparative Law*, 3rd edn (CUP 2022) ch 8.
[65] ibid 253.
[66] Whalen (n 50) 281.
[67] See, eg, Ran Hirschl, *Comparative Matters* (OUP 2014). Hirschl explicitly criticises the *verstehen* type of comparative law, arguing that idiographic comparative law does not cut it as: 'it has contributed significantly to concept formation and the accumulation of idiographic knowledge, it has, for the most part, fallen short of advancing knowledge through inference-oriented, controlled comparison', ibid 226.
[68] Uwe Kischel, *Comparative Law* (OUP 2019) 134.
[69] There may be differences between Europe and the US as scholars based at European universities are more likely to apply a comparative approach than is the case in the US. See for further discussion on this, Mathias Siems, 'The European Advantage of in Empirical Comparative Law' (2025) 2 *European Journal of Legal Studies* doi.org/10.62355/ejels.24727.
[70] In other words, there is 'a distrust of abstract scientific modelling', Geoffrey Samuel, 'Epistemology of Comparative Law' in Smits et al Vol 2 (n 50) 27–35, 33.

eye quantification suspiciously. Whalen describes this critique as thinking that quantitative approaches are unable to 'capture the rich nuance that is required to adequately compare different legal regimes, and they are thus unsuited to answer questions of comparative law'.[71] This is, in essence, very much a *verstehen* type of opposing argument.

To take an example, Alexandra Mercescu criticises the legal origins theory on the basis of a fundamental scepticism about quantification and measuring. In essence, this is very much also a Legrandian critique that sees law as something that cannot be quantified successfully. Another target of Mercescu's contrarian critique is generic constitutional law, which also builds on a cultural understanding of law and rejection of numerical comparative research.[72] This is an illustration of the deep hermeneutical roots of comparative law that is not based on the *erklären* type of research and its underlying belief in the many blessings of quantification and numerical approaches. The core idea of this critique is based on a deep suspicion of quantification, thus echoing the *Methodenstreit*. Along similar lines, Kischel says that the 'basic problem is the attempt to reduce the complexity of legal norms to simplistic assertions, which can then be expressed in simple numbers.'[73] Arithmetic appears to cause epistemic anxiety among the ranks of comparative law scholars.

Against the above discussion it seems possible to say that today's comparative law has opened somewhat towards quantification and numerical approaches.[74] Accepting quantitative methods as belonging to the toolbox of the comparatist is part of the new directions that comparative law has taken in this century.[75] This does not mean, however, that comparative law's hermeneutic foundation would have disappeared. As already noted, there are still those who are deeply suspicious about quantification in comparative law. Then again, those who speak for quantification do not argue that numerical approaches should or could replace more traditional approaches.[76] It is a question of supplementing the existing toolbox of approaches. I agree in part with Samuel, who describes the situation by saying that even though quantitative methods have become more commonplace and comparatists are ready to expand towards nomothetic research, '[a]t most they

[71] Whalen (n 50) 280.

[72] Simone Glanert, Alexandra Mercescu & Geoffrey Samuel, *Rethinking Comparative Law* (Edward Elgar 2021) chs 11 and 12 (both written by Mercescu).

[73] Kischel (n 68) 136.

[74] I have argued elsewhere that '[e]ven though the fundamental nature of comparative law is hermeneutical, it does not mean, however, that numerical or quantitative approaches cannot be utilised', Husa (n 43) 34.

[75] For a broader discussion on this, see Mathias Siems, 'New Directions in Comparative Law' in in Reimann & Zimmermann (n 44) 852–74.

[76] These kinds of ideas may, however, be seen as an implicit part of what Monateri seems to suggest: 'classical qualitative analysis of similarities and differences among legal systems is destined to give way to a new form of quantitative analysis; a major shift that implies a deep revision of terms and a rise in different approaches', Pier Giuseppe Monateri, *Advanced Introduction to Comparative Legal Methods* (Edward Elgar 2021) 109.

[numerical approaches] might offer a competing paradigm.'[77] No wonder, then, that even those who speak for quantification admit that 'the use of quantitative methods in comparative law is far from the perfect tool for legal comparisons.'[78] Indeed, despite its recent limited success one can say that numerical comparative law's results 'beg to be debated'.[79] Truth be told, much of what has been claimed by comparatists seems to have begged to be debated just the same.

All in all, today's comparative law seems to have left behind the heated collision between *verstehen* and *erklären* as comparatists have moved from contrarianism towards a more pluralistic understanding of their field. This conclusion comes close to what I have also argued in the above chapters, stressing the idea of a plurality of methods. Yet, taking into account the innate tendency of comparatists to be contrarians, it would be too much to expect that the collision between understanding and explaining would have disappeared for good.[80] There are reasons behind this state of affairs. It has been noted that there are enduring elements of traditional legal scholarship in general, regardless of certain diversification and expansion.[81] I suspect that quality versus quantity is like collisions on functionalism, legal transplants or legal families and, hence, like a jack-in-the-box.[82] This means that *Methodenstreit* may unexpectedly and uninvited jump out and give the numerical comparatist a contrarian surprise when epistemology and methodology are discussed.

[77] Samuel (n 50) 33.
[78] Monateri & Balestrieri (n 63) xi.
[79] Kischel (n 68) 136.
[80] As a countering factor against new directions Siems (n 44) 873 says that there are 'centripetal forces at work, rearming the traditional status quo of a more confined core of comparative law.'
[81] Susan Bartie, 'The Lingering Core of Legal Scholarship' (2010) *Legal Studies* 345–69.
[82] It might be mischievously noted that the jack-in-the box is based on a Catholic Saint named John Schorne who performed an exorcism by using an old boot. He caught a demon named Jack in a boot in 1290, and this is supposedly the origin of jack-in-the-box. The box, if one is to believe this story, is a tool for trapping demons.

11

'For I am nothing, if not critical'

Many collisions in the field of comparative law have to do, more or less, with the identity of the comparatist.[1] 'Who am I as a comparatist?' is a question that puzzles many legal scholars engaged in comparative law. Much of comparative law theory and methodology circles around the question which tribe to belong to or, more specifically, which subtribe to belong to. Despite belonging to the same tribe, we seem to gather around competing totem poles to cheer our heroes and to boo our scholarly pet peeves. We have seen this over and again in the preceding chapters. If one conceives oneself as a doctrinal or positive law comparatist, it produces a different kind of identity than if one conceives oneself as a socio-legal scholar or a law-and-economics type of scholar. Or if one is a comparative legal historian, then one sees oneself differently from someone who is an empirically oriented constitutional law comparatist.[2] All this is, of course, to be expected as the field is so diverse today.

In the above I have already investigated a number of collisions that are connected in one way or another to the question of identity and scholarly totem poles. An important issue that has not yet been discussed concerns the ways in which the comparatist sees the usage of their research results or, more generally, comparative law's aims altogether. Chapter three centred on the separation between academic and practical aims and concerned the purposes of comparative law. However, what was not discussed in chapter three concerns the particular nature of research results regardless of the intended purposes of comparative study of law. The question is: what happens after comparing, in the sense of what use are the conclusions? Some dimensions of the discussion on legal transplants (chapter nine) concern this but only in part. There is a clear difference between comparative law scholarship that seeks to be neutral and scholarship that underlines the

[1] The title of this chapter is a quote from Shakespeare's *Othello*, the line spoken by the character Iago (2.1.120).

[2] View from legal history, see Heikki Pihlajamäki, 'Merging Comparative Law and Legal History' (2018) 66 *AJCL* 733–50. For a view from constitutional law, see Niels Petersen & Konstantin Chatzia-thanasiou, 'Empirical Research in Comparative Constitutional Law' (2021) 19 *International Journal of Constitutional Law* 1810–34.

importance of being critical.[3] The ambition of neutrality – familiar from the scholarship of the 1970s and 1980s – is not difficult to grasp even though it is arguably an unattainable ideal. Unfortunately, 'critical' is a more ambiguous term as it has more than one possible meaning in terms of comparative law, as indeed we have seen in the preceding chapters.[4] For instance, discussion on functionalism (chapter eight) demonstrates certain ways of being critical about mainstream methodology.

Generally speaking, being critical means being inclined to search for and point out faults and defects. Critical legal studies, a school of thought that developed in the United States during the latter half of the 1970s, is one example of what being critical in the study of law means.[5] This movement highlighted the law's unavoidable connection to society and inherent social biases in the spirit of the mirror theory. In the case of comparative law there are abundant different kinds of critiques, which is not a surprise if we take into account the contrarian nature of comparativism. It is difficult, however, to pinpoint what 'critical' means in the context of comparative law. It seems, for the most part, to be a matter of the research-related attitude of the scholar producing a certain kind of academic genre.[6]

One way of having a critical attitude is based on the tradition of functional comparative law, meaning that 'the comparatist cannot deal with legal phenomena only from the viewpoint of facts' but needs 'to look for the reason behind the given solution too'.[7] Another way to define 'critical' is to see it as a method that is broadly connected to the hermeneutic approach, which is understood as opposite to the functional method.[8] Chapter six addressed the division between the West and the Rest, taking into account such critical forms of scholarship as decolonial comparative law and legal orientalism, both challenging the epistemic hegemony of Western law. These ways to conceive critical comparative law are, no doubt, possible and they also reveal what being a critical comparatist may entail. At the same time, the existence of different views only underlines the fact that 'critical' in comparative law is indeed an ambiguous term. If someone describes themselves as a critical comparative legal scholar, it begs the question: in what way are you

[3] However, it would be a mistake to claim that critical legal studies would not have had an influence on comparative law. See Ugo Mattei, 'Comparative Law and Critical Legal Studies' in Mathias Reimann & Reinhard Zimmermann (eds), *The Oxford Handbook of Comparative Law*, 2nd edn (OUP 2019) 805–25.

[4] 'Critique is a contested concept. As a result, "critical" comes with a plurality of meanings', Günter Frankenberg & Fernanda Nicola, 'Critical Approaches to Comparative Law' in Jan Smits, Jaakko Husa, Catherine Valcke & Madalena Narciso (eds), *Elgar Encyclopedia of Comparative Law*, Vol 1 (Edward Elgar 2023) 495–502, 495.

[5] One of the key ideas of critical legal studies is that the legal system supports the interests of those who create the law, which means that law is not neutral but has inherent social biases. For an overview, see Alan Norrie, 'Critical Legal Studies' in *Routledge Encyclopedia of Philosophy* (Taylor & Francis 1998) doi:10.4324/9780415249126-T003-1.

[6] 'It is important to note that the meanings and uses of critique vary dramatically across intellectual fields, disciplines, and schools of thought', Elisabeth Ancker & Rita Felski, 'Introduction' in Elisabeth Ancker & Rita Felski (eds), *Critique and Postcritique* (Duke University Press 2017) 1–28, 3.

[7] Balázs Fekete, *Paradigms in Modern European Comparative Law* (Hart Publishing 2021) 122.

[8] Yenny Vega Cárdenas, *Methodology and Epistemology of Comparative Law* (LexisNexis 2024) 168.

critical? Literature on the subject quickly reveals that there are many critics and critiques.[9] To that end, being critical is an element of scholarly contrarianism as those who consider themselves pragmatists show less interest in being critical.

In my reading, being critical in comparative law is yet another subtle indicator of the contrarian nature of the field. This is of course only natural as being critical means searching for and pointing out defects and problems. In essence, what can be labelled as deeply critical comparative law conceives itself as a kind of a negation because it stands not *for* something but *against* something. Peter Goodrich captures this essence when one of the adjectives he uses to describe Pierre Legrand's scholarship is 'contrarian disagreeability'.[10] Being against something in this case means the real or imagined mainstream, which the critical comparatist argues against and by doing so constructs their own identity as being an opposing counterweight, a voluntary dissident. Contraposition generates intellectual drive for the critic.

Thomas Coendet captures this tenet of critical comparative law by saying that: 'the safest thing that can be said about critical comparative law is that it directs itself against traditional comparative law, which it takes to centre around a positivist and functionalist framework.'[11] This form of critique, in essence, rejects the technical and positivistic view of comparative law as an innocent method.[12] In the eyes of critics, there is no innocence in comparative law scholarship. The deep critic reminds me of a quote attributed to Stalin's secret police head, Lavrentiy Berija: 'Show me the man and I'll show you the crime' or in the world of comparative law 'show me the comparatist and I'll show you the defects.'[13]

The discussion in this chapter focuses on a somewhat different dimension of criticality in comparative law, for two reasons. First, addressing critical comparative law as a form of opposition against the mainstream would end up rehearsing what has already been discussed in various contexts above. Second, I have not discussed the uses of comparative law except against the backdrop of the contradiction between practice-oriented and academically-oriented understandings of comparative law, which is only a part of the story. In what follows, I will focus on the role of criticality as concerning the end results of comparative study of law. This is also where the aim of comparative study meets the identity of the scholar. The caveat of the chosen approach is that some dimensions of scholarship that at least profess to march under the banner of critical comparative law are left out. Yet,

[9] 'The criticism comes mainly from legal theorists of various shades, international lawyers, sociologists of law, anthropologists of law and some comparatists who are interested in law and society and do not regard comparative law solely as a tool for the practice of law', Esin Örücu, 'Comparative Motley' (2021) 8 *Critical Analysis of Law* 9–26, 11.

[10] Peter Goodrich, 'Critique of Comparative Law: To Compierre' (2024) 51 *Journal of Law and Society* 130–42, 142 (book review essay of Legrand's book *Negative Comparative Law*, CUP 2022).

[11] Thomas Coendet, 'Critical Methods' in Mathias Siems & Po Jen Yap (eds), *The Cambridge Handbook of Comparative Law* (CUP 2024) 48–71, 50.

[12] Frankenberg & Nicola (n 4) 497.

[13] Ancker & Felski (n 6) 15 mention methodological orientation in critique that favours certain kinds of interpretations, hence leaving only little room for other kinds of views.

what is aimed at in this chapter is to provide some essential clues as to how 'being critical' can be understood in comparative law.

I. Being Critical According to the Mainstream

It is the hallmark of critical comparative law scholarship to assume that the mainstream - or traditional comparative law - would not allow criticality. This is a momentous assumption because the mainstream prefers to perceive itself as a field of scientific knowledge.[14] In turn, critical thinking is supposed to be part of science. Now, it is true of course that much of the mainstream tends to leave a rather technical and doctrinal impression and that certainly does not look like a critical way of doing scholarship. No wonder, then, that contrarian legal scholars - open to socio-legal and cultural dimensions - have chosen to oppose what they believe to be the mainstream. The logic behind this is simple: having an enemy makes it easier to attack, no doubt. Be that as it may, being uncritical is not quite true as traditional approaches do provide a certain - albeit narrow - corner for being critical. In order to address this, it is first necessary briefly to explain how the mainstream outlines the research process as criticality finds its place in a certain phase of that process.[15] I do this briefly as the same issue has been touched upon from various points of view in earlier chapters. Unfortunately, repetition cannot be fully avoided because issues are entangled in ways that defy a fully logical table of contents.

Traditional comparative law - that is, so-called mainstream - research starts like any comparative legal research by posing a research question. The research question is typically based on functional assumptions about law and - explicitly or implicitly - assumed essential similarities between legal systems in the core fields of private law.[16] Next comes a description of the legal systems studied and how they resolve the legal problem the comparatist is interested in - or how different systems resolve - what is allegedly the same problem. After that, the comparatist is supposed to ponder why there are differences and similarities in resolving what is allegedly the same social problem. Only in the final stage does the critical dimension step in as the comparatist is supposed to *critically evaluate* their comparative findings. Commonly, this includes an evaluation of which of the solutions provided by the legal systems is best in providing a legal solution to the same problem.[17] Comparative study of law is seen as an approach that seeks to identify

[14] I am fully aware that the notion of 'mainstream' is not overly clear. Here it refers generally to a kind of comparative law scholarship that shares most of the assumptions of Zweigert & Kötz.

[15] See also Cárdenas (n 8) 53–56.

[16] The modern version of this assumption holds that '[f]or a meaningful legal comparison to be carried out there must exist sufficient similarity with respect to social function, a form of conceptual commensurability is also required', George Mousorakis, *Comparative Law and Legal Traditions* (Springer 2019) 128.

[17] Konrad Zweigert & Hein Kötz, *An Introduction to Comparative Law*, 3rd edn (OUP 1998) 33–47. For a more concise take, see Jaakko Husa, 'Traditional Methods' in Siems & Jap (n 11) 15–31, 18–21.

the advantages and disadvantages of technically understood law.[18] To that end, comparative law is depicted as a quest for better law animated by the alleged spirit of pragmatism as an opposition to academic or overly scholarly comparativism seeking to understand law.

Of course, knowing what solution is best builds elementally on indirect criticism of other solutions. Regardless, in order to decide which is the best there needs to be some kind of a grading scale. This is a tacit form of critical comparativism as it hides itself and is challenging to detect because it dresses its evaluative character in the obfuscating vocabulary of 'better' or 'worse'. Yet, arguing that some legal solution is better than others implies a critique of those deemed 'worse' or 'inefficient'. This type of critique is closely related to the conventional aims of traditional comparative law, namely to provide critical policy evaluations.[19] Consequently, if we follow this train of thought, comparative law should be about a search for better solutions.[20] The obvious problem with this kind of comparison is that considering something as 'best' or 'superior' may merely be a result of a comparatist's personal subjective preferences not openly disclosed to others.[21]

It would seem that what mainstream scholarship says about critique does not require too much investigation. In the most influential description of the traditional comparative method, Konrad Zweigert and Hein Kötz deal twice with the critical dimension. It is easy to see that criticality plays a modest role in their methodological construction as the focus lies elsewhere. First, in the introductory part of their influential volume, in the chapter on method they provide initial considerations of the task of comparative law. Here they bring the critical dimension on board by saying that:

> Comparative law does not simply criticize what it finds, but can claim to show the way to a better mastery of the legal material, to deeper insights into it, and thus, in the end, to better law.[22]

In this view, comparison serves the practical aim of improving law. This aim enables criticism of 'worse' legal solutions by illustrating that there are, ultimately, better ones. According to this take, foreign legal systems are depositories of solutions to problems that can be resolved by legal means. Accordingly, the comparatist is like an explorer on the hunt for better rules or legal institutions. Striving for the use of comparative law to improve law is not easy to define but in essence it is about importing legal solutions from foreign legal systems in order to make one's own

[18] See, eg, Imran Ali, 'Comparative Legal Research' (2020) 26 *Journal of Legal Studies* 66–80 ('Legislation and legal reform are the main objectives', ibid 78).

[19] See for more detailed discussion on critical policy evaluation as part of traditional comparative law, Mathias Siems, *Comparative Law*, 3rd edn (CUP 2022) 26–29.

[20] Comparative law as a means to reveal weaknesses in law, see Leontin-Jean Constantinesco, *Traité de droit comparé*, vol II (LGDJ 1974) 302–06.

[21] Jane Stapleton makes this point against the backdrop of comparative tort law, 'Benefits of Comparative Tort Reasoning' (2007) 1 *Journal of Tort Law* 1–45, 45.

[22] Zweigert & Kötz (n 17) 34.

law better.[23] Of course, legal transplants are about this. The lawyer simply needs to look across borders with the tools they already have and learn, if necessary, from others and bring home foreign ideas. This is seemingly very much about 'doing it', not 'talking about it'.

Second, Zweigert and Kötz discuss what happens after the comparatist has done their research. Here, they advise the comparatist to proceed to a critical evaluation of what they have discovered. Again, this is connected to valuing some solutions as better and others as worse. According to them, the comparatist will often find that 'one solution is clearly superior'.[24] Comparison is the tool that reveals superiority and inferiority. Moreover, they deem the comparatist to be 'in the best position to follow his comparative law researches with a critical evaluation'.[25] To be sure, this is not being critical about comparative law itself but being critical about what the comparison may have revealed. It is about the research results of comparison and – though indirectly – about the very purpose of comparative law. The message, it seems, is that first one undertakes research and then there is room for some sort of criticism of the research performed. In other words, comparative research is not in itself critical.[26]

Another depiction of the traditional method – by Peter de Cruz – leaves less room for the critical dimension.[27] In fairness, de Cruz does not actually describe method in a technical sense but presents method generally as a blueprint that consists of different steps. These steps do not fall far from what Zweigert and Kötz say in their description of the method of comparative law. First, the comparatist needs to identify the research issue and state it. Second, the comparatist identifies and decides which legal systems are to be compared. The following steps are about collecting materials and arranging the data acquired. In the next phase the comparatist proceeds to map out possible answers to the research question(s). The critical dimension appears in the seventh step, where the comparatist is supposed to critically investigate the data in order to make sure that it is reliable. The eighth and final step involves drawing conclusions and evaluating them critically to make sure that they are correct. This description of comparative law research does not leave room for a critical dimension beyond a certain part of the research process and materials. Again – as with Zweigert and Kötz – critique is not self-critique of comparative law or its tacit assumptions but, rather, criticism of source materials and conclusions drawn on the basis of those materials. This sounds very much 'science-like' in the sense that it at least imitates the process of the (strictly) scientific research process.

A third description of a somewhat traditional method is provided by John Reitz.[28] According to this view, the comparatist needs to make explicit comparisons,

[23] See Mathias Siems, 'Bringing in Foreign Ideas' (2014) 8 *JCL* 119–36, 120–23 (discusses diverse ways to use foreign law in improving law).

[24] Zweigert & Kötz (n 17) 46–47.

[25] ibid 47.

[26] This may be related to the innate traditionalism of the legal profession. See, eg, Edgar Bodenheimer, 'The Inherent Conservatism of the Legal Profession' (1948) 23 *Indiana Law Journal* 221–35.

[27] Peter de Cruz, *Comparative Law in a Changing World*, 3rd edn (Routledge 2008) 242–46.

[28] John C Reitz, 'How to Do Comparative Law' (1998) 46 *AJCL* 617–36.

concentrate on similarities and differences, observe distinctive characteristics, push the analysis to broader levels of abstraction, consider reasons for similarities and differences, describe the legal profession in the systems compared, search for sources that can highlight possible differences between law in books and law in action, use the language and other non-legal skills needed, organise research around comparison, and carry out the research in a spirit of respect for legal cultures other than one's own. This is a broader and socio-legally more inclusive view on the comparative approach than the two discussed above. Regardless, even this description of the comparative approach does not seem to grant much space for being critical even though it is clearly more subtle than the two others discussed above.

However, Reitz also deals with the critical dimensions of comparative law by underlining that the comparatist needs to keep in mind that that outsider's critique is always suspect because of chauvinism. Accordingly, there is a reason to be 'cautious in criticizing foreign law, but it is much less of a problem when the same piece of scholarship levels the same or a similar criticism against the author's own legal system.'[29] He also notes that an outsider's critique is 'less likely to be dismissed as chauvinistic if it is supported by citation to domestic critics of the system.'[30] This discussion on criticality grows out of grasping the precarious epistemic position of the comparatist as it expresses methodological self-awareness. Reitz warns of the dangers that being critical about foreign law may bring about. He seems to be worried - quite rightly in my view - about how lawyers from the foreign legal systems compared will think of what comparatists say about their law. This misgiving, I believe, would fit well in the views of Zweigert and Kötz, as well as de Cruz. Presumably, every comparatist shares this worry – critical or otherwise.[31]

II. Being Critical According to the Anti-Mainstream

Critical views on comparative law itself and the methods it applies start from opposing what it paints as the mainstream. This diagnosis-based opposition is its vital spark.[32] Accordingly, critical comparative law is essentially contrarian as to its nature.[33] Critical views challenge many things but most importantly they oppose the hegemony of Western law, functionalism's idea of common problems, and the search for 'better' legal solutions that Zweigert and Kötz held in high regard as

[29] ibid 635.

[30] ibid 635.

[31] This is what Ernst Rabel meant when he was speaking of 'natives lurking under every bush with arrows' ('*unter jedem Busch Eingeborener mit Pfeilen lauert*'), Rabels, 'Deutsches und Amerikanisches Recht' (1951) 16 *Rabels Zeitschrift für ausländisches und internationales Privatrecht* 340–59, 340.

[32] cf Ancker & Felski (n 6) 4 (discussing the diagnostic quality of critique).

[33] The notion of critical comparative law is not settled. Typically, what is meant here by comparative law is discussed under the heading 'postmodern comparative law', see Siems (n 19) ch 6. In that chapter Siems, however, also discusses 'critical comparative law' noting that: 'it is best to use the term critical comparative law in a pragmatic way as including all comparative legal research closely related to such critical approaches', ibid 161.

one of the main aims of comparative law.[34] Another favourite target for contrarianism has been the assumption of similarity, which is supposed to exclude or at least play down the very existence of difference.[35] Günter Frankenberg, one of the key characters in critical comparative law, noted in the mid-1980s that 'the functional approach [mainstream] runs the risk of simplifying complex reality by assuming that similarity of problems produces similarity of results.'[36] In this view the mainstream's key defect is that it simplifies law, hence ending up with an overly mechanical view of the complex social phenomenon we call the law.[37]

In the eyes of critical comparatists, the mainstream is guilty of the epistemic sin of generalising that leaves aside law's *singularity*. Of course, this is very much the same critique that sprouts from the *verstehen* type of conception of comparative law, discussed in chapter ten above. However, the lines of battle here are not quite the same. Critical scepticism instinctively abhors the practical lawyerly mentality ('positivism') and seeks to shed light on the cultural and contextual factors that are to be found outside formal law. Quantitative methods do not really enter into this discussion. Accordingly, matters which lawyers educated in professionally oriented law schools and faculties are familiar with are placed in focus. We may depict the target of critique as 'lawyer's law' ensnared by legal positivism.[38] Paradoxically perhaps, the legal positivistic mainstream offers a breeding ground for scholarly contrarianism because of its focus on formal law and doctrinal tendencies. Mainstream performs intentionally, not by accident, which irritates the critics.

Importantly, critical comparative law rejects the very mentality of the mainstream comparatists.[39] Critical contrarianism builds on a certain kind of view of comparative law that brings on board not only analytical but also ethical and political implications that mainstream comparative law tends to neglect or simply chooses to ignore.[40] The mainstream, relying on technical mastery of formal law, is envisaged as blind to matters that surround the law and legal systems. The critical comparatist underlines that the choices comparatists make

[34] Frankenberg & Nicola (n 4) 496.

[35] 'contrarian challenge…advocates that the comparative lawyer be interested only in difference. In its extreme form, assuming an epistemological pessimism, there could even be denial of comparativism, as each culture is unique,' Örücü (n 9) 18.

[36] Günter Frankenberg, 'Critical Comparisons' (1985) 26 *Harvard International Law Journal* 411–55, 436.

[37] Of course, critical legal scholarship is by no means something that concerns only comparative law or legal theory. For example, it was noted at the beginning of this century that critical scholarship had by then infiltrated public international law and provided it with a novel sensibility and heightened self-consciousness. See Gerry Simpson, 'The Situation on the International Legal Theory Front' (2000) 11 *European Journal of International Law* 439–64.

[38] In the eyes of a critical comparatist, what legal positivists try to do is, simply, not feasible: 'impossibility of what positivists are desperately trying to do: to neutralize, albeit analytically, all extralegal incursions – notably politics, ethics, culture and the economy – on law-making and law-deciding,' Günter Frankenberg, *Comparative Law as Critique* (Edward Elgar 2019) 6.

[39] Fekete (n 7) 131 speaks of 'the general scholarly attitude in the comparative law community' from which Frankenberg's scholarship differs.

[40] Conventional methods, according to this view, reproduce what can be coined as scholarly/scientific standards and 'the accepted conventions of an epistemic community,' Frankenberg (n 38) 8.

are not only neutral academic (or lawyerly) decisions but shaped by their political and ethical views.[41] In other words, there is no epistemic innocence if we are to believe the critics. In particular, Anglo-Eurocentrism is the target here as this branch of critical comparative law seeks to deconstruct it and to broaden comparative law's horizons.[42]

From this intellectual position the critical comparatist detects 'the moral deficit that comes with routinely managing similarities and "othering" the foreign'.[43] In lieu of being an alleged advantage, the basic approach of the legal scholar is a weakness, not a strength. The basic approach is what one might describe as traditional black-letter-law-oriented comparative law scholarship that 'would not use any approach other than the reading of statutes, cases, parliamentary debates, and doctrinal works, believing description and identification to be the final stages of the inquiry', as Esin Örücü puts it.[44] According to this view, the basic approach is something that the comparatist should seek to unlearn or at least to become aware of.

Instead of focusing on differences and similarities and attempting to explain them, the focal point is on critical thinking in a rather broad sense. Critical scholars seek to shake off the shackles of the legal profession and the tacit assumptions of narrow-minded legal doctrinalists. This way to grasp criticality is more demanding than mainstream scholarship has the stomach for. The traditional approach and epistemic assumptions of the professional lawyer do not suffice for the critical comparatist as the aims are more demanding. Nicola and Frankenberg explain this aim of modern comparative law by saying that:

> from a critical vantage point, laws and legal rules are meant to order and protect matter because they sustain domination and discrimination. So, critiques of law, including comparative law, intend to unmake that project and its interpretive and legitimizing framework of ideas in order to reveal its ideology.[45]

This way of thinking holds that law – and by extension mainstream comparative law – is not above suspicion but an influence that sustains domination and discrimination. As a result, mainstream's attempt to find 'better' solutions is an attempt to uphold existing invisible power structures. Critical comparative law, in turn, seeks to unmask these qualities by revealing the tacitly integrated assertions that lurk under the surface of formal law and the mundane work of legal professionals. This form of comparativism does not seek to help lawyers in their profession but urges them to conceive law through critical lenses. Or – as Mathias Siems describes the critical ethos – the mainstream 'comparatist is merely interested in the technical legal response to a specific situation' while the critical comparatist 'is interested in

[41] cf Siems (n 19) 164.
[42] Frankenberg (n 38) 15–19.
[43] Fernanda Nicola & Günter Frankenberg, *Comparative Law* (Edward Elgar 2024) 15.
[44] Örücü (n 9) 17.
[45] Nicola & Frankenberg (n 4) 2. If this view is accepted, then it becomes difficult to uphold the boundary demarcating between comparative, socio-legal, and critical legal studies. See Lizzy Willmington, 'Permeating the Boundaries' (2025) *Journal of Law and Society* doi.org/10.1111/jols.70006.

changing society permanently'.[46] To an extent, this echoes the division between goal-oriented and theoretical scholarship, discussed in chapter five.

For the discussion here it is beneficial to bear in mind that the collision between limited mainstream criticality and critical comparative law is a longstanding disagreement. Being a critical scholar is, no doubt, a question of scholarly identity. In the path of broader criticality of mainstream scholarship, there have been turns and moves. Nevertheless, I would argue that some ideas of critical comparative law have been adopted in comparative law scholarship of today. According to the analysis by Frankenberg and Nicola, critical turns, in essence, support comparatists' attempt to estrange themselves from their own epistemic home base. This is about epistemic distancing from one's own assumptions which has - paradoxically perhaps - always been also at the core of traditional comparative law in the form of debates on methodology. Critical and traditional are, in this sense two sides of the same coin. Turns from the mainstream have taken place through competing perspectives coming from the directions of language, culture, history, and decolonisation.[47] It should be apparent at this point that criticality is a call to see beyond formal law and conventional limits of what lawyers understand a legal system to include. In a manner of speaking, it is an invitation to try to become, in epistemic terms, the Other.

Critical moves, in turn, can be seen as coming from the broad direction of hermeneutics. These moves share common features in the sense that they seek to 'unravel the power/knowledge connection to demonstrate how comparative law reproduces colonial, patriarchal, cultural, and market hierarchies'.[48] So, instead of strengthening existing hierarchies, critical comparative law is supposed to make them visible and thus open to critical evaluation. I would suggest that this does not fall very far from the way the mainstream sees the outcomes of comparative law research, as hierarchies are essentially something that is 'worse', even though the critical comparatist may not say what would be 'better' options in terms of positive law. This reveals an interesting imperfection in critical comparative law in the sense that attacking against the mainstream makes it a negative version of the mainstream.[49] I have argued that by placing the focus on difference instead of similarity - which is the underlying idea of criticism - risks making critical comparative law merely a negation of the mainstream because its contrarianism forces it to react negatively to the mainstream's assumptions and ideas.[50] Like a shadow, it projects the mainstream as its negation. On the other hand, if one's criticism is fundamental - like that of Legrand - then it is not bound by mainstream's assumptions. The key difference, it would seem, between Frankenberg's

[46] Siems (n 19) 162.

[47] Frankenberg & Nicola (n 4) 498–99.

[48] ibid 500. This form of criticality has potentially a very wide area of use. See, eg, Utkirbek Kholmirzaev & Manuchehr Kudratov, 'Rethinking Legal Transfers' (2026) 39 *International Journal for Semiotics of Law* 47–78 doi.org/10.1007/s11196-025-10331-7 (analyses the epistemological foundations of legal transfers in Uzbekistan).

[49] cf Coendet (n 11) 55.

[50] See Jaakko Husa, 'Methodology of Comparative Law Today' (2006) 58 *Revue internationale de droit comparé* 1095–1117.

and Legrand's critique lies in their nature as the first seeks to demystify whereas the latter deliberately attempts to do the opposite.

Another problem is caused by a strong contrarian spirit that fails to see anything useful or good in mainstream's way of doing comparative law. As Balázs Fekete notes, this kind of contrarian scholarship puts the comparatist at centre stage of the inquiry, which is problematic if we see comparative law more as a communitarian effort.[51] I would tend to agree with Fekete's critical point as comparative law is not only something that is done by individuals separate from their scholarly and professional communities. Moreover, it would not be quite right to argue that strong contrarian criticism would be the only way to do critical comparative law. Comparative law is a diverse field even when it comes to forms of doing what one may describe as critical comparative law.[52] No one holds a monopoly in critical comparative law scholarship, even though some central figures attract most of the attention. If we look beyond the central figures of comparative law critique, then we can see other forms of critique that are not political or existential as to their nature.

For example, it is quite possible to argue that what Mark Van Hoecke calls deep-level comparative law can also be seen as a form of critical comparative law scholarship as it opposes the mainstream's shallowness in understanding similarities and differences.[53] Additionally, Catherine Valcke's scholarship – in which she combines comparative law with legal philosophy in order to grasp legal systems on their own terms – may be deemed critical as to its nature even though it, too, avoids extreme formulations.[54] In a similar fashion, one could also conceive Geoffrey Samuel's comparative law scholarship as being critical in the sense that instead of black-letter-law it focuses on the internal structure of legal knowledge and methodology.[55] On the other hand, none of these scholars is critical in the sense of Frankenberg.

Seen in a broader light, it is also quite possible to argue that Siems's scholarship is critical in its relation to the mainstream as he clearly seeks to bring in a much broader palette of methods and approaches than does conventional comparative law scholarship.[56] In a similar fashion, I would be ready to argue that my own views on comparative law are also critical in their relation to mainstream views of methodology, functionalism, interdisciplinarity, or legal families.[57] And it does not stop there. Much of Örücü's scholarship falls in one way or another under

[51] Balázs Fekete, 'The Power of Negative' (2023) 18 *JCL* 379–90, 389 [Review essay of Legrand's *Negative Comparative Law*, CUP 2022].

[52] See Esin Örücü, 'Something Old, Something New in Comparative Law' (2015) 1 *Journal of International and Comparative Law* 323–36, 332 (she mentions Van Hoecke, Valcke, and Samuel).

[53] See Mark Van Hoecke, 'Deep Level Comparative Law' in Mark Van Hoecke (ed), *Epistemology and Methodology of Comparative Law* (Hart Publishing 2004) 165–95.

[54] For an overview, see Catherine Valcke, *Comparing Law* (CUP 2018).

[55] For an overview, Geoffrey Samuel, *An Introduction to Comparative Law Theory and Method* (Hart Publishing 2014).

[56] A good illustration is his textbook (*Comparative Law* 2022, n 19) which fits well in the modern diversity-embracing and methodologically open-minded comparative study of law.

[57] See, eg, Jaakko Husa, *Interdisciplinary Comparative Law* (Edward Elgar 2022).

the banner of critical comparative law.[58] To mention one more example, the same goes for Pier-Giuseppe Monateri.[59] This list could be continued further but the point is that there are, indeed, many kinds of forms of criticality in comparative law scholarship. In the final analysis, however, all these forms of critical comparative law appear less combative or radical than those of Frankenberg's or Legrand's views. Others are, I dare say, less contrarian and more open to balanced takes. For contrarians, I suspect, balanced takes are merely a craven practice of sitting on the fence, though.[60]

III. Fusing the Forms of Criticality?

How to make sense of all of the above? I doubt that a clear picture would be possible to draw as what I have called mainstream and critical comparative law are entangled in various ways. Attempts to make sense of critique in comparative law are faced with the difficulty caused by intertwinement. Indeed, it is virtually impossible to find a form of comparative law that would be completely lacking any form of criticality altogether. Nevertheless, some signposts are possible to erect for the present purpose. These signposts are not exact but at least they illustrate the space that is situated in between the contrarian extremes. My simple point is that a grey area can be found between black and white. Indeed, one can see comparative law as a way to understand law critically without having extreme views.[61]

An extreme illustration of critical scepticism is Legrand's claim, based on his philosophical view of law in general, that an insurmountable epistemic barrier separates civil law and common law.[62] It would seem that comparatists agree on the existence of the barrier, whereas Legrand considers the barrier insurmountable. This is a philosophically demanding idea of law and the way it is presented is theoretically merciless and epistemologically unforgiving. This kind of contrarianism seems to rely on the idea of law's cultural singularity, which is the animating thought in deeply critical comparative law. The assumption – which I think is too extreme to survive the test of what we know from our own experience – is that foreign law will always remain something that cannot be really understood (in a demanding philosophical sense) as law fundamentally relates to a different legal culture.[63] As such, this claim is probably supported by most modern lawyers. Importantly, though, the conclusions that comparatists draw from this separateness

[58] For an overview, see Esin Örücü, *The Enigma of Comparative Law* (Brill 2004).

[59] For an overview, see Pier-Giuseppe Monateri, *Advanced Introduction to Comparative Legal Methods* (Edward Elgar 2021).

[60] For radical contrarians, even Frankenberg's views are too close to the mainstream. See Simone Glanert & Pierre Legrand, 'Law, Comparatism, and Epistemic Governance' (2017) 18 *German Law Journal* 701–20 ('Frankenberg's critique is not as resolute as ours, it is less radical than ours', ibid 717–18).

[61] See, eg, Horatia Muir-Watt, 'La fonction subversive de droit comparé' (2000) 51 *Revue international de droit comparé* 1041–52.

[62] Pierre Legrand, 'European Legal Systems Are Not Converging' (1996) 45 *ICLQ* 52–81.

[63] See Günter Frankenberg, 'Stranger Than Paradise' (1997) 2 *Utah Law Review* 259–74.

are quite different. Despite its shortcomings, I argue that the mainstream's underlying assumption on the possibility to understand foreign law makes sense and fits into the scholarly life of most comparative lawyers. I find it very much a possibility that a common-law contract law specialist may understand German contract law sufficiently well or that the Swedish constitutional comparatist may understand American constitutional law sufficiently well. The heavy lifting here is done by the word 'sufficiently'. As the saying goes, perfect is the enemy of good in the sense that pursuit of an ideal outcome may hinder reaching a satisfactory goal. Crucially, at the end of the day, when it comes to being a critical scholar what counts is what one does, not whether one defines oneself as critical or not.[64]

As the extreme ends of the debate are so distant from each other, the question is: can there be reconciliation between these takes on comparative law? Are we doomed to think that there is no escape, and the comparatist will always remain between Scylla and Charybdis? That one is either uncritical or critical seems like a contrarian exaggeration. The reality of what comparatists do, however, seems more prosaic than choosing between the extremes.

Whereas the mainstream can doubtless be blamed for its legal positivism-based naivety and lack of criticality, critical comparative law may be blamed for its unforgiving philosophical or ethical contrarianism. The lines of battle are drawn in between similarity and difference, which is one of the key dividing lines in comparative law scholarship. There is no need to embark on this division separately as it runs through the fabric of most of the collisions addressed in the above chapters, especially in terms of the West and the Rest and functionalism. Besides, there is an excellent analysis by Gerhard Dannemann about the confrontation between strands of comparative law stressing both similarities and differences.[65] He makes it clear in a level-headed manner that comparative law cannot focus only on similarities or differences and that there needs to be a balance between these two dimensions. The call for equilibrium by Danneman is itself based on a balanced view as he sees the need for both. As far as I can tell, his conclusion makes perfect sense in its avoidance of mainstream's simplicity and critical comparative law's extremism:

> it is often the right mixture of difference and similarity which makes comparative enquiries particularly attractive, regardless of the methodological approach pursued. Finding difference in similarity can be as fascinating as finding similarity in difference. If any general advice is to be offered, it is to keep an eye open for both similarity and difference...[66]

Perhaps there is a lesson here as a similar kind of attitude might work if we try to mitigate between both extremes. Once again, we need to revisit the ethos of

[64] cf Thomas Wilhelmsson, 'Contextually Critical' in Maria Gran-Farley (ed), *Voices on Law and Activism* (Iustus Förlag 2021) 247–65, 263.

[65] Gerhard Dannemann, 'Comparative Law: Study of Similarities or Differences?' in Reimann & Zimmermann (n 3) 390–422.

[66] ibid 421.

modern comparative law that has slowly learned – or is about to learn – to embrace all sorts of pluralisms. Globalisation of law has led, perhaps grudgingly, to an increasing acceptance of legal pluralism.[67] If we are to abandon the ambitions of the last decades of the twentieth century regarding the idea of comparative law as an independent discipline having a regal role in legal academia and fulfilling the stern requirements of being truly a form of science, there is also a possibility of allowing different levels of criticality. I find it hard to draw any conclusions on this as there is always the innate quality typical of the comparatist: the contrarian spirit. There will always be scholars who want to be more critical or more radical than others in their criticality. At this point the question of criticality is trapped in between extremes and the debate has, more or less, failed to achieve resolution or even significant forward movement. In my view, critical and mainstream are overlapping, creating an inextricable amalgam.

The issue of this chapter can be described – following Van Hoecke – as the collision between epistemological optimism and epistemological pessimism. The mainstream tends to be blind to epistemic problems as mainstreamers believe that the comparative lawyer is in no need of theory, and they are perfectly capable of determining what are 'better' solutions. Deeply critical comparatists, in turn, may deny the possibility of comparing or the possibility of legal harmonisation as laws are such elemental social constructs of each individual legal culture. The problem is that both these extreme views fail to provide methodology even though they do provide interesting and potentially fruitful views on comparative law.[68] Contrarianism, in this case, leaves the comparatist at the mercy of extreme choices. Moreover, it makes methodological pluralism and interdisciplinarity unattainable. There is a risk that without criticality and epistemic sensitivity the comparatist is left with the basic approach of the lawyer. With sceptical criticality the comparatist faces either epistemic impossibility or theoretical demands that are too much for the scholar who is a legal scholar as broadly defined in chapter one and not a social scientist, anthropologist, economist or someone other than a lawyer. The bar is set so high that it acts as discouragement.[69]

For someone seeing the entangled lines of battle from outside the field, all this may seem confusing. Some fuzziness is probably unavoidable as critique is a form of rhetoric codified via such factors as style, tone, and vocabulary, thus making it a fluid constellation of discontinuous overlapping modes of scholarship.[70] In the end, I doubt whether the overall picture would be any clearer for those taking part in the debates. We are, it would seem, locked in our positions. Comparatists stand their ground that is clear, but does it suffice in order to go forward? By way of conclusion, I hope that there would be increasing movement in the grey

[67] See for a more detailed discussion, Jaakko Husa, *Advanced Introduction to Law and Globalisation* (Edward Elgar 2018).

[68] Van Hoecke (n 53) 450; cf Husa (n 50).

[69] Sometimes this is explicitly expressed by arguing that comparative study of law is indeed not for everyone, see Pierre Legrand, 'How to Compare Now?' (1996) 16 Legal Studies 232–42, 239.

[70] cf Ancker & Felski (n 6) 3–4.

area between the contrarian ends. Very few of us are either thoroughly critical or staunchly conventional. Finally, it is worth noting that, like other legal scholars, the comparatist is also forced to deal with uncertainties and often just needs to muddle through fully knowing the imperfections. Nevertheless, this diagnosis may seem like normalisation and domestication of critique so that it becomes defanged and part of the mainstream.[71] As I will demonstrate in the next chapter, globalisation has brought challenges that go beyond conventional comparativism and contrarianism.

[71] cf ibid 13.

12

Globalisation and Comparativism – Out of the Trenches?

It has become evident in the preceding chapters that a growing number of modern comparative law scholars seek to go beyond positive law and to study law in context. It is not, however, thoroughly clear what studying law in context means, although it is possible to provide some signposts.[1] Instead of zooming in on legislation, case law, and doctrinal writings, contemporary scholars are relatively open to taking into account societal, political, economic, linguistic, historical, and technological factors. The epistemic boundaries have expanded. I have conceptualised this change in the above chapters by speaking of theoretical and methodological *pluralism* and accompanying *diversity*. In contrast to the comparativism of the past century, the openness is different even though some comparatists still prefer to define law – the object of comparison – in a narrow formalistically oriented manner. This is hardly unexpected because there is no shared paradigm. As noted in the above text, today's comparative law is in many ways a broad church.[2] This author does not regard the diversity of the field as necessarily an insurmountable problem; perhaps quite the contrary. My argument is that diversity can act as an antidote to contrarianism.

In part, some of the scholarly transformation can be explained by a growing tolerance among modern comparatists for methodological flexibility and advancements in our understanding of what comparative study of law can possibly include and what its relation is to neighbouring fields of research. In addition, development of cyberspace provides new possibilities, approaches, and available sources. One indication of increased tolerance is that interdisciplinarity has become almost

[1] One way of trying to see what this means is to see what kind of papers have been published in the *International Journal of Law in Context* (www.cambridge.org/core/journals/international-journal-of-law-in-context) or what kind of books have been published in the Cambridge University Press 'Law in Context' series (www.cambridge.org/core/series/law-in-context/387EA14AA111E65AB-0120DA893AFAFCB). Both of these forums also contain comparative law scholarship.

[2] See, eg, Jaakko Husa (ed), *A Research Agenda on Comparative Law* (Edward Elgar 2024); and Fernanda Pirie, 'Global Comparative Law?' (2024) 44 *Oxford Journal of Legal Studies* 506–24.

a fashionable aspect of comparative law.[3] How much of interdisciplinarity is lip service and how much of it really manifests in actual research is unclear, though.[4] However, in my view it would be insufficient to try to explain the transformation exclusively by internal factors and causes. The simple fact is that the sub-tribe of comparatists is not a huge crowd even among the tribe of legal scholars in general. Like law itself, comparative study of law also has context(s) as it needs to adapt to the living realities of law around the globe. Comparative law does not exist in a societal or political vacuum – as is, of course, the case with all study of law. There is one noteworthy difference, though. Because comparative law cannot restrict itself to one legal system only, it is perhaps more sensitive in detecting global change than is the case with nationally oriented fields of legal study dealing mostly with one system only. Political, economic, cultural, and technological changes in the four corners of the world are reflected in law and by extension to comparative study of law regardless of the comparatist's scholarly preferences. Functionalists, contextualists, formalists, realists and all alike face essentially the same challenge, even though their responses are not identical.

What kind of changes are we talking about? Some of the changes in the contexts of law are fundamental in terms of their nature. We are not speaking of mere trifles here, that much is clear. For instance, when we read the scholarship of the past century, we can see that there is at least one elemental key assumption concerning *what* comparative law *can* compare. Past comparatists of all sorts assumed that legal systems – formal law – of states were the primary objects of comparative research. The units that were compared – with the exception of religious legal traditions, perhaps – were those of states.[5] This implied assumption – the overpowering centrality of the state – has been in retreat since the late twentieth century.[6] It needs to be pointed out that changes concern not only law but also, and more importantly, economy, rapidly evolving technology, world politics, and the changing climate.[7] Importantly, we should not overlook the undeniable fact that states have not disappeared even though their significance has to an extent done so. As Alessandro Somma puts it, '[e]ven in the times of globalisation the role of the State is not truly marginal'.[8] States are still powerful and significant legal actors

[3] I discuss this in more detail in Jaakko Husa, *Interdisciplinary Comparative Law* (Edward Elgar 2022) ch 1.

[4] See, eg, Christoph Engel, 'Challenges in the Interdisciplinary Use of Comparative Law' (2021) 69 *AJCL* 777–97.

[5] However, even though when religion was taken into account in macro-comparative law it has always been about the laws of others, as I argue in Jaakko Husa, 'Comparative Law and Christianity' (2024) 44 *Oxford Journal of Legal Studies* 54–73. Yet, as Pirie (n 2) 18 rightly points out '[c]omparative legal scholars have hardly dipped their toes into the vast and lightly charted waters of non-state laws'.

[6] There is no need here to engage with what can be coined as the Westphalian understanding of what states are and how they ought to interact according to public international law. For discussion on this see, eg, Stéphane Beaulac, 'The Westphalian Legal Orthodoxy' (2000) 2 *Journal of the History of International Law* 148–77; and Andreas Osiander, 'Sovereignty, International Relations, and the Westphalian Myth' (2001) 55 *International Organization* 251–87.

[7] cf George Mousorakis, *Comparative Law and Legal Traditions* (Springer 2019) 43.

[8] Alessandro Somma, *Introduzione al diritto comparato*, 3rd edn (Giappichelli 2025) 95.

but, in terms of creating norms, they are no longer the sole factors on the globe, due to globalisation.[9] This state of affairs changes things for legal comparativists' endeavour, too.[10]

I. Changing World

The withdrawal of the state as the sole creator of law has not gone unnoticed by comparatists. Consequently, it has been suggested by Mathias Siems that comparative law should extend its scope to objects not traditionally included.[11] This sensible suggestion recommends comparatists reach out in order to avoid theirs becoming a niche subject that, more or less, dwells in the past. According to this view, comparative law methods and insights can contribute to several areas of contemporary legal scholarship, including such fields as legal history and international law but also more distant fields, for example sociology and cultural studies.[12] Nevertheless, the most important factor that has more or less compelled comparative law to expand its reach is a phenomenon that has to do with the erosion of the state and the rise of globalised normativities and so-called transnational law.[13] Globalisation has generated novel objects for comparatists to compare in the form of different normativities or regimes, ranging from local to national and from regional to global.[14] Rapidly evolving AI is also one of the globally influential changes that comparative law cannot hide from, for better or for worse.

We need to tread carefully here in order to avoid exaggeration. Globalisation as a way to conceptualise the global transformation of law is not free of problems, but it does sketch certain features that are of special importance for the comparatist.[15] Some speak of globalisation, others of transnationalisation. The relationship between globalisation and transnationalisation is unclear as the processes of globalisation lead, in turn, to the growth of what one might label as transnational

[9] It needs to be kept in mind that global and globalisation are not innocent conceptualisations. It can be argued that they are anchored in a Eurocentric legacy that conceives space and time in a culturally conditioned manner. See Nikolas Rajkovic, 'What Is 'the Global'?' (2025) 21 *International Journal of Law in Context* 203–12.

[10] No matter what kinds of conclusions one draws, changes pose challenge to comparative law as the world of law has become more 'liquid'. See Domenico di Micco, 'La comparazione alla prova del mondo che cambia' (2020) 22 *Diritto pubblico comparato ed europeo* 3–25.

[11] See Mathias Siems, 'The Power of Comparative Law' (2019) 67 *AJCL* 861–88.

[12] ibid 887–88.

[13] See Jaakko Husa, 'Introduction: Globalisation, Comparison, and Legal Scholarship' (2021) 16 *JCL* 458–63 (introduction of a thematic issue with articles by Geoffrey Samuel, Matteo Nicolini, Michele Graziadei, Juha Raitio, Jennifer Hendry, and Paul du Plessis).

[14] Legal Globalisation refers here to the relative recent wave of legal globalisation, see Duncan Kennedy, 'Three Globalizations of Law and Legal Thought: 1850–2000' in David Trubek & Alvaro Santos (eds), *The New Law and Economic Development* (CUP 2006) 19–73.

[15] cf Mathias Siems, *Comparative Law*, 3rd edn (CUP 2022) 285–86. On definition, see Jaakko Husa, *Advanced Introduction to Law and Globalisation* (Edward Elgar 2018) ch 1 ('Legal globalisation means that organised normativities are de-territorialised, hence, power becomes networked and social systems like law are interrelated on a global scale', 5–6).

law or global law.[16] These novel post-Westphalian forms of law challenge state law even though they do not 'emanate from sovereign will', as Neil Walker puts it.[17] AI seems to accelerate these developments as it blurs all sorts of borders and opens new possibilities – but also potential threats.

As it is not the aim of my analysis to define globalisation or transnational law, it hence suffices to register that in today's world different normativities interact with each other, transforming the scene of comparative study of law from that of the twentieth century.[18] It is not clear what the relationship between global or transnational law is with comparative law or international law. That said, it is nonetheless evident that today's situation is different from that of the 1980s or 1990s.[19] Pluralism and diversity present a far more crucial dimension than they had in the past century. This is not to say that there was no legal pluralism before; bur, rather, to say that it is more commonplace and visible today, which in turn makes it increasingly difficult for the comparatist to leave it out.

It is, I admit, an exceptionally tall order to try to make sense of the numerous changes that influence comparative study of law. Yet it would seem possible to argue that the transformation involves ramifications of at least two kinds. First, comparatists have faced the need to reach beyond the legal orders of states. Second, those legal scholars who have not been much interested in comparative study of law in the past have now faced pressure to abandon – at least in part – the epistemic ivory towers of their home legal systems and enter into a new world. For the comparatist, these changes are essential. Indeed, one could argue that differences between legal systems (broadly understood) are the raison d'être of comparative law. For the comparatist the issue is crucial as the question is: what is there left to compare if transnational normativities create ever-expanding convergence? What if we end up having legal McDonaldization?[20] The resulting enigma is peculiar. As Horatia Muir Watt says, the relationship of comparative study of law to globalisation is essentially paradoxical. One of the reasons why it is paradoxical is because it 'could be seen either as the death of the discipline, or as an unsuspected source of renewal'.[21] A boon and a bane, if you like.

All this is at least relatively recent. The influence of globalisation on comparative law was not really an issue during the past century and it was only at the very end of the century that comparatists started to consider its impact on comparative law.[22]

[16] cf Mousorakis (n 7) 43–44.

[17] Neil Walker, 'Out of Place and Out of Time' (2010) 14 *Edinburgh Law Review* 13–46, 36.

[18] 'The relationship between law and globalisation is so multifaceted that the legal literature on this topic is extensive and fuels endless debate on the 'usefulness and harm' of these phenomena', Roberto Scarciglia, *Methods and Legal Comparison* (Edward Elgar 2023) 157.

[19] I discuss this in more detail in Jaakko Husa, 'Global Law and Comparative International Law' in Mathias Siems & Robert Schütze (eds), *Comparative International Law* (Hart Publishing 2026) 309–26.

[20] The term comes originally from George Ritzer who presented it in the early 1980s in his article 'The McDonaldization of Society' (1983) 6 *Journal of American Culture* 100–7.

[21] Horatia Muir Watt, 'Globalization and Comparative Law' in Mathias Reimann & Reinhard Zimmermann (eds), *The Oxford Handbook of Comparative Law*, 2nd edn (OUP 2019) 599–623, 599.

[22] See, eg, William Twining, 'Globalization and Comparative Law' (1999) 6 *Maastricht Journal of Comparative Law* 217–43.

International law scholars were alerted well before comparatists started to pay attention.[23] It was also realised early in the sociology of law that law plays different roles in the processes of globalisation.[24] From the late 1900s and the first decades of this century, globalisation and its relationship to comparative law gradually became an issue that increasingly found its way into comparative law scholarship.[25] I shall discuss the relationship in the following by first addressing the idea according to which we are all comparatists now and then move on to scrutinise if this really is the case. Though far from an exhaustive analysis, I hope that quick glances at the opposing views will shed light on these two aspects. Finally, I seek to strike a balance between these two colliding takes as to the impact of globalisation on comparative study of law and what it means for comparative law contrarianism.

II. We are all Comparatists – the More the Merrier?

Comparative law scholars have always been keen to define who is a comparatist and who is not. We have been tribal for a long time. Globalisation adds a new layer to this discussion. One does not need to be a globalist or someone who opposes globalisation – an anti-globalist if you prefer – in order to discuss globalisation, because its influence is hard to avoid. Indeed, (comparative or international) law is certainly no exception in this regard. The pressures that create the need for comparative law to adapt and improvise are well-known and the basic observation is that comparing domestic systems of the nation states or common law and civil law no longer appear sufficient for studying law comparatively. One might feel tempted to claim that this has always been the case. Nevertheless, I believe that some of the challenges are novel. The world of law has always been complex but today it is even more complex than was the case before, which in turn causes pressures for the comparatist. Roberto Scarciglia describes these pressures as follows:

[23] A seminal paper was published in the early 1990s by Martin Shapiro, 'The Globalization of Law' (1993) 1 *Indiana Journal of Global Legal Studies* 37–64 ('By globalization of law, we might refer to the degree to which the whole world lives under a single set of legal rules. Such a single set of rules might be imposed by a single coercive actor, adopted by global consensus, or arrived at by parallel development in all parts of the globe. Although the end of bipolarity and the cold war brings some comfort, surely we have not moved very far toward a regime of international law either through the establishment of a single global law giver and enforcer or through a strong nation-state consensus', ibid 37).

[24] See Klaus Röhl & Stefan Magen, 'Die Rolle des Rechts im Prozeß der Globalisierung' (1996) 17 *Zeitschrift für Rechtssoziologie* 1–57.

[25] See, eg, Annelise Riles, 'Wigmore's Treasure Box' (1999) 40 *Harvard International Law Journal* 221–83; Jean-Bernard Auby, 'Globalisation et droit comparé' (2006) 8 *European Journal of Law Reform* 43–52; Richard Buxbaum, 'Comparative Law as a Bridge Between the Nation-State and the Global Economy' (2009) 1 *Duke Law Center for International & Comparative Law Occasional Papers* 63–78; Maurice Adams, 'Comparative Law in a Globalizing World' (2012) 17 *Tilburg Law Review* 263–68; Mary Ann Glendon, 'Comparative Law in the Age of Globalization' (2014) 52 *Duquesne Law Review* 1–24; Ralf Michaels, 'Transnationalizing Comparative Law' (2016) 23 *Maastricht Journal of European and Comparative Law* 352–58; Jaakko Husa, 'Global Law and Comparative Law' (2017) 12 *JCL* 461–71; Michele Graziadei, 'What Does Globalisation Mean for the Comparative Study of Law?' (2021) 16 *JCL* 511–36; and Pirie (n 2).

> The leading cause of this insufficiency regards many heterogeneous sources that operate – and overlap – in the same legal space: supra-state and non-state, such as religious law, transnational law, chthonian law, customary law and other forms of *soft law*.[26]

The circumstances succinctly described by Scarciglia are familiar among the ranks of comparatists. We are aware that the world of law has new inhabitants, or at least inhabitants we did not consider in the past. Today is different in this regard. Mentions of legal globalisation or transnational normativities are not difficult to find from papers and books published by comparatists.[27] As Victor Ramraj points out, comparative law's traditional focus on state law is challenged by the rise of transnational regulators of which many are non-state actors.[28] This gives rise to certain premonitions of which some seem virtually self-evident. If the twenty-first century really is – as once envisaged by Esin Örücü – the era of comparative law, then globalisation is perhaps the main overall theme of this same century as every comparatist faces the challenges it brings to comparative study of law.[29] In fairness, some comparatists have shown more forethought than others, whereas many have remained less vocal about globalisation's impact on comparative law as a field. Regardless, any textbook on comparative law in the 2020s cannot exclude globalisation without being insensitive or downright blind.

So, globalisation exerts its influence on comparative law scholarship. The most interesting – and seemingly also the most influential – scholar has been William Twining, who has consistently claimed that in the world of today all study of law is in one way or another cosmopolitan.[30] I take it that 'cosmopolitan' in this context means pretty much the same as global.[31] Twining is making not merely a theoretical argument, as he builds from the fact that legal scholars, law students, and practitioners regularly need to consult sources, materials and ideas developed in various jurisdictions. Sources cross borders and, as a result, lawyers need to follow suit. Importantly, these sources of legal information originate from more than one legal culture. Accordingly, Twining holds, '[i]n that sense, we are all comparatists now'.[32]

[26] Scarciglia (n 18) 96.

[27] Of course, comparative law is not the only non-substantive law-focused field that is under the influence of globalisation. For example, legal history and legal theory are also influenced. See, eg, See Thomas Duve, 'Global Legal History: A Methodological Approach', Oxford Handbooks Online (DOI: 10.1093/oxfordhb/9780199935352.013.2); and Mikhail Xifaras, 'The Global Turn in Legal Theory' (2016) 29 *Canadian Journal of Law & Jurisprudence* 215–43.

[28] Victor V Ramraj, 'Transnational Regulation' in Mathias Siems & Po Jen Yap (eds), *The Cambridge Handbook of Comparative Law* (CUP 2024) 575–98, 575–76.

[29] Esin Örücü, *Enigma of Comparative Law* (Martinus Nijhoff 2004) 216.

[30] More about Twining, see David Sugarman, 'William Twining: The Man Who Radicalised the Middle Ground' (2020) 16 *International Journal of Law in Context* 475–80 (review of Twining's *Jurist in Context: A Memoir* 2019).

[31] Importantly, 'Cosmopolitanism rejects the view that there is an irreconcilable gap between "us" and "them", which would make it impossible to understand foreign ideas and culture', Mathias Siems & Po Jen Yap, 'Introduction' in Siems and Yap (n 28) 1–11, 6.

[32] William Twining, *Globalisation and Legal Theory* (Butterworths 2000) 155. More recent formulation: 'We are in an important sense all comparatists now, even if most of us lack sophistication in comparative method. Comparative law is increasingly more like a way of life than a marginal subject for a few specialists', William Twining, *Globalisation and Legal Scholarship* (Wolf 2009) 31.

The underlying idea, if I understand it correctly, is that the borders between legal systems and other forms of normativities have been weakened, thus creating an overlap that does not abide by the legal ideas and doctrines of the past century and our innate focus on the state. Legal systems and all sorts of normativities have become porous as to their nature. In turn, this porosity has generated a growth of non-nationally focused forms of legal scholarship. The same, more or less, has taken place outside the circles of comparatists because legal scholars seek to create distance between non-comparatist legal scholars and classic West-oriented international law and its underlying assumptions.[33] Growth of cyberspace and – more recently – AI have accelerated globalisation by making the flow of information smoother than it was before, even if anti-globalisation movements have gained momentum in other fields and political decision-making. Advancing technology has enabled faster communication and the flow of information across borders between legal systems, languages, and cultures.

It might be tempting to read Twining so that he would end up suggesting that comparative law as a field would be rendered somewhat useless. But this is not what Twining means in saying that all lawyers and legal scholars are now comparatists. He offers several justifications for the continued existence of comparative law, even in a globalised world. First, he points out that becoming a genuine comparatist requires 'a long apprenticeship and special expertise and sensibilities', but also ability to respect theory. This seems like an impediment concerning comparative law's ability to grow significantly from its current status. Second, because a scholar cannot truly be learned in many legal traditions or systems, there is always room for country expertise (see chapter seven above). Third, and most importantly, Twining outlines a special role for comparativism – because comparing is a central factor in terms of our ability to understand cosmopolitanised law.[34] For him, comparativism and globalisation appear to go hand in hand, even though not perhaps at the same pace. Instead of seeking to justify the scholarly position of comparative law as an academic field, Twining underlines a more general need for legal scholars of all kinds to think about law comparatively. I find it easy to agree with Twining's cosmopolitan diagnosis of law and the role it assigns to legal comparativism in general. Even if one were to dislike globalisation, his point is difficult to fully ignore.

In essence, Twining seems to suggest that, even though all legal scholars today are in some ways comparatists, they are not necessarily comparative law experts. As such, this makes sense as it is based on the simple observation that there are many kinds of overlapping normativities in the world. Choices of approach differ depending on what field one studies; the constitutional comparatist may deviate from the private law comparatist or comparative legal historian, and so on. Accordingly, there are many kinds of legal scholars equipped with varying

[33] One example is TWAIL scholarship. See for more detailed discussion, Anthony Anghie, 'Rethinking International Law' (2023) 34 *European Journal of International Law* 7–112.

[34] Twining (n 32) 49–50.

methodological toolboxes. As far as I can see, it would indeed be hard to convincingly argue against this view. It is not difficult to conceive Twining's points as belonging to a new kind of comparativist ethos that embraces the legal pluralism and diversity of law. Notwithstanding, this is not the kind of comparativism that eminent scholars of the twentieth century were hoping to construct. To be sure, this is not about the mature science of comparative law that the great scholars of the 1970s and 1980s dreamt about. Instead of a unified field, an autonomous legal discipline, all sorts of comparisons are taking place in different thematic areas.

In a broad sense, I count Twining among the comparative law pluralists, even though he tends to approach the issue from the point of view of legal theory. Then again, avoiding legal theory while discussing these issues seems virtually impossible. To that end, here we stumble once again on the issue of what one means by 'law'. We say that law is globalising – but what is it that we mean by 'law'? For the comparatist, there is no escape from this question as crossing the borders of legal systems forces them to define law in one way or another as they must decide what to include in their research and what to leave out. Moreover, today this is more complicated an issue than merely distinguishing between law-in-books and law-in-action (see chapter two). Globalisation has blurred the distinctions that comparatists have held dear for decades. As such, this may be beneficial for the attempt to study law comparatively and let the field grow from below instead of simply following the great names of the previous century.

How to understand law from the viewpoint of comparative law is not, I want to stress, a straightforward issue: subtleties are involved in the discussion. Even within the ranks of those who embrace non-traditional comparative law, there are views expressing a worry about defining law too broadly and being overly pluralistic. For example, Fernanda Pirie is concerned about what the law is that the comparatist should compare. She says that this issue becomes relevant when indigenous and non-state orders are studied. She continues by saying that '[a] huge body of literature has focused on the concept of "legal pluralism", which many, including myself, consider expands the category of law too far'.[35] What does that view tell us? Her point needs to be placed in context, though. This is not an argument flowing from conventional or mainstream legal comparativism, but an argument made by someone who speaks for broadening comparative law towards anthropology and legal history.[36] Regardless, she seems to be worried about going too far. She is not alone in this concern. Even those who seek to expand the scope of conventional comparative law are not ready to step too far from the mainstream. In a sense, this seems like a kind of unwillingness to collide too strongly with what lawyers in general understand by 'law'. In many ways, the same hesitation lies behind the impediments that concern interdisciplinarity in comparative law.[37] How far from conventional comparative law's assumptions are we ready to depart and still claim

[35] Pirie (n 2) 17.
[36] See, eg, Fernanda Pirie, 'From the Local to Global' in Husa (n 2) 39–60.
[37] I discuss this at length in Husa (n 3).

to be legal scholars is not an easy question to answer in a globalising world. In fairness, it was not easy even before, even if we might have believed so.

III. We are not all Comparatists – the Fewer they are, the Better they Fare?

Another way to meet the challenge of globalisation and blurring of borders embraces a narrower view of what amounts to 'law' as an object of study in comparative law. I interpret this reasoning to flow from the urge of comparatists to ensure that what they do does not drift too far away from law as a profession. This is a more subtle idea than law-in-books thinking entails. Yet, surprisingly, at least some of what Pirie argues appears to echo ideas belonging to conventional comparative law's propensity to define law rather narrowly. This view, even though modern and apparently free of the past century's somewhat simplified ideas, grows from a suspicion of pluralism gone too far. As if we would seek to erect at least some wall between law and non-legal fields (social sciences and other non-legal fields alike). Then again, though, the attempt to build walls seems to contradict the diversity-embracing spirit of today's comparative law.

Catherine Valcke – who is not against legal pluralism as a movement stretching beyond the traditional boundaries of law – recognises certain perils associated with legal pluralism.[38] All of these also concern the issue of globalisation's impact on comparative study of law. In other words, how much pluralism suffices and what would amount to a step too far? The question here is not whether globalisation influences law but how the comparatist should take it into account. To that end, Valcke identifies possible perils concerning the reach of pluralist views of law and their potential impact on comparative study of law. I read these perils against the backdrop of Twinings's idea on everyone being a comparatist in a changed world, as these two appear contradictory.

The first peril concerns avoidance of definitions by pluralists as they are, so she argues, 'known to dislike definitions.'[39] As far as I can see, this is by and large an accurate general observation about legal pluralism scholarship. Her critique assumes that definitions are unavoidable and, moreover, they do not constrain comparative study of law as such. In Valcke's view – which makes much sense to me – definitions are contestable propositions that in fact sharpen the understanding. Indeed, just by declaring oneself a pluralist does not free the comparatist from the necessity of telling what it is that one counts as 'law'. This is an epistemic risk worth identifying. Now, if accepting pluralism would mean surrendering to an 'everything goes' type of thinking, then it would indeed be a step too far. Accepting legal pluralism does not need to mean embracing full-blown relativism.

[38] Catherine Valcke, 'Three Perils of Legal Pluralism' in Seán Patrick Donlan & Lukas Heckendorn Urscheler (eds), *Concepts of Law* (Routledge 2014) 123–35.
[39] ibid 123.

The second peril concerns what Valcke calls the straw man syndrome. This concerns the tendency of legal pluralists to paint a picture of state law as if it were some kind of monolith or a rigid and unidimensional monster. The problem is that studying non-state law is not possible without taking into account how it is connected to the law of the state or official law.[40] These forms of law are interconnected. In essence, this idea is an important dimension of legal pluralist thinking, as much of it seems to be animated by a contrarian spirit in terms of the centrality of state law.

The third peril – also based on a one-sided view of formal law – holds that legal pluralism is not a very fruitful way to describe different systems as it is essentially unable to tell different forms of political organisation apart.[41] This, in turn, leads to a situation in which the comparatist conceives different systems through 'individualistic legality', which allegedly fails to act as an epistemic basis of comparative study because laws that are compared are not individualistic. Hence, 'legal pluralism cannot be recast as individual legality because, if it is truly individual it is not "legal", and if it is truly legal it is not "plural"'.[42] It may be the case that her critique finds its target less perfectly in terms of moderate comparative law pluralism, but it does make a fair point as it recognises some of the innate weaknesses of legal pluralism. Valcke's critique well hits the mark of radical legal pluralism as crafted by John Griffiths in the mid-1980s. Be that as it may, for the comparatist legal pluralism presents a challenge because dealing with non-state created normativities has never been the strongest feature of comparative law.[43] As soon as the comparatist leaves the comfort of their own law, they start to nurture epistemic doubts. For good reason, I would say.

In order to address the issue, it is useful to look back and see what Griffiths originally argued. For him, legal pluralism was, first and foremost, a theoretical framework that stands in opposition to what he coined as 'legal centralism'.[44] He collided with what one can consider a mainstream view about the law. Legal pluralism, as outlined by him, essentially opposes the idea according to which 'law is and should be the law of the state, uniform for all persons, exclusive of all other law, and administered by a single set of state institutions.'[45] The result is a non-normative legal theory that seeks to catch the empirical reality of any given system without being compromised by the normative fictions upheld by legal centralism. The core claim is that '[l]egal centralism is a myth, an ideal, a claim, an illusion.'[46] In my reading, this view entails a socio-legally turbo-boosted law-in-action type of theoretical framework. More recent forms of legal pluralism, like those of Brian

[40] ibid 129.
[41] ibid 131.
[42] ibid 132.
[43] See, eg, Somma (n 8) 33–39.
[44] John Griffiths, 'What is Legal Pluralism?' (1986) 24 *Journal of Legal Pluralism* 1–55. See also William Twining, 'Diffusion of Law' (2004) 42 *Journal of Legal Pluralism* 1–45, 14–15.
[45] Griffiths (n 44) 3.
[46] ibid 4.

Tamanaha, share much of the thinking with Griffiths but seem less combative.[47] Besides, Tamanaha's scholarship is later, hence he has also been able to take globalisation into account when writing about legal pluralism. The original formulation was not advised by globalised normativities.

For the comparatist, the collision with legal centralism is an important idea, no matter what one thinks about it, because it turns the focus from the state to other normativities not produced by states. Understood in this manner, legal pluralism is fundamentally a contrarian take as it presents an antithesis to conceiving law through an image of what law ought to be according to state-centred Western ideas. Importantly, legal pluralism is a contrarian concept that is today more pertinent than in the 1980s when the processes of globalisation had only started to get going:

> The legal reality of the modern state is not at all that of the tidy, consistent, organized ideal so nicely captured in the common identification of 'law' and 'legal system', but that legal reality is rather an unsystematic collage of inconsistent and overlapping parts.[48]

It is easy to detect that this view means taking a distance from what one might label as lawyer's law and a conventional view of the legal profession. The argument here is close to what Tamanaha has concurrently claimed: 'The longstanding vision of a uniform and monopolistic law that governs a community is plainly obsolete'.[49] What to make of this contrarian critique?

It seems possible to conceive legal pluralism in its relationship to conventional comparative law as a belligerent matrix that challenges some of the inborn ideas of a state-centred vision of what law is and what it should be. In the globalising world the anti-centrist view of law seems fruitful for the comparatist as it allows freedom from the limits of conventional views on law.[50] Consequently, the comparatist is able to take the contexts of law into account.

However, the problem with legal pluralism is that it is not a clear concept and seems to allow great room for flexibility even though its spirit seems to fit the age of globalising legalities. As Twining has noted, 'literature on legal pluralism is very diverse. It is dangerous to generalize about it, given the variety of its intellectual roots'.[51] Despite its obvious shortcomings, for the contemporary comparatist legal pluralism seems to have value as a broad methodological guideline that 'is broad enough to capture simple and complex legal configurations'.[52] The downside of legal pluralism, as handy as it may be, is that it is a very broad conceptualisation and seems to offer very little for practically oriented legal minds. To that end, even moderate legal pluralism pushes and stretches the boundaries of 'law' further

[47] See, eg, Brian Z Tamanaha, *Legal Pluralism Explained* (OUP 2021).

[48] Griffiths (n 44) 4.

[49] Brian Z Tamanaha, 'Understanding Legal Pluralism' (2008) 30 *Sydney Law Review* 375–411, 409.

[50] There are also views according to which globalisation causes the need for comparative law to become 'more scientific', Mousorakis, (n 7) 44.

[51] William Twining, 'Normative and Legal Pluralism' (2010) 20 *Duke Journal of International and Comparative Law* 473–517, 488.

[52] Franz von Benda-Beckmann, 'Who's Afraid of Legal Pluralism?' (2002) 42 *Journal of Legal Pluralism* 37–82, 40.

than conventional comparative law scholarship is able to approve. On the other hand, it seems to fit well in the study of globalised normativities as an underlying research-related mindset. Is this a cul-de-sac type of situation?

IV. Something Old, Something New, Something Comparative?

There is no point in trying to avoid the obvious: the world of law today does not seem too well organised, with consequences for all forms of studying law. Whatever we may mean by global law or globalised normativities, it seems indisputable that we are dealing with a fractured, fluid, permeable, and polycentric form of law different from traditional state law.[53] Because of its very nature, comparative law finds itself on the front line facing the changes. Staying stubbornly in the Westphalian trenches seems fruitless. Views differ on globalisation and its impact on comparative law. Some of these differing views collide with each other, while others are situated in between and stir no debate among comparatists. What is clear, nevertheless, is that '[g]lobalisation is of natural interest for comparative lawyers', as Siems notes.[54] There is no going around this simple fact even though much of comparative law would still frequently limit itself to state law.[55] From another point of view, one may conceive globalisation and transnationalisation as an anomaly that conventional state-bound comparative law has faced in this century.[56] At the very least, it has generated an epistemic shake-up. But the dice are still in the air.

At least two contradictory ideas are at play here. On the one hand, globalisation tends to impose a single legal-cultural model on the whole globe. Potentially, this is like a dream come true for harmonisers seeking legal unity across borders. Globalisation, understood in terms of harmonisation, contains a whiff of neo-colonialism.[57] For pluralists embracing diversity, this is no doubt a hard pill to swallow. On the other hand, the striving towards similarity is met with more pluralistic views that conceive law as being in dialogue with transnational, intercultural, and multilingual contexts.[58] These two views seem – at least at first sight – somewhat incompatible, as if comparativism's innate contrarianism would be categorically unavoidable.

Should one adopt a narrower view of law, then globalising normativities may be seen as a tool (see chapter three) to enhance globalising tendencies and

[53] See Larry Catá Backer, 'The Structural Characteristics of Global Law for the 21st Century' (2012) 17 *Tilburg Law Review* 177–99.

[54] Siems (n 15) 286.

[55] cf Uwe Kischel, *Comparative Law* (OUP 2019) 869.

[56] cf Balázs Fekete, *Paradigms in Modern European Comparative Law* (Hart Publishing 2021) 162.

[57] See Anthony Diala, 'Comparative Indigenous Law' in Siems & Yap (n 28) 693–712, 712.

[58] Elena Ioriatti, 'Comparative Law Method and Legal Formants' in Luca Siliquini-Cinelli, Davide Gianti & Mauro Balestrieri (eds), *The Grand Strategy of Comparative Law* (Routledge 2024) 39–54, 41.

harmonisation of laws.[59] To that end, comparative law would remain merely a tool for creating more uniformity. To put it more prosaically, this would diminish comparative law into a scythe of uniformity that cuts away legal diversity. Personally – I freely admit – such a future would be highly undesirable as I do not envisage the comparatist as the grim reaper of legal cultural diversity. Along similar lines, Geoffrey Samuel makes an important point in saying that linking globalisation and the future of comparative law would reflect a profound misunderstanding of contemporary comparative law.[60] Alternatively, one may see globalisation more in terms of a challenge for the comparatist because it poses diversity-generated interdisciplinary challenges.[61] A legal doctrinal approach alone has become more insufficient than ever it was. Accordingly, nationally forged doctrine is no longer – if it ever was – able to offer refuge to the comparatist if we truly live in a world of multiple overlapping normative communities.[62]

To be sure, challenges are not in short supply. Some of them have to do with substance, others concern the methods that comparatists are supposed to apply when trying to grasp new non-state normativities. In a world where humanity faces many thorny issues – ranging from climate change to migration and from wars to pandemics – both of these views are fused as both practical regulatory needs as well as deeper legal-cultural needs mean having to conceive law differently from the ideas of the past (twentieth) century. Some issues may be approached with the help of AI and the opportunities it offers, but at the end of the day it is hard indeed to replace the value added that creative and innovative comparative law can bring to the table. It may be the case – as Lutz-Christian Wolff suggests – that much future comparative law work will be AI-based.[63] This will not, I maintain, render comparative law obsolete, even though it will most likely bring new tools to the comparatists' toolbox. Comparative law's way of conceiving globalising law is not to conceive it as a field of law but as a way of grasping law free from borders and the doctrinal shackles of both international and domestic law.

There are at least two kinds of contributions that comparative law and comparatists can offer in terms of these issues. First, comparative law involves – as Twining has underlined for decades – talking comparatively about the importance of conceiving law and various forms of normativities. This, however, requires the comparatist to accept at least some of the underlying ideas of pluralism. There is no need to commit to radical legal pluralism even while accepting that some of its ramifications are virtually inevitable at the present time. Nevertheless, some sort of epistemic broadening is needed even if one would not eagerly embrace global legal pluralism. Moving beyond the conventional focus on state-based legal systems

[59] cf Eric Tjong Tin Tai, 'Global Law' in Jan Smits, Jaakko Husa, Catherine Valcke & Madalena Narciso (eds), *Elgar Encyclopedia of Comparative Law*, Vol 2 (Edward Elgar 2023) 171–76, 175.

[60] Geoffrey Samuel, 'Comparative Law and Epistemology' (2021) *JCL* 464–86, 486.

[61] See also Scarciglia (n 18) 160.

[62] cf Paul Schiff Berman, Global Legal Pluralism (CUP 2012) 3.

[63] Lutz-Christian Wolff, 'Artificial Intelligence ante portas' (2019) 7 *Chinese Journal of Comparative Law* 484–504.

and, in one way or another, acknowledging the existence of non-state actors and norms that also exert a regulatory influence is something that modern comparative law cannot avoid without becoming obsolete. As we saw above, this is all but a problem-free way to proceed, because pluralism is not a panacea.

Second, and more importantly, comparative law offers a critical contribution to globalising law and study of foreign legal systems. In one way or another, pluralism is a necessary part of what Twining argued about globalisation and the need for comparative law to abandon the epistemic safety of legal systems of Western conceptions of law and legality. This was addressed in chapter six above and there is no need to repeat what was said there. Another dimension that I find important – if not imperative – to take into account is the critical contribution that comparative law encompasses. Criticality refers here to both traditional and 'postmodern' forms of comparative law scholarship.

So, where are we with the claim that we are all comparatists now? There are reasons to believe that globalisation – or, if you prefer, transnationalisation – of law does not render comparative law useless. To be sure, the issue lies deeper than recognising new non-state bodies of law such as the new *lex mercatoria*, *lex sportiva* or *lex informatica*.[64] Moreover, while AI may change many things, it will probably not existentially threaten the endeavour of grasping law comparatively. Ralf Michaels notes – rightly in my view – that reports on the demise of comparative law are greatly exaggerated.[65] He notes that the critique of twentieth-century comparative law's parochialism is relevant even today, but he continues by saying that this is not enough for today's comparative law. In short, globalisation has raised the bar for what it means to study law comparatively, whereas technological developments may have made some of the endeavour a bit easier.

In essence, in my reading, Michaels encourages comparatists to also be critical when it comes to globalisation in the sense that moving away from the state-centric view may just end up being replaced by another kind of centric view. This something else is the universalising project of governance that seems to deny the importance of local cultures and experiences. This has been opposed by voices like that of Pierre Legrand, who has vocally argued against uniformisation.[66] Notwithstanding, the need for comparative law does not grow solely from the lawyerly desire to create more legal similarity by wielding the scythe of uniformity. I agree with Twining when he argues that:

> One of the main tasks of comparative law is to make us aware of legal systems other than our own; in future comparative law must extend this de-parochialising role to reducing our ignorance of non-Western legal cultures and traditions.[67]

[64] Kischel (n 55) 870 mentions these fields of law as systems that are claimed to be developed independently of states.

[65] Michaels (n 25) 352–58.

[66] See, eg, Pierre Legrand, 'The Return of the Repressed' (2021) 75 *Tulane Law Review* 1033–52.

[67] William Twining, 'Globalisation and Comparative Law' in Esin Örücü and David Nelken (eds), *Comparative Law* (Hart Publishing 2007) 69–89, 72.

Twining's point does not fall far from that of what Michaels is talking about. The sensible core assumption is that comparatists play – at least potentially – an important role in the sense that it is their job to ensure that knowledge of differences and similarities, and global legal diversity becomes known.[68] Even if similarities might be increasing because of globalisation, this does not mean that comparative law would be unnecessary, or that it would be universal in the sense that scholars working in the fields of global and transnational law would suddenly become comparative law experts. Instead, it is more probable that comparative legal methods become more relevant in different fields of law against the backdrop of globalising law.[69]

There is more to future comparative law than merely being a non-state centric form of legal scholarship or posing questions about foreign legal systems (in a broad sense) to AI. In other words, in opposition to Twining's key claim, we are not all comparatists now. Perhaps we should be but, alas, we are not. To that end, Michaels concludes, it would be 'dangerous to replace comparative law with something else, be it transnational law, global law, legal pluralism, new governance, or the like'.[70] All these phenomena influence comparative study of law, but they should not threaten the beating heart of comparative law. Personally, I cannot and will not envisage a future where borderless AI would threaten the heart of comparative law endeavour. However, my suspicion does not mean that technologically aided comparative law would not be a useful manner of dealing with new things such as non-state normativities.[71] My potential misgivings come from the methodological issues discussed in chapter ten above. Against the backdrop of comparative law's tendency to generate contrarian scholarship, it may be that fear of AI turns out to be exaggerated but, of course, this remains to be seen. My key concern is that AI – large language models especially – will look like a tempting shortcut to gain superficial or hallucinated information about foreign legal systems.[72]

In the end, debates circling around globalisation of law may prove that the comparatist of today finds themselves in a new situation in which being simply a contrarian no longer suffices. Polycentricity means that there are so many positions that opposing them in a coherent manner has become virtually unfeasible. Indeed, it may be the case that many of the binary positions discussed in previous chapters are less relevant in the comparative law of today and that of tomorrow. Then again, comparatists have been masterful in finding issues to disagree about and I do not expect drastic changes in this regard, no matter what. Even if we were

[68] David Nelken notes that globalisation of law is likely to produce simultaneously increasing differentiation and harmony, 'Legal Culture' in Smits et al (n 59) Vol 2, 436–43, 441.

[69] See, eg, Elisa Morgera, 'Global Environmental Law and Comparative Legal Methods' (2015) *Review of European and Comparative International Environmental Law* 254–63.

[70] Michaels (n 25) 358.

[71] See, eg, Catalina Goanta, 'Comparative Law and Cyberspace' in Husa (n 2) 177–196.

[72] Matthew Dahl, Varun Magesh, Mirac Suzgun and Daniel Ho, 'Large Legal Fictions' (2024) 16 *Journal of Legal Analysis* 64–93 (analyses the risks of using generic foundation models).

to have moved from the era of globalisation to post-globalisation, nevertheless the influence of border-crossing non-state normativities continues to exist.[73] All this is, I believe, conducive to mitigating the loneliness of the comparatist.[74] Whether this is acceptable for contrarian loners is a different matter altogether. Perhaps we prefer to dwell in our own tribal corners after all.

[73] See for further discussion on post-globalisation, Victor Roudometoff, 'How Should We Think About Globalization in a Post-Globalization Era?' (2025) 1 *Dialogues in Sociology* 13–26 ('While some declare that globalization is dead, others suggest that prevailing counter-globalization tendencies represent solely the current moment', ibid 14).

[74] See for a broader discussion, John Henry Merryman, *The Loneliness of Comparative Lawyer* (Kluwer 2001) 1–12 ('our domestically focussed colleagues at home are good talkers and excellent critics, but they have only a limited interest in our work in foreign law. Is it, perhaps, the fault of our scholarly tradition? Do we suffer from a disabling *deformation professionelle*? Are we committed to a mode of academic scholarship that only other comparative lawyers, similarly deluded, value and the rest of legal academia rightly considers trivial or irrelevant?', ibid 11–12).

13

Outlook: Sailing the Seas of Diversity and Pluralism

Before concluding, I need to state the obvious. No part of this book claims that scholarly contrarianism would be exclusively a feature of comparative law. Many fields of law, legal theory, legal history, and sociology of law have had scholarly collisions. Comparative law has absolutely no monopoly on scholarly contrarianism. To argue otherwise would be foolish. Notwithstanding, what I argue in this book is that contrarianism has been an innate feature of comparative law scholarship. Importantly, this feature has directed the transformation of the field. In other words, nothing is said about the collisions of other fields that study law even though many of the above chapters discuss issues that overlap with other legal disciplines. The story told in this book is the story of modern comparative law scholarship. Another caveat is that most of the literature cited is in English and a smaller portion in other European languages. This limitation made it possible to follow the English-speaking mainstream, but it does leave aside various national comparative law traditions.[1]

Reading comparative law literature is a curious experience as it is a patchwork quilt sewn loosely together and consisting of many pieces of scholarship in different designs, schools of thought, and methodologies. Comparative law builds upon the work of previous generations of comparatists, with each era, each culture, and every scholar posing their own questions. Each comparatist seeks answers to their questions both as individuals and as members of a border-crossing community of scholarship. Their research may be animated by new judgments or legislative changes as well as by new technologies, available data, methods, and novel questions which

[1] The fact that English has become comparative law's lingua franca means that several problems are not discussed in this book. For discussion on this, see Erika Arban, Maartje De Visser & Jeong-In Yun (eds), *The Language of Comparative Constitutional Law* (Hart Publishing 2025). Even though the book focuses on constitutional law it applies to comparative study of law more generally. See also Gary Bell, 'The Civil Law, the Common Law, and the English Language' (2019) 14 Supplement 1 *Asian Journal of Comparative Law* 29–49 (makes the point that English is nowadays the lingua franca of civil law legal scholars in Asia).

are key to renewal and topicality. Without a shadow of a doubt the comparatist is obliged, in one way or another, to follow their time and discussions in their field. Even the most waspish members of the comparative law community do this because not even the most erudite and disagreeable comparatist can undertake scholarly work in a vacuum.[2] Yet, at the same time, opposing requires something to oppose. By way of conclusion, I maintain there is no sense in remaining in the trenches if there is no real enemy to fight. Globalisation and the growth of transnational legal normativities have made it more difficult to find things to oppose as so many potential opponents are out there. Diversity and pluralism function as a counterforce to sharp contrarianism. But it would not be right to think that pluralism in law would be without its problems even though it may work as a general methodological and epistemic inspiration.[3] Nevertheless, it is beneficial to grasp that the call for pluralism is not unproblematic and certainly not a panacea. Comparative law will most likely remain a field of dissenting academic entrepreneurs.

One of the shortcomings of this book is that this tale of comparative law scholarship is certainly not an exhaustive one. However, I hope that what I have managed to do is to narrate a story that is woven in a manner that resembles the story about an elephant and blind men. This is a story of a group of blind men who have never come across an elephant before. They try to learn and imagine what the elephant is like by touching it. Each of the blind men has their own limited experience based on them touching only one part of the elephant, meaning that they arrive at very different understandings of the creature: wall, snake, spear, tree, and fan are all possible explanations based on their limited experience of touching. The lesson is that each man tends to believe that their perception is the accurate truth about the elephant. Only the spectator with the ability to see, having a sort of God's-eye view, notices that each individual observation reveals only the partial truth. In much the same way, I am fully aware of the risks that telling the story of modern comparative law involves. That said, in order to avoid the problem of the blind men, I have told the story through many points of contact spanning from legal realism and formalism to private law versus public law, science versus practice, and so on. This story is certainly not perfect but at least it has several points of contact, meaning that the story told may not be too far from a relatively believable reconstruction. The problem I cannot avoid is that comparative law is always on the move as a field of legal study. Tracing its movements always comes too late, like 'The Flying Dutchman' - doomed to sail the seas forever but never to reach port.

It is crucial to realise that, as a field of legal studies, comparative law will never reach any final stage. It is always in the making, there is no endgame. I have argued

[2] I borrow the word 'waspish' from Peter Goodrich, in Peter Goodrich, 'Critique of Comparative Law: To Compierre' (2024) 51 *Journal of Law and Society* 130-42 ('Pierre, however, must also admit that he is part of the target discipline, a most hesitant comparatist, and a waspish member of the guild, yet nonetheless belonging, howsoever oppositional his stance', 139).

[3] See, eg, Alexis Galán & Dennis Patterson, 'The Limits of Normative Legal Pluralism' (2013) 11 *International Journal of Law in Context* 783–800 (review essay of Berman's *Global Legal Pluralism* 2012). See also Sally F Moore, 'Legal Pluralism as Omnium Gatherum' (2014) 10 *FIU Law Review* 5–18 ('too general a category to be analytically useful', ibid 5).

in the previous chapters that comparative law has never become 'the science of comparative law'; it has never reached its mature scientific state as an autonomous legal discipline. Like law itself, comparative study of it is in constant motion even though the motion may sometimes be hard to detect. As contrarians, we may also think that the motion is going (or has gone) in the wrong direction.

Regardless of the pace of change, the comparatist constantly balances the familiar and the foreign, struggling not to lose their essence as legal scholars (academic as well as other legal experts and judges) who zoom in on differences and similarities. It is this very balancing act that tacitly entices the comparatist to be a contrarian legal scholar. Contrarianism, I tend to believe, is a result of two key features. First, comparative law research will never become ready as it is in constant motion. Consequently, we keep asking because we must. Second, each comparatist needs to find their own way as there are no unanimously accepted models. We build frameworks again and again as each study creates different kinds of methodological needs. This is, in essence, like the work of Sisyphus. But – unlike Sisyphus – the comparatist is free to choose both the hill and the rock they push uphill.

Without arguing for the existence of strong path dependence we can, nevertheless, see continuity and layering. Crucially, the manner in which the comparatist perceives the familiar and the foreign depends on the work of past and present generations of comparatists even when we choose to disagree with them. Our field is like a patchwork quilt: a thing that involves sewing together different pieces. However, we are not in any way obliged to repeat what past generations did. We can – indeed, we should – diverge when we see the need. We can add our own pieces. Then again, it would be foolish not to learn from past scholarship or from other schools of thought (even those one disagrees with!). At least, we can try not to repeat their errors and add pieces that we think work better. But, in a world of globalising legalities and ever evolving technology the challenges have multiplied even though, at the same time, developments provide new tools and data for comparatists, as indeed AI and cyberspace demonstrate. Regardless, it seems safe to claim that comparative law has been a field of contrarians. The above analyses show how scholarly collisions have shaped the field into what it is now.

It is the disagreement, the spirit of opposition, that is an important portion of the academic quality of someone who has chosen to study law comparatively. It is my belief that comparativism itself feeds the fire of contrarianism and there is no problem in that. Quite the contrary. As a result, comparative law may look like a jungle when looked at from the outside. Understandably, many would instinctively prefer what an earlier generation of comparatists dreamt of: a neatly organised garden. But diversity and polycentrism are hard to avoid in today's world. This is not a problem if we accept that there is no Holy Grail of comparative law; it is the quest that counts. The quest has been animated by contrarian legal scholars engaged with comparative study of law driven by the conviction that it offers valuable insights into the nature of law and legal cultures. Despite all the disagreements, this remains a worthy and inspiring belief.

INDEX

www.ingramcontent.com/pod-product-compliance
Ingram Content Group UK Ltd.
Pitfield, Milton Keynes, MK11 3LW, UK
UKHW020816290926
15470UKWH00003B/1198

9 781509 985562